Stop Fighting About Money

Stop Fighting About Money

How Money Can Make or Break Your Relationship

Corinne Sweet

Hodder & Stoughton
LONDON SYDNEY AUCKLAND

British Library Cataloguing in Publication Data
A record for this book is available from the British Library

ISBN 0 340 74621 1

Typeset by Avon Dataset Ltd, Bidford-on-Avon, Warks

Printed and bound in Great Britain by
The Guernsey Press Co. Ltd, Channel Isles

Hodder & Stoughton
A Division of Hodder Headline Ltd
338 Euston Road
London NW1 3BH

To Clara:
my little moon and star

Contents

Acknowledgments   ix
How to Use This Book   1

Part One: Why Couples Fight about Money

1 Emotional Money Baggage   7
2 Money Patterns and Money Relationships   31
3 Power Games and Money Addiction   53

Part Two: Making a Money Match

4 Dating and Mating   77
5 Living Together   96
6 Getting Married   119

Part Three: Money Relationship Crunchpoints

7 Having a Baby   141
8 Life Crises and Life Changes   164
9 Splitting Up, Divorcing and Starting Again   186

Part Four: Stop Fighting about Money

10 Building Your Money Relationship   209

    Appendix: Money Patterns Quiz   223
    Further Reading   229
    Useful Organisations   231
    Index   238

Acknowledgments

Thanks to Carole Blake, my astute literary agent, for making this book happen and to Judith Longman, at Hodder, for excellent editorial support and encouragement. Heartfelt thanks to Rufus Potter for inspiring and supporting this book in every way possible; and to Hayley Baker, for daily help and ideas. Thanks, too, to Corinne and Albert Haynes, Susan Quilliam, Virginia Ironside, Sarah Litvinoff, Chris Blackie, Sue Pratt, Marika Denton, Rupert Firth, Johnny McKeown, Margaret Evans, Sally Morgan, Penny and Jerry Deans, Lizzie Smith, for plenty of brain-picking and letting-down of hair.

How to Use This Book

When love flies in the window, money flies out the door.

An old saying

MONEY. Love it, loathe it, hate it, crave it: money is an essential part of life, and therefore of our love relationships. Money colours our relationships, our love and sex lives. Money has become the number-one issue that couples row about. A national survey in 1998 by Relate, the couples' counselling organisation, found 44 per cent of couples fight about money, with spending priorities causing the most friction. Recent research by Jan Pahl of the University of Kent warns that the new forms of 'electronic money' now available, such as PC/Internet banking and cashtills, is also causing more friction, greater secrecy and financial inequality between couples.

One bed, two heads

Women's increased equality since the 1960s – at work, at home, in public life and in bed – has led to households having two heads. Instead of couples simply pooling their money and living as one, relationships are often supported by two earners with very different views and needs. In the 'bad' old days money was seemingly straightforward in relationships – men controlled both their women and the finances, and marriage was for life. Today, serial monogamy is the name of the relationship game. Life and love is much more complicated and most of us enter our relationships with a great deal of emotional and financial baggage in tow from other loves and marriages. We might even have children in tow as well. Most people also live together before marrying, and even though the divorce rate is high (one in two marriages end in divorce today), we try to succeed again and again by dating, living with or marrying new mates after a relationship fails. Lone parenthood is also on the increase and set to rise as the twenty-first century progresses.

However, all this means that money is more complicated than ever within love relationships. It can cause a great deal of strife and upset because it represents freedom, power and control. Money can become a measure of equality, trust, commitment, love, honesty and care to the couples involved. Yet, money remains a taboo topic to talk about as it's generally felt to be more private and personal than sex. So when couples try to talk about money they can both fly off the handle while love flies out the door.

Why couples fight about money

This book is meant to help you talk to your partner about money so that you can resolve your differences and improve your love relationship. If you have picked it up because you are at loggerheads about money and are fighting constantly about who spends what, where, when and how, then it will be worth your while reading Part One, which is about 'Why couples fight about money'. It explains where our money problems come from, psychologically speaking, and how they can operate in our current relationships. It also helps you identify what I call Emotional Money Baggage and Money Patterns, so you can understand yourself and your partner better. People often play power games and have money addictions which put a terrible strain on relationships. However, even though it may feel impossible to raise the thorny issue of money right now, you should be in a better position to take the boxing gloves off and start talking about money by the time you have read this book.

Making a money match

Part Two deals with 'Making a money match' and is particularly aimed at helping you see the way in which you and your 'ex', your partner, prospective partner(s), or spouse may be hooking together about money. This section looks at issues like dating and mating, living together and getting married. Having a baby and being parents can also put an enormous financial and emotional strain on your relationship. However, there are things you can do to diffuse the money fights when they are about to explode. It takes two to tango, as the saying goes, and it takes two to fight about money. If you get wise to the money games you are playing with your ex, your partner or spouse (or they are playing with you), you can start doing something to change the situation for the better.

Money Relationship Crunchpoints

Part Three is about what I call 'Money Relationship Crunchpoints', and tackles the thorny ups and downs involving money in our love relationships. Few of us go through life without experiencing some kind of crisis, like losing a job, having an accident, getting ill, even having a breakdown; and most of us experience swings and roundabouts in love and life, when one partner wants to retrain, or drop out, or when one of you wins or earns substantially more than the other (especially when the woman earns more).

Stop fighting about money

Part Four focuses on what we need to do to stop fighting about money – for good. This doesn't mean you won't argue about money from time to time, but if you want to stop everyday niggles from becoming domestic nuclear explosions, then it is crucial to notice the warning signs, understand more of what your rows are really about, and turn what is often very destructive behaviour into something which is positively constructive.

3

What's love got to do with it?

This book is not about money management; for that I direct the reader to the Help section at the back of the book. Also, it is not assumed that all couples are heterosexual – money fights occur in all love relationships, whether straight, gay or bisexual. Couples can also come from a wide range of cultures, classes and backgrounds. However, this book is for anyone who feels love is ebbing out of their relationship as the money fights take over. It is aimed at anyone who feels despair about ever really trying to get through to their partner or spouse about money; to those who feel trapped in a cycle of repetitive fighting over supermarket bills and credit card spending; or those who feel money is a well-gnawed bone of contention in their relationship, and that love and patience are wearing pretty thin.

Sort out your money problems together, and your love relationship will blossom; tackle your relationship difficulties and/or your own emotional problems, and your money difficulties will gradually straighten out. Do both together and you're onto a love-relationship winner: bigger, better and more satisfying than any lottery scoop.

Please note
Names of the couples and individuals cited in this book have been changed as most said they felt money was too personal and revealing a subject to go public on.

Part One

Why Couples Fight about Money

1

Emotional Money Baggage

Love gives naught but itself and takes naught but from itself.
Love possesses not nor would it be possessed;
For love is sufficient unto love.

Kahlil Gibran

Jessica and James are barely talking. The atmosphere in their beautifully designed and maintained house is so tense that sparks are virtually fizzing out of the walls. They are in the middle of one of their interminable fights about money, which my visit has sparked off. 'I'm sorry,' Jessica explains embarrassedly, 'but he's just been really horrible to me about our money situation.' She goes on to explain they have fallen out over her spending and debts. Jessica has recently found out she owes over £2,000 to the tax man. As she works part-time she says all her income from freelance cookery demonstrating goes on childcare and maintaining herself and Susi, their two-year-old child. James pays for the house and its maintenance, plus most of their social life expenses, including holidays. They are not married, however, although Jessica longs to be. She explains: 'James doesn't believe in marriage, although I really do, especially now we have a child together.' Her private fear is that he's keeping her at a distance because 'he doesn't really want me to get my hands on *his* house which he owns outright and is worth around £500,000, or his hard-earned savings.' If they were legally married she would automatically be entitled to half. 'But I don't think that's fair as I've done all the decorating, plus I do the cooking, shopping, washing, gardening and organise the cleaning and childcare. Surely that's worth something?'

Crunchpoint

Jessica and James' relationship is at a Crunchpoint. They are so rigidly locked in argument with each other that neither can move towards the other.

Throughout this book we will be examining common Crunchpoints about money in relationships and how to handle them. Crunchpoints are usually caused by something happening outside the relationship – such as Jessica's tax bill – which creates a clash between the conflicting viewpoints of each partner. The crunch comes because a decision has to be made – sometimes a very big and expensive decision – and both partners need to be able to communicate clearly with each other so that a mutually agreeable deal can be struck. Things come to a crunch when partners have not been able to negotiate or resolve sensitive money issues during their relationship. Crunchpoints are usually an accumulation of money niggles, misunderstandings and hidden resentments which can build up over months, even years.

Things have come to a head now Jessica has asked James to lend her the £2,000 to cover her tax bill. He has refused point-blank (she says he usually charges her interest on loans 'to teach me a lesson', so she can't understand why he is drawing a line this time). As a stockbroker, and working full-time, James earns about five times more than Jessica. 'It's not that he is mean,' she explains defensively, 'it's rather that he says he's fed up with bailing me out.' In desperation, and perhaps in retaliation, Jessica has asked a mutual close friend to lend her the money, which has made James explode. 'James is furious that I've revealed so intimate a matter to an "outsider".' Yet, to Jessica it is natural to turn to a friend for support and to talk about everything to do with her relationship, including money. She can't understand why, for James, revealing anything about their financial life to others represents the ultimate betrayal.

Embarrassed, Jessica explains that I will have to interview them separately, not together. She begins by telling me her side of the story. 'I know I'm bad with money, but I do a lot of unpaid work around here. To me it all balances out in the end.' She says she's extremely worried about how their constant money fights are affecting Susi: 'I heard her say "fick off" to her teddy yesterday and I was horrified to realise she was mimicking me shouting obscenities at James.'

Our interview had been agreed a month ago when I met Jessica at a social event. I had explained the book I was writing was for couples constantly fighting about money and her eyes had lit up: she had leapt at the chance to talk. Not so her partner, who at first felt very defensive about talking about something so 'private'. However, when Jessica explained to James that I was a counsellor as well as a writer, he eventually agreed to meet me: perhaps a sign of how secretly desperate he was feeling himself about their embattled money situation. Indeed, when James emerged from his den to talk to me alone, he was surprisingly open about how despairing he felt about their money problems. 'I began letting Jessica use my credit card a few months ago for emergency purposes only. But now each month when I get my bill it's like opening Satan's jamboree bag. There's all these items I know nothing about: expensive haircuts, designer clothes, smart lunches out in town. I even pay her business phone bill.'

A little further digging reveals that things are more complicated with Jessica and James than they initially seemed on the surface: they are caught in a mesh of secrets and lies about money. Clearly, they are coming at their financial situation from very different perspectives, which is complicated by their inability to communicate effectively with each other. They have never been able either to discuss or agree how money is distributed between them as a cohabiting couple, which is crucial, given James' substantially larger salary. They also have a child to provide for: hence the current Crunchpoint. 'I basically feel I'm losing control,' James admits honestly, 'I feel manipulated by her going to our friend for a loan. I can't tell you how it grates – I just don't know why she can't handle her own money properly.'

Money: the main cause of relationship fights

Jessica and James' frustration with each other has led them both of late seriously to consider splitting up. Their situation is not unusual, however, as money has become the number-one issue couples fight about today. The national Relate/Candis survey in February 1998 found:

- most couples argue about spending priorities, especially if not working;
- low-income couples are more than twice as likely to argue over money than middle/high-income families;
- money arguments are more common if the couple have children under ten;
- more women than men are likely to argue over trust and secrecy issues related to money;
- equal proportions of men and women argue about lack of money.

More recent national research by Hamilton Direct Bank (September 1999) has echoed the Relate/Candis findings, with 37 per cent of couples saying they believe they are 'simply financially incompatible'. It also found that couples with separate bank accounts were 'far more likely to disagree over money than couples who share a joint account'. Simply, a love relationship which does not recognise or accommodate the needs of two distinct and separate individuals is not going to last.

What's love got to do with it?

A relationship which is not happy about money will not be happy in love; similarly, a relationship which is not happy and loving will be lousy on the money front. When a couple, like Jessica and James, are fighting about money all the time, their love is eventually eroded by strife. Patience, compassion and care is replaced by resentment, irritation and distrust. Money is symbolic of so many things in our love relationships: power, independence, choice, freedom, sexual desirability, value and worth. When we fall in love, we tell ourselves and each other money doesn't matter – but it does. Right from the first date, money is exchanged and used in the process of getting to know one another. We make all sorts of assumptions about who we are going out with, what they are worth, how they equate to us financially, even if we don't consciously admit these things to ourselves. Some people want to 'marry into money', others feel 'money can't buy me love'. Whatever, money will soon insinuate itself into the dynamics of a relationship and need to be consciously clarified by a couple to their mutual benefit – otherwise love will not flourish. (For more on this, see chapter 4, 'Dating and Mating'.)

Power struggle

When couples, like Jessica and James, make money the battleground the argument it is not always about money itself. Usually it is about power, about working out who is on top in the relationship, who is the winner, who the loser. And where the sexes are concerned there is always an added edge to these money fights. It's a typical power struggle, the age-old battle of the sexes played out over credit cards and cash tills. One woman told me that her wealthy boyfriend 'makes me feel like a prostitute when he gets out his wallet and flashes his cash around. He's a real show-off.' Recently he produced £3,000 cash in front of her in a showroom to buy a motorbike. 'I was so embarrassed, but I knew he needed to show me how wealthy he was – it was yet another sign of his power.' It was also another nail in the coffin of their relationship. Every time she tried to raise the issue of their financial inequality he simply changed the subject: 'He wanted me to be dependent on him, but I couldn't bear the price I had to pay. He wanted to control everything I did or we did together. He could never do anything simple, like enjoy a pub lunch, it had to be a grand dinner out. I tried to talk to him about it, but he would just shrug it off. In the end I felt I'd lost myself and my self-respect, so I left him instead.'

Breaking the last great taboo

Generally, it's easier for most couples to talk about sex than money. In *The Real Meaning of Money* (HarperCollins, 1998), Dorothy Rowe, author and psychotherapist, confirms this oddity of modern life: 'I mentioned this difficulty to a friend who works in a large publishing concern. She suddenly realised that while she knew all the scandal about the sexual activities of several of her senior colleagues, she had no idea what they earned.' Coming clean about earnings, investments, assets, savings and debts is like breaking the last great taboo.

Too private

Researchers who seek to understand how peoples' private money lives work can find themselves up against an impenetrable wall of secrecy. Money remains intensely private with a capital 'P' and people can be easily affronted by any intimate questions about the state of their finances, especially from 'outsiders'. One woman I interviewed, whose husband of twenty years had cheated on her by having an affair (which led to their divorce), felt she couldn't possibly reveal anything about her ex-husband's finances to me, an outsider: 'I feel it's terribly personal,' she said, defensively, 'and even though he betrayed me sexually I still feel loyal to him over his most private business.' In other words, she felt more protective about revealing his earnings and assets than his sexual misdeeds (which she told me all about). This confirms Dorothy Rowe's perception of the taboo nature of talking about the intimacies of money: 'I saw bankers turn white when all I wanted was for them to tell me a little about their work.'

Money and couples: uncharted territory

Jan Pahl, author of *Money and Marriage* (Macmillan, 1989) and Senior Research Fellow at the University of Kent, believes that the whole issue of how money is managed within marriage (and cohabiting relationships) remains largely uncharted territory. Jan Pahl found her studies hampered by peoples' inability or unwillingness to talk about money: only 52 per cent of interviewees contacted for *Money and Marriage* agreed to talk about money. According to Jan Pahl, 'the high refusal rate [48 per cent] seemed to reflect partly the fact that money was defined as too private a topic for discussion with a stranger, and partly the fact that both husband and wife were to be interviewed.'

Gender difference

There was also a gender difference, in Jan Pahl's study: typically, 'men were more likely to refuse than women'. One explanation for this is that women are simply used to relating to others more openly about personal issues and have wider support networks than men (friends, family, colleagues, neighbours). This phenomenon is well documented and women's magazines are filled with articles asking 'Why won't he talk to me?' or 'How can I get my man to open up?' Men as a species to be studied and considered separately from women has spawned a wide range of insightful self-help books over the past decade, including bestsellers such as John Gray's *Men Are from Mars and Women Are from Venus*, Susan Jeffers' *Opening Our Hearts to Men*, or Susan Qulliam's *Stop Arguing, Start Talking*. Also, men are so well conditioned to compete it is almost like laying themselves open to attack, psychologically speaking, if they talk to other people in a vulnerable and revealing way about earnings, assets and all things financial. Who knows, the person they are talking to might just earn twice as much, and that would be devastatingly emasculating to contemplate (especially if it's a woman who earns more).

Alvin Hall, the US financial whizz and co-author of *Money for Life: Everyone's Guide to Financial Freedom* (Hodder & Stoughton, 2000) agrees that 'money is inextricably linked to our self-image and hard-wired to some of our deepest emotions'. Which explains why, when a couple try to discuss something like a credit card bill, they can 'veer sharply into an argument about their joint finances, escalate into a shouting match about responsibility and end with a sulking tirade about the mixed joys and doubts of commitment'. However, Alvin Hall believes it's essential for couples to break the taboo: 'Learning to talk about money, especially about joint finances, is one of the most difficult but important challenges in sustaining a relationship. Frank financial conversation allows you to get to know your partner intimately, warts and all, and forces you to consider your own strengths and weaknesses.'

Lesbians, gay men and bisexuals' money fights

It is important to note here that not all love relationships are heterosexual and money battles also occur within lesbian, gay men's and bisexual relationships. One lesbian (who had been married for ten years previously) told me that in her view the fights about money can be even more vitriolic in gay rather than in heterosexual relationships, because they are so symbolic of power and social acceptance. Because of this, gay men and lesbians can experience a great deal of relationship insecurity and wrangles over money and property. Money can become heavily symbolic of trust, commitment and love. Discrimination (such as not being able legally to pass on a pension or an estate to your gay male or lesbian partner) increases the stress on a long-term relationship. Perhaps we need to look to more enlightened cultures, such as California, where gays and lesbians can declare their relationships in legally recognised ceremonies. The public legitimacy this would give may provide more relationship security and decrease money fights.

Money language

Few of us have had the chance to develop the necessary language to talk about money with each other in our most intimate relationships. Most of us are unused to articulating our deeply held, often confusing, or even conflicting, feelings about money, so it can simply seem too difficult an issue to talk about. It can also seem 'self-evident' to some what is 'right' or 'wrong' on the financial front and they can't understand why other people simply don't see it the same way.

This lack of language and feeling of taboo means we look for clues, literally for signs of wealth, when we meet somebody new. Meeting someone at a party you probably ask 'What do you do for a living?' or 'Where do you live?' But it is still considered extremely impolite in the UK to ask 'What do you earn?' In some cultures, such as the United States or Hong Kong, this reticence over revealing your earnings is quite baffling as one of the first questions there might well be 'What do you make?' Yet, even if few of us ask other people directly how much money they earn or have, most of us look for a range of non-verbal clues which represent wealth (or lack of it) – clothing, cars, neighbourhood, etc. We scrutinise these things, almost unconsciously, trying to pinpoint each others' social position and thus level of wealth.

However, first impressions are often misleading, or belie the truth, as so many of us are caught up in creating an illusion of wealth through appearance or material goods. One man I spoke to said he deliberately hid his inherited wealth from his new girlfriend: 'I wanted to make sure that it was me she was interested in, and not my money.' It's the stuff of fairytales: two paupers fall in love, only to discover that the man in rags is a prince. However, it does happen in real life, especially with the National Lottery which has created nearly a thousand millionaires out of 'ordinary' people.

Life and love gets very complicated when money gets in the way and when there is no easy way to talk about what it all means in our most intimate relationships.

Parental role models

If we haven't experienced our parents or carers being able to talk calmly and openly about money, and/or we haven't observed them reaching amicable, rational solutions to money problems affecting them as individuals or the family as a whole, then we are personally devoid of role models in this highly sensitive, but crucially important, area of everyday life. One woman I interviewed told me her mother used literally to run out of the room crying if her father raised the subject of money. She simply refused to talk about anything from the price of peas to planning a holiday. Consequently, the woman I spoke to found it impossible to talk about money in her current relationship. Instead, she felt a feeling of dread, even fear, and would find herself avoiding the subject at all cost.

Opening the floodgates

The taboo nature of money and our lack of language and experience talking about it intimately can lead to a strange phenomenon. It seems once people have broken the last great taboo by talking openly about money – often with someone in authority (and not their partner/spouse) – it can open the floodgates to talking, often inappropriately, about other sensitive issues. 'People use us as confessors,' explains Richard Murphy, a chartered accountant of twenty years' experience with his London accounting firm. 'Once clients have talked to me about their money problems it seems they feel they can talk to me about anything and everything. I've had some asking me for abortion advice or help with intimate marital problems. It's as if once you bare your innermost soul by talking about money, which seems to be a subject of great secrecy and obsession, you might as well bare all.' For some of us, keepers of money wisdom – accountants, financial advisers, bank managers, debt counsellors – have become the wise extended family that many of us miss and long for in modern industrial society. They are almost like the ersatz mothers and fathers of our modern age.

Flashpoints

The lack of positive experience and appropriate language about money in family relationships mean couples are often groping in the dark when they try to talk through their money problems. Money can be the tip of the emotional iceberg: arguments occur over money because feelings are running high and then explode. People often try to talk about money at the wrong time, in the wrong place and in the wrong way: tired, stressed out, or with the bailiff banging on the door. Money problems can then feel insurmountable, and talking about them with a partner to find a solution impossible. These moments become relationship 'Flashpoints' in everyday life. Throughout this book we will note Flashpoints and suggest what to do about them.

Overall, the best remedy is to be aware of which elements in your own relationship will create a Flashpoint and then try to think round or through them during a calmer moment, either alone or together with your partner. Becoming aware of your own and your partner's Flashpoints can help you reduce the number of money fights you have, which is particularly important if they are of a repetitive and destructive nature and you have children.

Emotional Money Baggage

Whether couples are homosexual or heterosexual, arguing about money points to more general psychological and emotional issues. Whether we are conscious of it or not, each of us enters our intimate love relationships fully equipped with our own Emotional Money Baggage. Psychologically speaking, your Emotional Money Baggage comes from your upbringing, life experience, class values, culture and personal beliefs. These include:

- how your parents or carers talked about or coped with money;
- whether you experienced poverty or plenty (or somewhere in between);
- what you were taught was 'right' or 'wrong' about handling money, from pocket money onwards;
- personal experiences you have had with family, friends, colleagues, ex-partners/spouses and bosses about money (from sharing an inheritance with siblings, to being cheated of joint savings by an ex-spouse, to lending a friend money and never being paid back);
- how much information you have about money, what it is, how it works, how it is used, what it is for;
- your own personal ability to work with numbers: for many people money, and anything to do with figures, holds great terror; for others playing with a calculator and doing sums brings nothing but pleasure. Many of us muddle along somewhere in between, counting on fingers, tapping on calculators and adding up shopping lists in our heads;
- any particular religious or belief systems you were immersed in as a child, young adult or adult;
- whether you've developed a 'prosperity-consciousness' (the universe will provide) or a 'poverty-consciousness' (there's never enough to go round) frame of mind.

Understanding your own Emotional Money Baggage

Understanding your own Emotional Money Baggage, where it comes from and how it works, will enable you to articulate much more about why you view and use money the way you do. Money as an issue is packed with emotion and meaning, and unpacking it will therefore help you and your partner understand where you both, literally, are coming from. This book will have only a few strategic 'quizzes' to help shed light on your entrenched ideas and beliefs about money. It is worthwhile taking a few minutes to think about the following questions for yourself (and your partner/spouse) because it is a way of making your unconscious views conscious. If you want this book to make a real difference to helping yourself and your partner, it will be worth writing your answers either in a private notebook or on a confidential computer file, so you can come back to it later and think about the implications. If you feel you can be open with your partner about identifying your Emotional Money Baggage, it could be extremely helpful to do this quiz together (preferably in a relaxed way, sober and when there is time to talk). However, if you and your partner are at daggers drawn with each other about money, then try and think about your own Emotional Money Baggage first, so you can absorb what it tells you about yourself, your attitudes and beliefs. Perhaps you could write down your answers separately and then swop notes and read each other's answers if talking is proving difficult?

Quiz: What's your Emotional Money Baggage?

Take a moment to ask yourself these questions and then write down your honest responses. (If you skip this bit as you read, it will definitely be worth coming back to it later.)

Understanding your past:

1   What is your earliest memory connected with money in any way at all?
2   What was your mother's role/attitude regarding money? Did she have her own money?
3   What was your father's role/attitude regarding money? Did he have his own money?
4   Did you see your parents negotiate openly and successfully about money issues? If not, what did you see?
5   Did your parents agree or disagree about how money was spent? What did you learn were 'right' and 'wrong' things to spend money on?

6   How did your parents 'teach' you about money? What were the main messages you learned about it?

7   Growing up, did you feel poor, well off, rich? Did you have pocket money? If so, how much, when did it start, how did you feel about it? Did you have more or less than same-age friends and siblings?

8   If you had siblings, did you get treated fairly regarding money? If not, how not? If you were an only child, how were you treated regarding money?

9   What memories do you have of Christmas and birthday presents, treats or gifts? Were you disappointed, overwhelmed or were they just right?

10 When did you get your first job and why? How much were you paid? What did you do with the money?

11 Did you ever steal money (from your mother's purse or father's wallets)? If so, were you caught? Did you steal from anyone else?

12 Are there any big events which have coloured your view of money (like a father's redundancy, an inheritance, unemployment, winning the lottery, losing or gaining money in your family, bankruptcy)?

13 What were you taught money was for? Saving for a rainy day? To enjoy living in the moment? The root of all evil? The solver of the world's problems?

Look back over your answers and think what they tell you about your own family history, your values, beliefs and ideas about money. In particular, how have your beliefs about money and love relationships been shaped?

Understanding your present:

1   How has your parents' relationship affected your perception of money? Are you more like your father or mother on the money front? If so, who and how?

2   What money lessons from childhood do you apply to your current (or past) relationship?

3   Do you now think of yourself as poor, well off, comfortable, scraping by, rich? Is it similar to or different from how you were, financially speaking, in your childhood?

4   Do you find yourself attracted to partners who are similar or different to you regarding money? If so, how different?

5   Do you see yourself as 'good' or 'bad' with money? If good, what are your strengths and weaknesses? If bad, what are your weaknesses and strengths?

6   Looking at your relationship (or last relationship), do you or did you play a specific money role? Is or was it like your mother or father's roles? How?

7   Do you choose new partners and then end up in the same old money tangles? Is there anything you can learn from this?

Rebelling against and repeating the past

Overall, ask yourself how your past Emotional Money Baggage is still affecting you in the present. Are you in rebellion against it? Or are you repeating it? Maybe a bit of both. Perhaps your father lost money, so you must always be prudent? Perhaps your mother had no money of her own, so you must always have some? Maybe your parents were moderate and unadventurous and you are too? The more you can clarify what your Emotional Money Baggage is, and where it comes from, the better equipped you will be for handling whatever comes up in your closest relationship on the money front. After all, knowledge is power.

Jessica and James' Emotional Money Baggage

We saw at the beginning of this chapter that Jessica and James were at a Crunchpoint over money. Both told me, in private, that they loved each other passionately, adored their daughter and wanted things to work out, but were utterly despairing about trying to talk to each other about their money situation. They were so frustrated with each other that they both were beginning to threaten to leave the relationship as money seemed an intractable problem to solve. In fact, they were both bashing each other over the head with their unsorted Emotional Money Baggage, hoping the other would eventually 'get' the point if they bashed hard enough. What needed to happen was for both of them to be able to sit down and rationally unpack their respective Emotional Money Baggage and take a long, cool look. First at their own, then at each other's.

Jessica's Emotional Money Baggage

'I can remember fierce money fights when I was a child,' remembers Jessica; 'my father withheld money, although he earned well as a country vet. He would drive round in a flash car, while my mother rode a moped.' Jessica comes from a middle-class, southern English, rural background and she and her two brothers all went to private schools. Money was very tight for mother and children: 'My mother had to pick us kids up one by one from our schools on her moped at the end of term because my father had his car to himself and wouldn't lend it to her.' Jessica also saw her father being mean with the housekeeping: 'My mother never had enough money, so she worked as his receptionist. My father would buy himself "treats" like a new hi-fi, car or clothes, while my mother saved out of her meagre wages to buy a washing machine, which he simply wouldn't pay for.' Jessica and her brothers had pocket money and their father would suddenly buy the boys extravagant presents like motorbikes. Her own pony was paid for over years from her mother's earnings, marking a difference in the treatment between the boys and the girl.

Although Jessica comes from a fairly privileged background (which James admits to envying), it was a pretty miserable one. Jessica saw her parents fighting constantly over money in everyday life: 'My mother would get people round to do the DIY or gardening and take money out of the joint account. But my father, who was a pillar of the community, would blow up because things would always cost more than he could stand. Even so, I remember my mother carrying planks of wood and bricks and trying to do everything on the cheap.' She also borrowed money from her own family to tide things over when necessary – meaning she was often in debt to relatives.

Jessica's parents finally divorced when she was twelve, but the story didn't end there. There were acrimonious rows about property, inheritance, savings and debts. 'My father's father died intestate and my father was forced to sell his part of the family estate. Unfairly, his brother got a massive amount of money because he was the favourite, while my father got nothing, which fuelled his fury over money. My father had to sell the marital home to pay my mother off which meant he was bitter and she had a fairly poor settlement.' Both parents remarried and Jessica's mother became a farmer, ploughing her divorce money, literally, into a tenant farm which then went bankrupt during the 1980s recession. As a consequence her mother now lives relatively poorly, although Jessica's father has started to amass his fortune again. 'My mother's OK just as long as she has enough money for her daily wine and gin. She gets her clothes from Tesco's and lives in ripped jeans and rugger shirts.' Jessica's mother works hard, but still has to borrow money to survive. Ironically, 'my mother threw me out of home when I was seventeen just before my A Levels because I spent £10 on sausages and she was furious.'

What Jessica learned from her parents' marriage was that men had money, but withheld it; and women had to scrimp and scrape, while taking responsibility for the children. Her parents were not a team, they were at war, with the man or boys always having the lion's share. Jessica's upbringing also told her that money was something to fight about, noisily, violently, repetitively, pointlessly. She saw adults wrangling all the time over the price of peat or paying for petrol and she also learned the culture of borrowing (from watching her mother's money struggles) as a means to get by. Jessica absorbed the notion, either through her father's financial selfishness or her mother's punitive poverty, that money was somehow more important than love, understanding or human kindness.

James' Emotional Money Baggage

James' upbringing was, on one level, totally opposite to Jessica's. 'My father was practically a Victorian, Scottish policeman,' explains James. 'He was working class and very, very careful with money as we didn't have a lot. My mother had a flair for spending it on frivolous things. On the one hand my father was ultra cautious about everything and on the other my mother was saying 'Oh, blow it, you only live once'. When the Depression hit Edinburgh in the 1920s James' father migrated to London to find work, which meant leaving any supportive family networks behind. James was an only child to what he calls 'elderly parents' (his mother was forty-three, his father forty-six, when he was born). Unlike Jessica's parents James never saw his parents fight about money although 'they rowed about most things'. Like Jessica's parents, they had a passionate, fairly volatile relationship (he saw his father hit his mother and they often shouted abuse at each other). Also like Jessica's parents, 'My father held the purse strings. He would give my mum housekeeping and she would manage it. But it all happened behind the scenes.'

As an only child, James has been left solely responsible for his aged mother, who is now eighty-two and in a home. His father died nine years ago: 'I realised I had to look after my mother because when I sorted out my father's affairs I saw there wasn't much left after an entire working life.' He sold his parents' house to pay for his mother's upkeep in a home. 'I learned from my parents that money is a precious commodity, not to be wasted. I save money because I've learned to accumulate rather than spend it.' James' rather dour, penny-pinching, only-child upbringing has left him with an over-riding sense of responsibility. 'My maxim is like Dickens', you know, "Income 3d, Expenditure 2d, Result: Happiness".' He saw his father, somewhat isolated, tough, Victorian, working hard and being cautious about money (like him), while his mother was a bit more 'frivolous' (like Jessica). 'I've never been overdrawn in my life and I like to know where I am,' says James proudly. Whereas Jessica's maxim is 'I love to have money, I like it, want to live comfortably, but can never keep hold of it because I fear it. I'm always overdrawn, and what's wrong with that?'

Jessica and James' Emotional Money Baggage has left them with very different patterns of behaviour: she spends too much, he hoards; she fears money, he embraces it. Instead of being able to work together as a team towards a common goal while acknowledging they have very different perspectives, they are at war, like their parents before them. This war is fuelled by their individual past experiences: Jessica saw her father being mean while her mother struggled. She felt this was intensely unfair and confusing (poverty in the midst of plenty). Now with James she is repeating her mother's past: being the poor woman with a seemingly withholding man (he's actually been far more generous than her father, because he has given her money many times). Equally, James is being like his father: prudent, penny-pinching, cautious, and has adopted his father's disdain for his mother's spending habits (although she did live within their means). Symbolically, Jessica has become like his mother in his eyes (which she isn't because she earns more than his mother ever did and is far more independent generally). However, he has adopted a stance which echoes her mean, withholding father's role accord-ingly: they are playing out their parents' roles.

Jessica and James' Flashpoints

Whenever they remind each other of their respective parents' behaviour a relationship Flashpoint occurs: Jessica's 'reaction' to James is fuelled by her fury at her fathers' injustice to her mother; James' 'reaction' to Jessica's spending is like his father's reaction to his mother's spending. Flashpoints happen because we are emotionally on automatic; we are feeling a range of conflicting emotions rather than thinking rationally. Jessica and James regularly flare up with each other not because it is Jessica and James in the boxing ring, but because there are two sets of parents in there with them, slugging it out. Two's company, six is definitely a crowd.

How parental relationships affect us

We not only have relationships with each other as individuals, but we are also relating to each others' mothers and fathers as well (like Jessica and James, above). When we form love relationships we are hardly conscious this is happening, until we reach a Crunchpoint (usually after many Flashpoints) about money.

Internal mothers and fathers

Growing up we all 'internalise' our mothers and fathers on a psychological level. We are immersed in our parents' language, feelings, attitudes, viewpoints, prejudices and behaviour from the moment we are conceived. Watch any toddler and they will be carefully mimicking what mummy and daddy do and say. We take these role models inside ourselves and they become what we feel is 'natural' to be male or female. When we reach our teens many of us rebel against these internalised models of behaviour in the process of becoming independent individuals. Separating from parents, physically and psychologically, usually occurs over late teens and twenties and provides a focal point for living an independent life. Often we react so violently (especially if parents have been exceedingly strict or chaotic) that we adopt a totally opposite kind of behaviour. There are, of couse, many aspects of our internal parents that we embrace and think of as the 'natural' or 'right' way to think and behave. By the time we reach adulthood many, but not all, of us will have begun to become our true selves, completely separate, in a psychological sense, from our parents. However, for many of us this is a process which can take a long time, even a lifetime in some cases. Internal parents obviously live inside of us on a psychological and emotional level, but there are also real live relatives who have an external effect on how money works in our closest love relationships.

Controlling in-laws and out-laws

Obviously, in-laws and 'out-laws' (if you're not married) can be fantastically financially supportive to a couple finding their way together in today's expensive world. However, in some relationships in-laws and out-laws may actually try to control the couple on the money front because it is a way of wielding power: advising, lending or borrowing, buying property, using inheritance or monetary gifts as 'golden carrots' to shape behaviour, so that the couple is not alone, working things out or fending for themselves. Money can be used to manipulate behaviour or to make children or others feel beholden. This can create emotional complexities because it is unclear who is in charge in the couples' money relationship.

Stepfamilies and lone parents

This gets even more complicated if there are stepfamilies, lone parents, ex-partners/spouses, foster or adoptive parents involved as there are more sets of Emotional Money Baggage to handle. In *His. Hers. Theirs: A Financial Handbook for Stepfamilies* (National Step-family Association, 1995), Tobe Aleksander explains the emotional complexities involved in family life today:

> Stepfamilies may feel that they are at the constant beck and call of someone else – perhaps your or your partner's ex and their new family. Stepfamilies [would] rather break away completely from the threads that bind them . . . they may have the sense that someone outside the immediate family unit has a stranglehold over the financial situation and therefore over much of the way they live.

Similarly, lone parents can find themselves borne down upon by parents, ex-partners, former in- or out-laws and current lovers' expectations concerning money. 'My boyfriend refuses to pay anything towards my two children, even though we've been together a year,' says Lois, a single parent with two sons under five. 'He simply says they are not his responsibility, but it does make life difficult when we want to go on holiday as I have to pay for three against his paying for one.' Lois explains he comes from a traditional Hindu culture, where the birth father pays, and therefore he feels himself beyond any responsibility to care for children which are not legally his. This may be understandable in terms of being what his forbears believed and handed down as right, but it is difficult in terms of having a relationship with a woman in the twenty-first century who is struggling to bring up children alone.

Sandra and Jim's story: handling a controlling father-in-law

If in-laws are controlling a couple, either literally through loans or through Emotional Money Baggage, the couple need to take charge of the situation for themselves – otherwise love dies. Sandra, now divorced, explained how her father tried to control their relationship by giving loans to her ex-husband, a freelance musician. 'My father is quite wealthy and when I mentioned my husband was finding it hard to earn enough and needed money to set himself up in an office, he offered to lend us some money. Although I had reservations about this, Jim leapt at it. After a while I realised my father was actually setting the terms for my relationship with Jim and it was interfering with our marriage. I decided then that it was inappropriate for me ever to go to my father again to borrow as it kept both myself and my husband in a childlike state, not only in relation to my own family, but also in relation to each other.' Sandra's 'internal father' (she had always identified with him, rather than her mother who was a traditional 'housewife' and had no money of her own) was exceedingly anxious about money, while Jim's 'internal father' was largely absent, his own father having died when he was three. 'I realised that Jim had absolutely no role model of a man making money. He just kept saying "the universe will provide", and that universe was me and my family,' says Sandra ruefully. 'Jim's own mother had brought up a family of four boys single-handedly in the 1960s. So what did I do? I ran our relationship financially speaking and single-handedly, too. I was just like my dad and his mum, and he was like my son.'

Sandra and Jim's Crunchpoint

When they borrowed a large amount of money from Sandra's father on the promise that Jim would repay it once his business got going, they reached a Crunchpoint after a year when it was clear Jim would never pay his way. Unable to talk about money constructively together, the relationship didn't last once Sandra became aware of what was happening. 'I'd supported him for so long I was getting resentful. Eventually I said "It's my turn" when I wanted to retrain as a journalist and he point-blank refused.' Jim was not ready to become a responsible adult or an equal partner in his own right. Finally, Sandra felt she had to free herself from the shackles of an over-dependent husband and a controlling father who tried to run their marriage from the outside. Jim and Sandra subsequently divorced.

Handling your own Emotional Money Baggage

Like Sandra and Jim, we all have Emotional Money Baggage because we are all brought up in families, by carers, and/or in institutions, like schools, even children's or foster homes, which teach us specific things about what money means in our relationships. As we have already seen above, Emotional Money Baggage is made up of our particular life experiences, according to class, culture, religion and gender. It also reflects our feelings, beliefs and ideas about how money should be handled in couple relationships. Jessica and James, whom we met at the beginning of this chapter, and who were totally embattled about money, were finally able to sit down and write each other a letter (at my suggestion) about their difficult money situation.

How Jessica and James started 'talking' about money

Jessica wrote honestly and warmly to James about her early child-hood memories of money, about what money meant to her and how sorry she was always to be in debt. Because her letter was thoughtful and reflective, not attacking and blaming, James was able to read it and empathise with her situation. He understood more about her

Emotional Money Baggage. Consequently, he wrote a letter back to her about his austere childhood, revealing his fears for his mother's welfare in an old people's home and the stress of living with unknown credit card bills (incurred on Jessica's shopping sprees). Again, he didn't blame or attack, but told Jessica clearly how he felt – which enabled her to understand his viewpoint and feelings better. In their letters they both made it clear they loved each other and wanted to stay together. Being able to read each other's letters calmly and in private opened up a channel for communication. Of course, not everybody can write letters expressing the intricacies of their emotions, but it is possible to write something about your history which explains more about who you are and where you are coming from, to your partner.

'I suppose I didn't realise how much my behaviour was affecting James,' admitted Jessica afterwards when I visited a second time. 'I guess I'm a bit of a free spender and I hate planning, so that must be very hard for him. I know it would be hard to live with me if I were him.' James had visibly softened because Jessica had taken the brave step of owning up to her own difficulties with money. 'I suppose she never learned to deal with money properly in her crazy family,' he said warmly, 'her parents divorced and she had a lot of unhappiness which, I suppose, I felt was compensated for by her coming from a more privileged background. But I can now see that's not the case. I guess I'm a bit rigid, which is foreign to her.' Less angry and defensive, James was also able to admit that he could go out and splurge money himself on golf clubs, designer clothes, even cars, when the mood took him, so he knew the pleasure of spending. The only difference being he had the money to do so (because he saved and planned his money), whereas Jessica did neither.

Clearly their problems were not over: issues such as getting married and planning her big bills were still unresolved, but they had made a start on the more pressing everyday problem of managing their money together. More importantly, they were beginning to be able to talk more calmly about the dreaded subject of money, rather than fight all the time. This meant their rows had abated not only in their frequency, but ferocity. This doesn't mean they won't continue to experience money Flashpoints, but it might mean handling them differently so Crunchpoints also diminish. People usually only attack or explode with each other when they feel utterly exasperated.

Communicating more openly and honestly about money can help save a relationship from the destructively repetitive ups and downs of money crises and fights. This means one or both partners have to learn to count to ten and put themselves in their partner's shoes before launching into the usual speech or sulk. Developing an effective means of communicating with each other in a positive, non-judgmental, empathic way about money is crucial to stopping money fights. Of course, it takes time, determination and some basic listening and negotiating skills to do this. (We will return to this in more detail in chapter 10.)

Emotional Money Baggage leaves each of us with our own particular Money Patterns, or dominant types of behaviour, which represent the ideas, attitudes, assumptions and values we have developed as a way of surviving in and negotiating the world. When we characterise ourselves or others as 'mean' or 'generous' or 'thrifty' or 'foolish with money' we are describing Money Patterns. Understanding what these Money Patterns are, how they work and how they affect our closest love relationships is examined further in the next chapter.

Emotional Money Baggage checklist

This chapter has been about identifying your Emotional Money Baggage (EMB) about money. As a final check, ask yourself the following (and write down your answers in a notebook or on a computer file if it's helpful):

- Who am I more like, my mother or my father, in terms of EMB about money?
- Does my partner/spouse/ex remind me of my mother or my father in terms of EMB about money?
- How do/did we hook together?
- How am I not like my mother and/or father regarding money?
- How is my partner/spouse/ex not like my mother and/or father regarding money?
- What one thing could I do to stop fighting about money?
- What one thing would I like my partner/spouse/ex to do to stop fighting about money?

- What's the main thing I have learned about myself about money?
- What's the main thing I have learned about my partner about money?
- How would I like our relationship to be about money?
- What am I going to do about it?
- What would I like 'us' to do about it?
- What's my next step?

2

Money Patterns and Money Relationships

If this be not love it is madness, and then it is pardonable – Nay yet a more certain sign than all this: I give thee my money.

William Congreve

Money Patterns

Tightwad, spendthrift, skinflint, golddigger, tightarse, squanderer, meanie, prodigal, scrooge, big spender – there are endless (usually pejorative) words which describe our Money Patterns. If money makes the world go round, our Money Patterns can make us go round relating to our nearest and dearest concerning money in a unique, but fairly robotic, kind of way. We saw in chapter 1 that our Emotional Money Baggage is the sum of our individual experience in life (good and bad) and we tend to lug all sorts of unsorted emotions, beliefs and ideas about money into our current relationships as a consequence. Our Money Patterns, on the other hand, are the main way we *behave* in everyday life on the financial front. 'He's a miser' we say of a friend who is careful with money; 'She's a spendthrift' we say of someone who loves going shopping.

Know your Money Patterns

If you are reading this book because money is a source of strife in your current (past or last) relationship, then becoming aware – fully aware – of your own Money Patterns can be a major step towards gaining greater clarity and, hopefully, harmony in love. However, it is necessary to understand more about just how you and your partner's Money Patterns may be fitting together if you want to stop fighting about money.

For the purpose of this book I have identified nine main Money Patterns. Of course, a brief description of a Money Pattern does not do justice to the complexity of human psychology. A Money Pattern is really a caricature because it is a sweeping description of a behaviour. Nonetheless, it is possible to describe certain patterns of behaviour generally as there will be a grain of truth at the core. You may or may not be aware of what these are exactly either in your own or your partner's case. And even if you are aware, you may not fully understand what they mean in terms of your relationship. Nevertheless, it can be extremely helpful to identify and think about what kind of Money Patterns both you and your partner *mainly* manifest when you are trying to disentangle why you keep fighting about money with each other. The main ones are:

- Planners
- Hoarders
- Spenders
- Worriers
- Gamblers
- Golddiggers
- Doormats
- Ostriches
- Eco-Warriors.

If you would like to do a Quiz to find out more about your Money Patterns, turn to the Appendix on p. 223.

Nine main Money Patterns
Planners

Money means business. Planners are shrewd with their money. They make sure they read the financial pages of the newspapers and invest their money wisely. Planners take calculated risks while being prudent on a day-to-day basis. They can be hard-nosed about money and are good at bargaining. Their boundaries are rock solid and they can't be taken for a ride. They always know the going rate for the job or commodity. Planners seem unemotional about money, but in actual fact their very dryness may denote having been brought up in financial stringency or chaos. Planners need security and make a virtue out of being a financial whizz. They like being in control and find it hard to trust.

Hoarders

Hoarders are very careful about what they spend and always save, no matter how little they earn. Hoarders put 'value for money' above everything else. When purchasing they go for durability and quality, while keeping an eye on the price. Tough bargainers, it almost hurts hoaders to be generous (and even when they are, they feel somehow it's been extracted from them). Cautious by nature, hoarders will probably have been brought up either in relative poverty or at least will have had monetary values rammed down their throats by thrifty parents. Conversely, they might have been brought up in chaos, which has made them react by hoarding. At one end of the spectrum, they can be prudent savers, at the other, downright mean and obsessive. In Oscar Wilde's famous words, Hoarders tend to 'know the price of everything and the value of nothing'.

Spenders

Nothing makes a spender happier than splurging what they haven't got. Spenders live for the moment, enjoy having new things and being generous to others. However, they are often overcome with remorse and guilt having splurged. Consequently, they hate planning ahead and loathe opening statements and bills as they fear burgeoning debts. Unfortunately, not facing mounting expenditure means the problem gets worse while Spenders will continue to deny there's a problem (often until it's too late). At root, Spenders feel very insecure and are often trying to buy love, security and self-esteem.

They seldom have savings, usually only debts. They can be from poor, middling or rich backgrounds, the origin of their spending usually lying in a sense of emotional, rather than material, deprivation. The Spenders' maxim is: 'When the going gets tough, the tough go shopping' – so the going gets tougher.

Worriers

Basically, worriers fear money and feel they have no real control over it or access to it. They often worry about minor details and lose sight of the bigger picture. Often lost in the past, full of regret, Worriers tend not to face the present and fear thinking about the future. Worriers fear being poor (and have 'bag lady' or 'dosser' nightmare fantasies), yet also fear investing. They can get very stuck and stubborn in relationships. Worriers can be exceedingly thrifty, but don't really save wisely or plan for the future properly as they fear the unforeseen, including facing death. They tend to live minute by minute, buried in anxiety. They don't trust themselves, so would never have a credit card or take a risk.

Gamblers

Gamblers are eternal optimists, and live, like Spenders, very much in the moment without thinking of the consequences. They enjoy the endorphin and adrenaline high of taking risks: at the dogs, on the Lottery, betting down the pub, in the office sweepstake, at the roulette table and in business. They believe they will bounce back, even when they lose large sums; they think it will all come right in the end (even when it doesn't). They dislike being broke, but can ride losing everything because they simply start all over again – with the next risk.

Golddiggers

Not always obvious to prospective partners, Golddiggers believe the world owes them a living. Both Golddigging men and women attach themselves to others, hoping to be kept, fed, nurtured, housed and spoilt. Deep inside Golddiggers are both angry and empty, and are actually taking revenge on their past through hurting someone in the present. Often Golddiggers don't feel grown-up enough to be totally responsible for their own survival, so they want others to do it for them (the world owes them a living). Often having lacked adequate parenting, they seek substitute parents to look after them in adult life. Golddiggers find it hard, if not impossible, to love; instead they trick others into feeling they are needed by them.

Doormats

Doormats don't have any healthy boundaries about money. They give away what they have, often in the hope people will like them. They don't spend on themselves, like Spenders, but they will splurge on others happily. Doormats share everything they have, and more, without being able to hold back what they need for their own lives. They can be very gullible to sales patter and end up putting all their savings into non-existent things or bad investments like timeshare funds. They are prime targets for Golddiggers and Gamblers of all kinds.

Ostriches

Ostriches dig a little hole, bury their heads in it, and hope against hope that money problems are going to disappear – all by themselves. They fear looking money issues straight in the eye, never open bills or bank statements, seldom consider the consequences of either spending or hoarding, believe everything will work out in the end (magically) and blame others (and governments) for making life so hard. Ostriches almost deliberately keep themselves ignorant about money matters and can be infuriatingly naive in relationships. In fact, they just don't want to know about filthy lucre. Other people can do that for them. If a partner wants to talk with an Ostrich about a money problem, they run away: 'Problem? What problem? It'll sort itself out.'

Eco-Warriors

Eco-Warriors are serious about changing the world and its destructive behaviour based on greed and capitalism. Eco-Warriors rightly believe it is possible to heal the earth's damage by each of us taking responsibility for consuming less, especially in the West and industrialised nations. They can be extremely frugal and worry a great deal about what they consume and how. Their boundaries are very strong concerning spending on frivolities, reading labels on jars, being vegetarian and thoughtful about consumption. However, they can verge on the obsessive and be judgmental if partners are less disciplined. They can also suffer guilt if they spend on something which is less than 'PC'. They like being in control and are often fuelled by rage at others' over-consumption and cruelty.

Patterned streaks

Although our Money Patterns denote the main, overriding characteristic concerning money, it would be simplistic to say people are solely one thing or the other. Most of us have 'patterned streaks' of different types running through us, like a proverbial stick of seaside rock. A Hoarder may have Spender, Worrier or Ostrich patterned streaks, where occasionally they splash out on something special for themselves or a loved one, live in fear of the consequences of spending too much or simply want to forget all about it; whereas a Planner may live life in a wonderfully ordered way and burst out and go wild and take a financial risk typical of a Gambler. It's more than likely that you will have a mixture of more than one type of Money Pattern, even though one will probably predominate. It's also possible that your 'type' may change over your lifetime, not only according to your circumstances, but also in relation to whoever is your current partner and/or what your family or work situation is like. It is useful to understand which patterned streaks accompany your individual Money Pattern, as this explains why you or your partner sometimes do things which seem to be confusingly 'out of character'.

Mirror-Image relationships

Some couples seem to choose each other because they simply reflect each other, like mirror images. It's the 'two peas in a pod' syndrome, where you get two happy Hoarders together, who love being thrifty, always make their own sandwiches on a day trip out and get excited about saving elastic bands; or two Spenders, who always spend up to and beyond their plastic limits on a regular basis and couldn't save a penny if a gun was pointed at their heads. People who mirror each other may well be happy because there is seemingly little conflict. They often believe they are one person joined at the hip in a 'two-hearts-that-beat-as-one' kind of way. However, they may feel frustrated and bored by the other over time because they secretly desire one of them to break the Money Pattern mould and either splash out or start saving. It can also threaten the relationship if one of them wants to change either themselves or how they operate together: individuality is not usually encouraged or even tolerated.

Sue and Dave's story

Sue and Dave both come from manual working-class backgrounds. Sue, thirty-five, works in a post office on the stationery counter and is good with figures; Dave, thirty-seven, works in a local garage as a mechanic. They don't have any children as both come from large families and feel they want to enjoy holidays, their house and garden, hill walking and bike riding, without parental responsibilities. Dave spends a lot of time tinkering in the garage – he collects 1950s cars, strips them down, does them up and sells them – or in their extensive vegetable garden. Sue keeps house and loves sewing. As a sideline, she makes children's clothes for relatives' children and for private customers – the money from sales going into their annual holiday fund.

Dave and Sue met at school when they were fifteen and have been a couple ever since (apart from one short split after ten years when Sue thought she had fallen out of love). She hadn't, and after living together for a further five years, they eventually married five years ago. 'I suppose we just have very moderate tastes,' explains Sue as she sews on the kitchen table, 'I was brought up not to waste food or money and as my mum brought up eight of us single-handedly I think it's stuck.' Dave's family was similar, if different, as both his parents looked after four children together: 'My dad was a factory worker and my mum stayed at home,' he says, 'but we always had food on the table and clean clothes.'

Dave was a 'red-nappy baby' as his father was a socialist union organiser and imbued his family with a strong sense of social responsibility. 'I remember my dad coming home and putting his wages on the kitchen table and he and my mother parcelling money up into different shoe boxes. We always saved for this and that – holidays, Christmas, clothes, shoes. I saw them talking about money – yes, and worrying about it at times – but I never felt there was any unfairness at home.' As a consequence, Dave's Emotional Money Baggage is fairly unencumbered. He has always worked, saved and striven to think clearly about money. His predominant Money

Pattern is that of a Planner, but he has Hoarder and Doormat streaks. 'I don't know much about high finance, but I do know money doesn't grow on trees,' he says wryly, 'and I find it hard to spend on myself.'

Sue's Emotional Money Baggage is more loaded having seen her mother's endless battle to make ends meet. Sue got her first Saturday job at twelve and knew she had to leave school to earn a crust at sixteen – further or higher education being out of the question. Sue is more fearful about money and admits she's probably mainly a Worrier, with Spender and Ostrich streaks. 'I suppose I saw my mother struggling hard to look after us and we never had holidays,' she admits. 'Once the eldest two went to work they had to bring money home. I suppose I felt you had to be very careful with money or you wouldn't survive.' Even so, Sue and Dave say they are very happy with their lot. Neither have been embroiled in other long-term relationships and neither have dependants or debts. 'I sometimes would love to throw caution to the wind though,' says Sue, laughing, 'I feel we're very boring really. We have a week in Scotland or Wales each year and that's it. Sometimes I'd love to splash out and go somewhere exotic, because I feel I've missed out on a lot of exciting things in life, but we could never afford it.' And neither of them would ever be happy to put a foreign holiday on a credit card. 'Anyway, I'd never sleep again worrying about paying it back,' says Sue candidly.

They have fought about money on occasion, however. Sue's worrying irritates Dave who strives to stay rational at all times; and his planning tendencies have annoyed her when she's wanted to splash out. 'I have gone and spent on a pair of expensive shoes before now and Dave has gone nuts,' says Sue honestly, 'and then I've worried about telling him for days afterwards. I think we get things out of proportion sometimes because we're so careful most of the time.' This is typical of their occasional Flashpoints. However, they are usually able to talk things through (or Sue is able to control her spending) so they have never yet come to a Money Relationship Crunchpoint.

Dave agrees: 'The bottom line is I can trust Sue as she would never go totally berserk and bung things on a credit card without talking to me first.' Mirror-Image partnerships can be very blissful as both partners easily understand and agree to the financial rules by which they live. Both usually hate strife and can trust each other enormously. However, Mirror-Image relationships can become stifling, especially if one of you wants to change the ground rules or do something a bit more adventurous, as in Sue's occasional breakouts.

Chalk-and-Cheese relationships

Conversely, the 'Chalk-and-Cheese' dynamic occurs when partners choose each other because they are fascinated by someone who is diametrically opposed to themselves: the old 'opposites attract' adage. This can create a very strong relationship: for instance, a Golddigger and a Doormat fit nicely together because their roles feed each others'; a Spender and Hoarder may fight, but they may also help to keep each other in check by striving to balance each other out financially; an Ostrich and a Gambler can pair perfectly as the former ignores the latter's monetary excesses. Again, it's useful to bear in mind that within any main Money Pattern there will be patterned streaks of behaviour, so couples in conflict ought to look beyond the predominant Money Pattern and see what they've got in common or even identify what is different.

Deepak and Irene's story

Self-made businessman Deepak, thirty-seven, is a Gambler. Nothing turns him on more than a risky deal or starting a new enterprise. He left a secure job in the retail industry five years ago, taking a good redundancy package (his firm was 'downshifting') and, ever the optimist, he saw it as a once-in-a-lifetime chance to 'go it alone'. Deepak has been married to Irene, thirty-three, who trained as an occupational therapist, before they had their two children, Joshie (eight) and Sophie (five). Irene is mainly a Hoarder and shivers visibly remembering Deepak's risk-taking antics. 'When we'd just had Joshie, Deepak came home with a new BMW. I couldn't believe it. We needed nappies and he'd used all our savings on a flash new car. I hit the roof.' But Deepak smoothed this Flashpoint over with his usual charm and optimism: 'How else should I celebrate the birth of my first son?'

'Deepak doesn't tell me much about his business because he knows it worries me,' explains Irene. (He is burrowing away at his work in their large loft conversion and says, charmingly, that he may be able to spare me a few minutes later.) 'Deepak's always evasive when I ask him about money,' Irene says. 'In the early days he tried to explain things to me, but I was always pinning him down to detail. He likes talking in broad strokes and jargon, I want to know how much is coming in and when.'

Linguistic barriers about money are not their only difficulty. When they decided to have children, Irene made Deepak promise he would go and get a 'proper' job if they couldn't make ends meet. 'He lost a huge contract that he'd worked on for ages just as I gave birth to Sophie,' Irene remembers with a wince. 'He had to take out a huge business loan, which I was terrified of. I have no idea now how much he owes as he won't tell me, but I often have nightmares about the house being repossessed.' Irene clearly has a lot of Worrier streaks. She comes from what she calls a 'lower-middle-class' background, where her mother worked in a shop (a branch of Debenhams) and her father was a clerk in the civil service. Money was always tight and Irene's Emotional Money Baggage is clearly geared towards creating financial security through being prudent and saving regularly.

So why end up with Deepak? 'It's crazy, but I met him at a disco held at the hospital I was working in and Deepak was a friend of a consultant and came that evening for a laugh. He was so handsome, such fun, so full of life, energy, confidence, I thought "Wow, I'd like some of that".' For Irene it was love at first sight. Deepak was dating someone else at the time, but, true to character, he ended the relationship abruptly as the whirlwind romance took off with Irene. 'I was literally swept off my feet with champagne, dinners out, perfume, trips to Paris. I thought I'd found a millionaire.'

Deepak emerges for a ten-minute coffee break and I try to get him talking about money. He is definitely charismatic, rather than classically good-looking, and has a forceful, energetic personality. 'I hated my job, felt totally stifled, and I guess I'm one of those people who if their butt's not on the line feels bored to death.' Does he worry about failing? 'Never.' Not even in the dead of night when there are bills to pay and a contract's not been signed? 'Nope, I leave the worrying to Irene.' He says growing up in the Hindu religion has stopped him worrying as he simply lives in the present and leaves things to fate. Irene grimaces, then smiles: then their eyes meet and they both laugh.

Clearly still besotted with each other, Irene is a down-to-earth foil to Deepak's heady risk-taking. For them the chalk-and-cheese tension keeps their marriage alive. 'The bottom line for me is the children, their security and their futures,' says Irene adamantly. 'I've just gone back to work part-time and I see it as my duty to save for their education. Deepak thinks I'm crazy because he thinks money comes and goes and he can always find some, but I'm not so sure.' Deepak doesn't feel inclined to reveal much about his background in the few minutes we meet, but Irene fills me in. 'In fact Deepak's father is a bit of a failure,' she explains, 'he was a wealthy businessman who emigrated to Britain from Uganda in the 1970s when Idi Amin was killing Asians. He lost everything and was heartbroken, finding it hard to start again in a cold and strange country. His health suffered, he made some bad deals and even turned to drink. His family helped him sober up, but Deepak says he never really recovered his former power. I personally think Deepak wants to show his old man how it can be done – and in this country which has been so hostile sometimes – it's some kind of macho thing. Plus, his mother is a terrible worrier, like me.' Deepak's Emotional Money Baggage is pretty loaded up with the spectre of his father's failure and decline and the weight of his mother's incessant worrying. He also had to support his family (including four brothers and sisters) from a young age. Yet, instead of seeking security in his own adult life, he is almost repeating his father's situation (taking risks, starting again), while trying to prove he can do it better; at root, he is motivated by basic male competition and fear of failure.

Deepak and Irene haven't come to a Crunchpoint yet, although they have survived several serious Flashpoints recently. 'I have contemplated leaving him when we've had some awful money fights. The last one a few months ago was after I'd found out his personal overdraft was £15,000. I was utterly shocked, I thought it was about £3,000. I had absolutely no idea it was that big. Deepak reassures me the business will cover it and I just have to believe he knows what he's doing. He knows now though that the bottom line is that if he damages the children or puts their future at risk in any way, then I'll leave.'

Unravelling feelings about money

When couples fight about money they are usually brimming over with feelings of fear, outrage and frustration. One partner simply can't understand why something which seems so blatantly obvious to them is completely foreign to the other. Trying to understand your own and your partner's Emotional Money Baggage and identify your Money Patterns can be a major step towards unravelling why your emotions are so intense about money in your relationship. Recognising how you and your partner's Money Patterns fit together can also help ease tensions. The first question I asked all interviewees about money was simply 'What do you feel about money?' The response was telling: 'I hate it' or 'I love it' or 'It makes me sick that it's so important' or 'I want loads of it'. One thing is clear: the subject of money is a subject full of feeling.

What sorts of feelings get attached to money?

Ask yourself which of the following words fit your feelings about money (tick as many as you like):

- evil
- exciting
- essential
- thrilling
- wonderful
- frightening
- pleasurable
- sickening

- necessary
- corrupting
- lovely
- numbing
- sexy
- painful
- fun
- stupid

- empowering
- nauseating
- worrying
- elusive
- luxurious
- terrifying
- healing

Look carefully at what you have ticked. What do they tell you about your feelings about money?

Self-esteem, value and worth

We attach feelings of self-esteem, value and worth to money, believing it is literally either the root of all evil, the meaning of life or a source of pure joy. It is, in itself, none of these things. In a society which is driven by money it is easy to lose sight of the fact that money is a mere commodity, a means to an end. Our own Emotional Money Baggage and Money Patterns make money into something fraught and loaded (literally) with meaning. Your feelings about money will dictate how you see yourself, your partner and how you choose to live. Money connects us all to the crudest of our survival drives. Obviously, you need money to live. Without money in our highly industrialised society, life is an impossible, miserable struggle. But to measure yourself and your worth entirely by what you earn and own is to restrict your emotional and psychological growth as a person. This is why people on low wages, unemployed, staying home with children, or underemployed because they are disabled, are often treated by others (or see themselves) as valueless. We forget this is society's judgment, rather than a true measure of what any human being is really worth as a unique individual. True value cannot be measured in money, even thought most of us have 'bought' the false notion that it is.

Yet, some people who overvalue money and what it means for them as a measure of themselves and their worth can end up playing psychological games with their partners as a means of wielding power. These power games and accompanying addictive behaviours are often the cause of money battles, which can be damaging not only to the people involved, but to the relationship as a whole. (We will return to this in chapter 3: Power Games and Money Addiction.)

Conflict

Conflict occurs in relationships for all sorts of reasons: we feel misunderstood, judged, hurt, intolerant, mistrustful, irritated. Feelings brim over to the point where each person is no longer able to think, and a row ensues because we feel provoked into defending ourselves or need to attack to feel better. Some people hate conflict and avoid it at all cost; others relish it as it makes them feel closer to the person they are fighting with. Most relationships can tolerate a certain level of conflict, otherwise they would be completely dead. However, conflict can be destructive if it is repetitive and especially if it becomes violent. Because money brings up such strong feelings about survival and personal worth, money fights can be extremely heated. People can feel betrayed, abused or cornered, because fear and anger is at the core of their feelings. Of course, a lot of the feelings vented in rows tend to be loaded with past Emotional Money Baggage.

Conflict about money tends to occur because:

- our Money Patterns conflict: we simply cannot understand why the other person is behaving as they are – so we can't empathise with them;
- we can't understand why the other person doesn't agree with our own viewpoint – we feel hurt by their lack of empathy;
- we are intolerant of differences: we have a firm belief that our Money Pattern is 'better' and that we are 'right' and our partner is 'wrong'. We expect the other person to be like ourselves and are baffled that they are different;
- our Money Patterns cause us to dislike ourselves. We want our partner to sort us out and are furious when they don't;
- our love is conditional: we find it hard to accept our partner for who they are and try to change them – trying to make a Gambler into a Hoarder or a Spender into an Eco-Warrior. Love is given only on the condition that the person changes (a recipe for disaster);
- Emotional Money Baggage is running the relationship, rather than the individuals involved ('My last girlfriend stole my money, so I'm not trusting you'; 'My ex was mean, so I'm spending your money fast').

Conflicts about money can only begin to be resolved in relationships if you start from understanding that:

- the other person is an entirely separate person from you in every way, no matter how romantic your love is, or how long you've been together or married;
- your current partner is a completely different person from your ex, no matter how much they remind you of them;
- no two people think or act the same way (even if they seem very similar);
- people change over time, so don't make assumptions that what you've always done will continue to be so;
- you are not your mother/father (or in their position) even if it seems very similar or familiar;

- you learn to respect the other person's difference;
- you listen to their viewpoint without judgment or criticism.

Money Relationships

When two distinct individuals come together and fall in love something unique happens: they create a third entity, their relationship. If a relationship is working well, it will be controlled and managed by neither party: it will have a life of its own. Similarly, when two people come together in a close, loving relationship, they will also be creating their own particular Money Relationship. This will reflect the relationship as a whole as well as the individuals concerned. The whole process of working out whether you are compatible with someone or not takes a lot of understanding, patience and negotiation on the money front. Couples have to:

- learn about each other's histories and to trust each other;
- communicate about sensitive or difficult feelings;
- work out their individual and common goals;
- put up with (or ignore) each other's irritating habits;
- handle and accept each other's families, friends and even children;
- agree the relationship's money goals.

Nurturing love

A good Money Relationship is crucial to the success of a love relationship and is something which needs nurturing, like the relationship itself. Of course, some relationships work better than others, simply because of the combination of individuals with their respective Money Patterns and Emotional Money Baggage. The trick is to learn how to identify them and then work with them constructively to help love flourish.

Relationships where this happens can be relaxed, joyful, fun, purposeful, productive, sexually satisfying, supportive and mutual. Of course, there will be everyday tensions, misunderstandings, even rows, but these can usually be sorted out fairly constructively. Indeed, in a healthy relationship these arguments can create an opportunity for both parties to gain insights into each other and themselves. The relationship will grow because they get closer through sorting out a misunderstanding. In these sorts of relationships co-operation is the mainstay. No one calls the shots, but ideas emerge from one or both partners and then are negotiated.

Understanding your Money Relationship

A Money Relationship is tested when a couple make a decision and want to implement it. It might be moving in together, or buying a flat or house, trying for a baby, or saving to travel round the world. If a Money Relationship is working well, the couple will be able to work as a team: planning each step of the way, negotiating difficulties, working together towards a common goal, making personal sacrifices where necessary. The type of Money Relationship you have will affect not only how these decisions are made, but how they are implemented. For example, imagine a couple are living together and want to buy a house. What might happen?

Mirror-Image couples' Money Relationship

Her: 'Look, it's nuts paying such high rent for our flat now – why don't we take out a mortgage and buy our own place?'

Him: 'You know, I've been thinking that, too, recently, but it's quite a step.'

Her: 'I know, but let's at least find out what it costs.'

Him: 'OK, why not, let's go for it.'

Her: 'Shall I look for good deals on the Internet, I've got access to a PC at work?'

Him: 'Yep, and I'll look in the papers and phone round some mortgage companies.'

Her: 'Great.'

A satisfactory conclusion. Their Money Relationship has an agreed agenda and they are able to negotiate successfully. This kind of conversation is typical in a Mirror-Image type of relationship, where couples tacitly understand each other and neither has to 'win'. When it comes to buying a house, these couples usually manage to work out sensible ways of handling money which benefits them as a team working together for a common goal. Co-operation is the name of this money game.

Chalk-and-Cheese couples' Money Relationship

Conversely, there are Chalk-and-Cheese couples where they usually have completely diverse ideas and find it hard to agree. These relationships create the most friction, with neither really being able to give way to, listen to or understand the other.

Her: 'Look, it's nuts paying such high rent for our flat, why don't we take out a mortgage and buy our own place?'

Him: 'You're crazy. We haven't got that kind of money, I've got to pay off my overdraft and credit card bill. Anyway, I thought we were going on a long holiday this year?'

Her: 'But it doesn't make sense to pour money down the drain – we're not investing in our future at all.'

Him: 'Hey, I like having a landlord, it takes all the responsibility for maintaining the place off our shoulders and we can move on whenever we feel like it.'

Her: 'But we can't go on like this for ever – I thought we were going to make some plans for the future?'

Him: 'Well, we've got plenty of time to think about all that long-term stuff. I think we need a good holiday first, blow the expense, before we start getting bogged down in buying property.'

No real conclusion. Their Money Relationship has two separate agendas and they can't agree what is to be negotiated. Stalemate. This kind of Chalk-and-Cheese discussion can end in tears very rapidly as both partners have distinctly different spending priorities and ideas about money and therefore find it hard to reach each other across the abyss. Fierce individualism is the name of this money game.

Positive and negative Money Relationships

The Money Relationship of the first couple is compatible; the Money Relationship of the second couple is incompatible. Your Money Relationship is a third entity, like your relationship itself, reflecting how the dynamics in your relationship really work. The more intimate, trusting, harmonious and open a love relationship is the healthier the Money Relationship will be as there are no awful secrets or repetitive money wrangles, which can be a constant drain on the energy of the couple both as individuals and as a unit. A relationship which is built on mistrust, tit-for-tat, secrets and lies and lack of intimacy will probably have an unhealthy Money Relationship, reflecting that fact. This doesn't mean everyone has to be a Mirror-Image couple to agree – that would be both impossible and boring. But it does mean understanding why you and your partner come at money so differently.

Acknowledge your differences

Sometimes a relationship which seemed to be based on a couple being mirror images of each other turns out really to be Chalk-and-Cheese. We often fail to see a person as they really are *because we see what we want to see*. Sometimes a change in personal circumstances or external pressures helps to reveal all. If you are desperate for a relationship to work, especially if one or both of you wants a baby, to buy a house or set up a business, it is quite easy to ignore the aspects of the person you don't like because you hope, in time, they will change. This is a major mistake: people are who they are and we form relationships on the basis of who we are, in the here and now. It usually fails if you enter a relationship with a hidden agenda, thinking you can change somebody and tailor them to your needs. As couples get to know each other better they begin to see who the other person really is, and who they are in relation to them. Disappointment can set in. This only usually happens if you have painted some kind of rosy glow over your partner's foibles or if you have tried to make them into your psychological twin. If you can see your partner as different from yourself, right from the start, you will have more possibility of relationship success. This means Chalk-and-Cheese relationships can work just as well as Mirror-Image ones (or even better), as there is an acknowledgment from the start that you are two separate individuals. You can complement each other, rather than live in permanent conflict, because you can learn to appreciate and work with each other's different or opposing viewpoint, especially over the touchy subject of money.

In summary (and whether Mirror-Image or Chalk-and-Cheese):

- *Some Money Relationships are positive.* They are constructive, fruitful, healthy, thriving, productive, even fun and relatively easy to manage. Money isn't really a problem in these relationships. This is especially true of couples who love each other as separate individuals, who respect each others' differences, and who remain fairly separate, emotionally speaking. They usually have commonly agreed goals and compatible Money Patterns.
- *Some Money Relationships are negative.* These Money Relationships are often unhealthily lop-sided, with one partner's Money Patterns dominating the other's. Lack of communication, trust and the unequal power at the core of this kind of relationship is usually reflected in the nature of the Money Relationship. Negative Money Relationships are fruitless, argumentative, unhealthy and hard to manage because there is little or no communication.

Main causes of money fights

Of course, most of us have Money Relationships somewhere in between, with both positive and negative elements. However, if you are fighting about money it may well be that the negative aspects are dominating the positive ones. You need to stand back from your relationship as a whole and ask yourself:

- Do I trust my partner/spouse's judgment about using money?
- Are they fair to me? Our children? Themselves?
- Do I know my partner/spouse's salary/wages/assets? Do they know mine?
- Do I know my partner/spouse's debts and dependants? Do they know mine?
- How easy is it to communicate about money? Very easy? Easy? Difficult? Impossible?
- Is our Money Relationship more positive or negative overall?

Look at your answers. Do they tend towards the positive or negative? If you feel your Money Relationship is fairly positive, are there any areas you'd like to improve? If, however, your Money Relationship is fairly negative, what needs to change? Couples can get very embattled trying to change each other's Money Patterns, particularly if they are in a Chalk-and-Cheese relationship. It's important to remember that you chose each other in the first place, perhaps because you were similar or maybe because you were so different. Your Money Patterns will be creating Flashpoints in everyday life. If unchecked, your Flashpoints can accumulate and escalate into a major Crunchpoint, whereby your relationship is threatened with falling apart completely. Thus, if you are fighting about money constantly then you are going to have to stand back and understand clearly how your Money Patterns are hooking together and your Money Relationship is operating in both negative and positive ways. You will need to eliminate the negative and build on the positive to move forward together. (We will return to this in chapter 10.)

Money Relationship goals

If a relationship is not going to stagnate, it is important that you work out short-, medium- and long-term money goals together. These may only evolve over time, especially if a relationship is new and you are not sure whether it is just an affair or is going to turn into something longer and stronger. All relationships are unique. However, if you reach a point where you have acknowledged you are in love with each other and you want to make a commitment, this is the time to start thinking about your Money Relationship goals. Sometimes it will be just deciding to go on holiday together, or it might be one of you wants to retrain or study full-time. Perhaps you are moving into the flat or house of one of you, or have decided to buy property together. Whatever, it is important to set, say, a three-month goal and see if you can reach it together. If you are unable to agree, or neither of you sticks to the plan, or one of you sabotages it, it will tell you not only a great deal about the state and nature of your current relationship, but also the problems you may be up against in your Money Relationship. If rows escalate once you have agreed goals, this will also tell you how your Money Patterns are working (or not working) together.

Setting goals

Just how people set goals is unique to them. For some, it occurs over a beery chat in the pub; for others it happens late at night on the pillow after love-making; for yet others it happens over steaming mugs of tea at the kitchen table or in front of a computer spreadsheet. The main thing is to be clear what your goals are and stick to them, without policing each other. Write them down, put them somewhere safe, and get on with life. One woman told me she had supported her boyfriend through his study course for three years while she worked as an English teacher. 'Then I wanted to become self-employed. We were living in a rented room together. I thought it would be fine, as he was now working full-time, until he looked at me aghast and said "No way".' She thought their relationship was set up on mutual lines, whereas for her partner it was a one-way street. Needless to say, she left the relationship soon after, somewhat broken-hearted, but much wiser about how she would approach her next relationship on the money front. If a relationship can't get past this kind of Crunchpoint it is usually going nowhere and the sooner you find this out the better.

Money Patterns and Money Relationship checklist

This chapter has been about identifying your Money Patterns and type of Money Relationship. It looked at the main ways you behave about money – and the feelings they evoke in your relationship. It also discussed the type of Money Relationship you might have – Mirror-Image or Chalk-and-Cheese, positive or negative. Ask yourself:

- What have you identified as your main Money Pattern?
- What is your partner's/spouse's/ex's main Money Pattern?
- Are you a Chalk-and-Cheese or Mirror-Image couple?
- What are your patterned streaks?
- What are your partner's/spouse's/ex's patterned streaks?
- Would you like to have a different Money Pattern? If so, what?
- Can you see how your Money Patterns together create conflict?
- Are you able to work as a team positively or do you defend your positions as fierce individuals?

- What money decisions would you like to make as a couple in the next three months, six months, year?
- What's your next step?

3

Power Games and Money Addiction

For money has a power above the stars and fate to manage love.
Samuel Butler

Imagine what it would be like to be able to meet a prospective life partner and say 'Hey, I'm a terrible spender, I'm £10,000 in debt and want to find someone to bail me out and help me learn to handle money. How about you?' 'Me? Oh, Scrooge is my middle name. I recycle all my tea bags ten times over and never have the heating on before 1 December. I'm a real killjoy. Nice to meet you.' Wouldn't it be so much easier if we could lay out all of our Emotional Money Baggage and Money Patterns – like wares on a market stall – and choose each other for a Money Relationship on the basis of a best fit? Indeed, that's what well-meaning friends who set up blind dates, dating agencies and arranged marriages do to some extent. We could have money CVs or relationship inventories telling of our debts, bad investments, penny-pinching or squandering ways. Instead, we're left trying to find a partner in a kind of romantic lottery. It's notoriously difficult to see someone new clearly for who they really are when you first meet, particularly when you are in the first flush of lust or love. 'How was I so taken in?' we cry as we are flung back on the relationship ropes, bleeding after fifteen rounds with a penny-pinching love-rat. 'He seemed so wonderful at first, showering me with roses, perfume, champagne – how did he end up making me walk home when I didn't have my taxi fare?' Or maybe, 'She found me so sexy and desirable at first, she couldn't keep her hands off me, so how was I to know it was my Gold Card she was really after?'

Money games people play

The psychological games people play about money tell us a lot about them as individuals. Of course, not everyone plays games and some people pride themselves on being straightforward, fair and honest about money. These people usually have a good time financially in relationships because money has not become a battleground, although they might row about other contentious things with their partner instead. However, even though one partner might be very straight about money, it doesn't follow that the other one will be. Which is why it is important to understand the money power games people can play as they are often an indicator of a partner's

- *status* – social standing, class, cultural importance;
- *success* – having money is being a success, not having it signifies failure;
- *intelligence* – having money means being smart, shrewd, clever, streetwise;
- *sexual attractiveness* – having a big wad denotes being sexually potent, whether male or female. Money has definite pulling power.

Power games can become a source of deep grief and pain in a mismatched relationship. They may not be headline-grabbers, because the amounts of money involved are small, or the outcomes not particularly dramatic. But they can be destructive, even though they are quite subtle or hidden and would take some therapy to reveal. We need to understand money power games for two main reasons. First, they are a breeding ground for money fights in relationships and therefore it's essential to get wise to them: forewarned is forearmed. Second, once you understand the games which are being played out in your relationship you can do something about them. One of the first and most popular psychology books, *Games People Play* (Penguin, 1964) by Dr Eric Berne (which is still in print), explains how mind games are handed down in human relationships:

> Games are passed on from generation to generation. The favoured game of any individual can be traced back to his (sic) parents and grandparents, and forward to his children; they in turn, unless there is a successful intervention, will teach them to his grandchildren. Thus game analysis [what Berne does in his famous book] takes place in a grand historical matrix, demonstrably extending back as far as one hundred years and reliably projected into the future for at least fifty years.

The key phrase here is 'successful intervention', for it is true that if Money Patterns (and therefore Emotional Money Baggage) are handed on unaware from generation to generation, nothing will change. However, it is within reach for each of us as individuals to change our lot – we are not robots running on tracks. We have all sorts of powers which we can wield if we want to – the power of decision, the power of making a difference, the power of changing our family's money 'curse' or bad habits. To do this we have to be willing to face things head-on about ourselves and money: some things we will need to accept, others we will need to understand and change.

Understanding your money power games

Understanding how you feel about money and what games you play will help you disentangle problems in your Money Relationship when you come to having Flashpoints and facing Crunchpoints. The games we play are so often buried in our unconsciousnesses, we simply don't know we are playing them. We just feel irritated with our partners when they do or say something about money or have a feeling of dread when a bill or statement arrives. By making unconscious processes more conscious it is possible to unravel why you end up fighting with your partner about money, simply because you are also unravelling your own money power games.

Three things are important to note here:

- money games reveal much more about the player than the played upon;
- if you feel you need to play games, it means you find it hard to:
  - trust another person;
  - be honest about your needs and expect them to be met;
  - give, take or both;
  - be intimate (fear of being known);
- it takes two to tango: money power games only work when both people participate. If one of you stops colluding, the game naturally falls apart.

Money power games are a way of keeping the other person at a distance, by keeping them guessing, not telling them the whole truth, manipulating them for your own ends. The most common games played out about money are often about competition. One partner wants to dominate the other and needs to 'win' battles over money. They sense their partner is a bit gullible and manipulates them into being generous. One woman wrote to me telling of her husband's draining of their joint account: 'He has several credit cards and in total owes somewhere in the region of £5,000 for electronic gadgets and watches and such, but nothing for the house. I work and spend little, so I am funding his spending.' Other games can be about withholding money (making a partner wait or even suffer, or making them 'earn' or 'deserve' money). Some partners try and guilt-trip the other, by wearing down-trodden heels, frayed shirts or looking generally dowdy or scruffy as a 'badge' of being hard done by. The desire to do this to a loved one will be rooted in a painful past and you can be sure that anyone who plays money power games will in fact be feeling very powerless (otherwise they wouldn't need to play games). The Emotional Money Baggage of a power-game player is usually loaded with a lot of resentment, anger or envy about their past treatment by parents or carers. Their predominant Money Patterns will probably be that of Golddiggers, Planners, Gamblers and Doormats: manipulation is the name of the game.

Melanie and Simon's story

Melanie was far too trusting when she was caught out by the money power games played by her unscrupulous fiancé, Simon. Her 'true story' was reported in *Best* magazine by Justine Marklew (6.10.98).

Melanie, then twenty, was celebrating a friend's twenty-first birthday party in London's Covent Garden when she spotted Simon, twenty-three, a hunky New Zealander, serving behind the bar. 'We were really drawn to each other,' she explains, 'he seemed just as smitten as me.' The passionate relationship developed rapidly and within two weeks they were living together. They decided to have an exotic wedding in St Lucia and Simon persuaded Melanie to take out a £4,000 loan to pay for it (on top of her existing £3,000 loan) as neither had ready cash. Although Simon said he was a plumber he stayed at home while Melanie worked full-time as an office administrator.

Then they had their first Flashpoint: Melanie was horrified when a telephone bill for £170 plopped onto the mat and Simon had no cash to pay for it. But being wildly in love she forgave him, especially when he said he was 'lonely at home and needed to call friends "back home"'. By the time they were in St Lucia for their dream wedding their relationship had deteriorated. They were arguing all the time and although Simon protested his love for Melanie she was having serious doubts about marrying him.

Now they were at a Crunchpoint. He remained 'committed' to their marriage plans although she had never met his parents (being in New Zealand). Then while on holiday Simon said he had received a call saying his grandmother had died, leaving him £10,000 so he could repay Melanie all he owed her. Melanie felt relieved and relaxed, although she still declined to marry him as she was no longer sure if she loved him: 'I was beginning to regret coming on holiday. We were sharing a room, but that was all. I avoided him wherever possible, but when we did meet it was only to argue.' Returning home, unmarried and barely talking, Melanie rushed to the travel agent to claim the £400 refund for the cancelled wedding, only to find Simon had got there before her. 'I felt so angry and betrayed that he'd had the nerve to claim my money,' she said. Then Simon's mother called: not from New Zealand, but from Gillingham outside London. 'I told her Simon had gone and she asked if he'd left me in debt. I couldn't believe my ears when she told me her son was a conman.' Simon wasn't a plumber, had never worked (except for occasional bar work) and all his grandparents were alive in the UK. By now Melanie had £10,000 of debts: the £4,000 new loan, £3,000 old loan, £600 phone bill, overdraft and other unpaid bills. The debts were all in her name, so the police couldn't prosecute. As she earned only around £13,000 a year, it would take her many years to repay her debts. 'Simon was nothing but a money-grabber, but I was so in love I didn't see it,' admits Melanie.

This is an extreme story, of course, but it is a good example of unscrupulous Golddigger meets gullible Doormat.

Emotional Money Baggage

As we have already seen, when two people come together they bring with them more than just heated-up hormones and poignant passions. They bring their whole life history in the shape of their Emotional Money Baggage and specific behaviours or Money Patterns. When two sets of Money Patterns meet they have to work out how they will operate together. In Simon and Melanie's case above, his Money Pattern (a Golddigger) was saying 'Give me what I want [money] in exhange for me making you feel loved, sexy and wanted,' while Melanie's Money Pattern (Doormat) was saying 'I'll do anything for you, make me feel special and please don't leave me because I need you.' These two Money Patterns hooked together perfectly and could only be unhooked by Melanie consciously taking charge of the situation once Simon's true colours were revealed.

Some other examples of money power games are:

- *Gambler* 'Give me all your money to invest, if you really loved me you'd trust me.'
- *Planner* 'Money can't buy me love, so don't try and impress me with your flash cash.'
- *Hoarder* 'If you think I'm splashing out my hard-earned cash on you, you've got another thing coming.'
- *Ostrich* 'We don't need money, our love is enough. Anyway I can't pay, but things will sort themselves out somehow in the end.'
- *Spender* 'Darling, I'll give you the moon, just ask me and I'll buy you anything (so long as you love me/are truly grateful and beholden).'
- *Worrier* 'I can't decide whether to buy that dress or not, please make my mind up for me . . . No, no I couldn't possibly accept

your money... Ok, thanks, you're a sweetie, but are you really sure you can afford it?'

- *Eco-Warrior* 'I'm sure you could live on less ... are you sure you really need to buy that? Anyway, the universe will provide, if only you will trust it.'

Money = self-esteem

In the heady early days of romance our attention is usually caught up in making ourselves as attractive as we can and working out whether we fancy the other person as much, or more, than they fancy us. We need all sorts of clues and make assumptions about the person's character and wealth. How someone handles money and their attitude to it reveals a great deal. During the first hours, days, weeks and months of getting to know someone new, money becomes a very important sign to watch about their psychological make-up. We often need to talk to friends, family or colleagues about them in the process of working out where they are on the money front and what it could mean if things got really serious (we return to this theme in chapter 4).

One friend said to me of a new boyfriend, 'Oh, he's a tightwad,' after they'd only met a couple of times. When I asked what she meant she explained he was careful with his money. 'How does this make you feel?' I asked. She stopped to think: 'I don't know, but I feel he ought to be more carefree in terms of spending on me.' 'But you'd be careful if you were spending on him.' 'Yes, I know,' she said, 'but all the same I want to feel he has enough money or at least he should think it's worth spending on me.' Already these two were locked into a money power game and they hardly knew each other. In fact, his attitude to money was a mirror image of her own prudence and my friend was beginning to see that she actually wanted something different, maybe a Chalk-and-Cheese match with someone with money to burn or who at least had a generous nature and who made her feel special. In fact, she really wanted her self-esteem to be boosted by a man making her feel she was worth spending money on.

Emotional hidden agendas

It's important to note here that our feelings about money and the games we play about money are totally irrational. Some people, especially Planners, claim they can look at money dispassionately and objectively (however, where their own money is concerned it's usually a different story). Because money is often used as a way of expressing our deepest needs and feelings it is very hard to be rational about it. Becoming clear about your own particular emotional 'hidden agendas' will help you understand money power games you might be playing or participating in. Fred, a 73-year-old man I spoke to on a long train journey about the forbidden topic of money, was still burning with bitterness about his lack of inheritance, fifty years on.

Fred's story: colluding with his family's money power games

From a working-class family of ten, Fred had been promised a slice of the family assets after the Second World War as a 'bribe' to stay in the UK. He had been in the army and his father ran a rural fish shop, which was a solid family enterprise. Fred, the eldest, had absented himself for ten years from the age of fifteen. 'When I demobbed my mother said, "Listen, Fred, you've been off round the world all these years fighting for King and Country. It's time you settled down and stayed near your family to do your bit." ' Fred felt guilt-tripped into putting off his plans to emigrate to Canada (he'd fallen in love with a Canadian female soldier and they planned to marry) and he went to work in the shop.

However, things didn't work out. 'I just couldn't get on with the old man and eventually I got a job in a local print works.' By then Fred had given up on getting to Canada and eventually settled down in London, about fifty miles from his family home. However, when his parents died (he was in his thirties with three children of his own), not a penny was left to him. 'By the time all the savings were divi'd up between us all there was very little, a few hundred pounds. My parents left the business proceeds to my next sister, Gwennie, so I never got a penny of what I was promised. I felt truly cheated.'

Fred felt a victim, but in fact he had colluded with his family about money. Fred allowed himself to be bribed by guilt, but couldn't really put his heart and soul into making the family business work. Had he taken charge of his life and gone to Canada as planned, he would probably have made 2,000 per cent more money and had a happier life. When I asked him why he hadn't gone, he said he'd felt he 'ought' to stay: he felt duty-bound to his family. But he also felt he didn't want to miss out on his inheritance – which of course, he eventually did, because his whole family was playing out a rather mean and manipulative money power game.

Collusion

This kind of destructive power money game only works if both parties agree to collude. If you are hanging in there trying to extract money from a mean partner or parent, you will play all sorts of games yourself as a consequence. You have to ask: Is it really worth it? In love relationships people play games, such as allowing a partner to hit them or have sex with them as a 'repayment' for money or security that money brings. Some people's hidden agendas make them feel they have literally 'bought' the other person's loyalty or silence about their bad or anti-social behaviour. If you recognise elements of collusion in your own closest relationship it's a good idea to get professional help from a counsellor or therapist, so that you can start working out what you want, how to free yourself from being manipulated because of what you think you deserve or 'ought' to do.

Fear of intimacy

One reason people play power games about money is fear of intimacy. It takes a long time really to get to know a new partner and even in longer-term relationships people change over time due to circum-stances or other reasons. (Which is why making friends first and becoming lovers second can be such a good idea.) Destructive money power games may only emerge over time, and usually once one partner has become secure in the love of the other. We all know that we show our worst aspects to those who are closest to us simply because we feel safe enough to do so. What makes it more compli-cated is some people deliberately put on a front or hide parts of themselves which they don't want the other person to know about (like the conman, Simon, above). Most of us do this, to some extent, as we can be frightened of a new or potential lover seeing our insecurities, fears and bad habits. We want them to think the best of us, or feel sorry for us, or admire us, or think we are impressive, and that can lead people to play games with each other. Some people play psychological games without really knowing they are doing it. They've done it all their lives – those little white lies, small exaggerations, being 'economical with the truth'. In other words, they fear being intimate.

Who holds the purse strings?

'He who pays the piper, calls the tune' is an old saying which really means, in relation to this book, 'He who holds the purse strings has the power'. Because some money games are subtle and confusing it's not clear exactly who is in charge. In the bad old days few women had money of their own and were necessarily deemed dependent on their men (if they had them) for survival. Today, most women work and although, according to the Equal Opportunities Commission, women still only earn 80 per cent of what men earn (and only get 70 per cent of what men get for the same job), there are nonetheless a significant number of households where the woman earns more than the man – sometimes when a man is retired or unemployed, or a woman does more than one part-time job or is better educated/ qualified. (We return to this in chapter 8.) The change in men and women's financial relationships has created some new power games. For instance, a man whose partner earns more may well feel emasculated by her; a woman whose man earns more than her may feel infantalised by him. It's not easy getting the balance right.

Sally's story: looking for a financial saviour?
We also think money will be a cure-all in relationships. The idea of the filthy-rich partner who will solve all our problems and save us is in the realm of childhood fantasy, where we are princes and princesses and go off into the sunset to live happily ever after, without every having to earn a crust. The reality of pursuing a financial saviour can be somewhat disappointing as an article by Marie Lunn in *M*, the *Mirror*'s weekly women's magazine (19.10.99) reveals. Sally, thirty-eight, a graphic designer from Southampton, saw James

aboard a 40-foot yacht in a nearby harbour. She ended up sailing with him for the day, only to discover that James, a wealthy barrister and businessman, owned the fabulous yacht. There was an instant mutual attraction: 'I couldn't believe my luck,' says Sally, although she was conscious the boat 'was probably worth £150,000 – eight years' wages for me . . . I was working for a publishing firm and earning just under £20,000, so I was doing all right but I'd never mixed in wealthy circles.' Sally wasn't a Golddigger exactly, as she hadn't hunted down a man with money to solve her problems, but nonetheless she found herself fantasising what life with money would mean for her. 'My mind was racing. What couldn't we do with that kind of money? We could be happy together, travel the world, stay in the best hotels whenever we liked.' In fact, James could be her financial saviour.

The romance developed as Sally was whisked off in James' TVR sports car (the Aston Martin left at home) to country mansions and eating meals of smoked salmon and caviar with bills amounting to £200 each. 'His jacuzzi and sauna were bigger than my small terraced house.' It was a whirlwind affair and after nine months James asked Sally to marry her. However, his money was beginning to cause a strain in the relationship. For a start he always had to pay: 'He always insisted on picking up the tab, even when I offered to pay.' But James had made his millions from investing and when the market took a dive he went into overdrive: he had no time for Sally.

James called the shots all the time, cancelling dates and holidays, fitting Sally in briefly between meetings. She soon began to realise that the fantasy life of living high would always be marred by his fanatical need to make money: he was a typical Gambler, 'taking four or five calls on his mobile before we even got to the restaurant'. Even though she had been mesmerised by his wealth and lifestyle, Sally, who wasn't enough of a Golddigger to stay the course, saw the light. 'I knew he loved me, but I also knew I was second on his list of priorities.' James also knew he couldn't put love before money as his Christmas card was signed 'to the one who's always there from the ratfink who never is'. Finally, Sally left the relationship and all the trappings of wealth, because she needed someone who didn't play money power games. James and his wealth wasn't going to save her like a fairy-tale prince, after all. She was heartbroken, but philosophical, as she's now explained to her new boyfriend, who is far from a millionaire. 'Sometimes he panics that he won't match up but I tell him that being happy is what matters most. It's a cliché, but all the money in the world can't buy happiness.'

Money addiction

Some people truly believe that money not only can buy happiness, but can also repair the damage of a wasted life or brutal childhood. People who are addicted to money – and that includes gamblers, risk-taking businessmen like the shamed politicians Jeffrey Archer and Jonathan Aitkin, shop-lifters and the estimated two and a half million shopaholics in the UK – all feel that having more money than they actually need will solve their problems. Money addiction affects relationships in the same way as any addiction, like alcoholism or drug addiction. It saps the relationship of vital energy, making both partners bend to the whims of the addiction. Of course, there are people who have nothing – or very little – who steal for sheer survival. These are distinct from the significant number of people who actually have enough to survive, but who simply *feel* they have hardly anything and certainly not enough.

Frozen needs

Why do people feel impoverished even in the midst of plenty? On an emotional level this can be explained by the notion of 'frozen needs', whereby the past dominates the present. Frozen needs were real needs which were not met adequately, or not at all, when we needed them to be in the past: so they are frozen in time. If you were left alone to cry as a baby, without any affection or reassurance, and you had physical needs (hunger, thirst, a dirty nappy) or emotional needs (want of a hug, reassurance, comfort, love) which were not met, then they can become 'frozen' psychologically. In teens and adulthood this manifests itself as emotional patterns which say 'Nobody loves me, I have to do everything for myself' or 'No one is ever there when I need them'.

If this experience of isolation and disconnection is repeated many times during babyhood and childhood, and there has been no space or encouragement to deal with the underlying feelings of rage, fear, grief, panic, then the likelihood is there will be chronic 'frozen need' patterns of isolation and mistrust in adulthood. It may feel impossible to ask for help or get close to others because you never learned to be vulnerable or to trust.

If a child also experienced deprivation at the same time (such as not having enough food, money or warmth), there can be a 'frozen need' for these things in adulthood. Many people with eating disorders, those who steal or gamble compulsively, have experienced extreme deprivation in childhood. They are permanently needy babies. As adults we all try to fill our frozen needs in all sorts of ways – ranging from having treats to wholesale theft or embezzlement. Some people have 'stealing patterns' and seem incapable of resisting trying to get something for nothing. These people may even steal from partners and husbands: 'Whenever my husband leaves his wallet on the sideboard, I help myself to some notes or coins,' confesses Trudi, a hairdresser. 'He's got more than me and he's mean with the housekeeping, so I see it as a way of balancing things between us.' Actually, Trudi feels very angry that Jason spends money on his hobbies, but won't go on holiday with her. 'He thinks nothing of spending money on his blasted motorbike and going scrambling. His idea of a great weekend away is being up to his neck in mud in a freezing field.' Trudi's fantasy of the perfect weekend is being sunk deep in a downy double bed or bubbling jacuzzi with a glass of champagne in hand. 'I do feel bad about helping myself, but he never notices because he's such an old skinflint.' Trudi, meanwhile, is playing a powerless money game, which could backfire long-term.

In relation to money, frozen needs are the root of many people's money games. There is a desperate drive to fill up, numb out or compensate for a yawning inner emotional emptiness: this is the root of all money addiction. A disproportionate number of famous 'celebrities' frequently tell tales of unloved childhoods, indifferent absent parents, foster homes, drafty boarding schools, even sadistic physical, sexual or emotional abuse. The unquenchable thirst for fame and its accompanying financial rewards is a desperately addictive drive to fill frozen needs, which can never be filled, only grieved over. This is why when fame and fortune comes, it's never enough. People still feel empty, and so up the stakes, trying to fill the emotional void with drugs, drink, workaholism, compulsive shopping . . . anything at all, just to feel loved and compensated for the deprivation of their past. Unfortunately, these addictive behaviours sometimes overtake, even destroy, the person who fails really to benefit from the fruits of their fame. A significant percentage of the fortunes of Billie Holiday, Marilyn Monroe, Elvis Presley, Jimi Hendrix, Kurt Cobain and Michael Hutchence were splurged on self-destruction and self-sabotage, as if early emotional damage could be simply mended with money. As a consequence, few famous and driven people can really enjoy and relax into love relationships, because they never know if their partner is after them or their money and fame (like Madonna and her string of past lovers). This is why celebs of similar wealth tend to hang out with each other (like Madonna and Guy Ritchie) – at least they feel their partner is not after their money for once.

Frozen needs in relationships

In relationships we often try to meet our frozen needs by being ultra-generous with our partners, while secretly hoping they will pay us back equally or more. In fact, this is a way of trying to control the other person, which is now commonly recognised as being 'co-dependent' behaviour. Co-dependency was first understood in the 1960s when Alcoholics Anonymous analysed why love relationships broke up once drinkers became sober. It wasn't necessarily that the ex-drinker could not cope in the relationship; it was rather that the other partner – who had inadvertently propped up and fed off the other's addiction to alcohol – could not cope with their newly sober partner. They no longer had a 'saviour' or 'policing' role and they had to face their own problems instead, which felt extremely uncomfortable. There are co-dependent people who literally need their partner to continue to be a drinker, drug-taker, womaniser, spendthrift, miser and so on, to give their life meaning and focus.

People who are co-dependent:

- wrap themselves round addicts or people whom they perceive as 'needing' them;
- disempower their partner by thinking for them (double-guessing them, finishing their sentences);
- step in and rescue them, when in fact it would be better for them to work out for themselves what to do;

- are actually very needy themselves, but fear owning up to their own needs – so put their needs onto someone else. They fear their needs because they never learned to articulate them in the first place and/or fear being let down if they ask for their needs to be met, and are ignored;
- control the relationship from within while appearing a victim to the rest of the world;
- are deeply disturbed when their partner takes charge and sorts themselves out – the co-dependant has nothing to do and turns away, usually to find the next helpless victim who needs their 'help'.

For more on this subject read, *Facing Codependency: What It is, Where It Comes From, How It Sabotages Our Lives* by Melodie Beatty (Harper & Row, 1989).

Money and co-dependency

Money plays a special role in co-dependent relationships. The co-dependent partner may bail out the other whenever they get into debt or money trouble, so they remain in control of the Money Relationship. They make the financially dependent partner feel beholden and that they couldn't live without them, as they dish out money to feed their addiction. This is very destructive because it is boundaryless behaviour and encourages the addicted partner to stay addicted. Relationships where one partner is 'hopeless' with money and the other is a 'coper' are set up on a premise that the coper (co-dependant) will sort out the helpless one (addict). In fact, both are addicted to the relationship being out of balance and both play a destructive money power game accordingly.

Love or need?

In such relationships, which are driven by frozen needs rather than mutual love, care and affection, couples keep score and measure how generous one partner is towards the other. (A bit like Edward Albee's famous play and film *Who's Afraid of Virginia Woolf?* where two alcoholic couples slug it out and keep score mercilessly.) These couples only give as good as they get and take revenge when they feel hard done by. They are often deeply disappointed by and with each other, without really understanding that their disappointment lies in their Emotional Money Baggage from parents who let them down, or past partners who abused them, or with the unreal expectations of a perfect love which they foisted onto the relationship in the first place. They may have grown up in a household without love, but with plenty of money and therefore will have attached affection to material things over people, or may hold material things in contempt and live frugally instead. Or they may have grown up with little financial security or affection, and therefore feel material gain is the only way of gaining status and love in the world.

Shopaholism: the ultimate power game

Shopaholism is on the increase within the UK. During 1999 it was estimated that we spent £134 billion in credit and debit cards and still owed £28.5 billion at the end of the year. It's much easier to be extravagant and secretive using plastic cards and computer terminals for Internet banking – much easier than lifting cash out of the jam jar or siphoning off the current account.

Rachel and Barny's story: a shopaholic nightmare
When I visited Rachel and Barny's beautifully decorated terraced house in Manchester the bailiff had just departed and they were right in the middle of a major Crunchpoint. Ashen with fear and rage, Rachel shook as she sat at the kitchen table, steaming mug of tea in hand. 'I just opened the door and there they were,' she explained tearfully, 'I let them into my house and had no idea they were sizing up my worldly goods.' The bailiffs had been sent by a local loan shark to recover an unpaid debt of £6,000. 'It was like being interrogated by two Mr Potatoheads. I said, "You don't need to send heavies, you don't need to make me feel like a criminal. Here I am making cookies in my kitchen and my son is lying ill in bed. I'm not a criminal, I just owe you some money." It was so humiliating.' Rachel is an articulate, upper-middle-class self-employed trainer and mother of two boys. She is married to Barny, who is a (resting) actor, from a lower-middle-class background.

Rachel admits she's horrendous with money. Her earnings are

erratic and she finds it hard to keep track of what she owes. She saw an ad in a local paper for cheap loans and, without telling Barny, she got one. 'I felt so relieved because I was at the top of my overdraft and didn't know what to do.' She didn't feel she could go to Barny, who had thrown up a secure job as a junior solicitor in a law firm to pursue his acting career. Talented and hard-working, he found an agent who has not yet got him his 'break', but, ever optimistic, he sincerely believes 'the big time' is just round the corner. Rachel's not so sure: 'It's been just round the corner for two years now and it's sending me round the bend.'

So why is Rachel deep in debt? 'I spend,' she says conspiratorially, 'I just spend and spend.' This hasn't always been the case, but is something which started just after her father died a year ago. 'I've always liked nice things, but could never afford them,' she explains, calmly, 'and we had the boys [two, now nine and five] and I stopped working for a while, but Barny was working then and we sort of scraped by.' Her father, who had been a 'domineering tyrant' in her words, left her £50,000 in his will. 'And I spent it, I went out and spent the bloody lot in six months, much to everyone's horror.' Having spent the money, Rachel continued to spend, filling credit card after credit card to the limit. 'I've lost count now exactly, four or five. I know I owe over £10,000 altogether,' she says flatly. 'I find it unbearable being a responsible grown up. I feel I need all the things I've been buying, beautiful boots, wonderful bedspreads, fabulous curtains, things for the boys. I feel, deep down, all these things will make it all better. I obsess about them – that jacket, those shoes, that cricket bat or a camera. I want them and can't relax until I've got them.' After that, there's the let down. 'I just feel flat, a bit sordid, afraid. I hide things until I'm ready either to take them back or start all over again.'

Why did her father's death trigger it all off? 'How long have you got?' she asks with a wan smile. Rachel's father was a wealthy, Jewish academic, who had escaped from Central Europe during the Holocaust to make money in America and South Africa. 'He loved the high life, he lived in another city during the week and came to live with us at weekends. He always drove a BMW or Mercedes and dressed beautifully.' Rachel's father was brilliant, an athlete, an entrepreneur – and extremely sexist. 'He kept my mother on a tight reign and always gave her the exact same amount of housekeeping.

We lived poorly, she shopped at C&A, we hardly had enough to eat while he lived the life of Riley.'

Consequently, Rachel's mother was bitter and angry. She denied her husband sex, so he had affairs. He also sexually abused Rachel, ritualistically, with her mother's acquiescence. 'I was the family's sacrificial lamb. I had sexual contact with my father, as if I were his wife (my mother refused sex with him). So I existed in this false relationship with him where I was his golden child, his baby, the one that he loved and who understood him. It was a special relationship and I wanted it to stay like that. I didn't want to deal with reality.' Rachel still doesn't, even though she is now furious about how her childhood was taken away from her. Rachel's spending went berserk when her father died because the mass of unresolved and unbearable buried feelings came to the surface. Now the tyrant was dead, she could breathe free. Or so she thought. She felt flexing her plastic was a way of taking revenge, of revelling in her freedom. Spending her inheritance at lightning speed was like ridding herself of blood money. 'Barny was amazed and I think utterly furious, and helpless, because he's quite pragmatic and he could see us paying off our mortgage and being sensible shoes.' But Rachel's emotions dictated her actions, she was not able to stop and think. It was a Spender versus Doormat dynamic, with Rachel's Money Patterns dominating Barny's.

'We fought about the money, and my spending it, but what could I really do? This inheritance money was an utter curse, so I got rid of it. What Barny doesn't know is that I replaced it with credit cards and, to be honest, I have no idea what to do next. I'm at the limit on all of them and the bailiff's at the door. Help.' Help indeed. For that is Rachel's power game: 'Help me, I can't do it on my own. Save me, I'm only little, I can't do it for myself.' It's the cry of a broken and abused child, only she's now a fully-grown adult, with adult responsibilities. Within her relationship she holds the power strings; Barny, at present, is a passive onlooker. He's playing a powerless money game of 'It's not my responsibility, I just want to be a star'. When he was earning, he was more of a player. Now he's looking to Rachel to carry things financially, which she finds utterly unbearable. Intellectually, Rachel wants Barny to fulfil his dreams, but her behaviour is taking them in the opposite direction, whereby he will probably have to return to the law to earn 'proper money'. He would resent this enormously and it might cause a major relationship Crunchpoint as a consequence.

The positive thing going for their relationship is a deep knowledge and love of each other and their two boys. However, once the total truth about Rachel's spending emerges, which it will once the bailiffs return, it will take a ton of patience, understanding and love for them to pull through the impending Crunchpoint. 'I know I'm living a secret life within our relationship, but I guess that's what I've always done,' says Rachel candidly. 'I'm like my father on that front – I know Barny loves me, but the test will be: will he still love me when I've revealed all?' Abused people often test others in this way because they can't trust. However, it's just a destructive money power game at root.

Self-sabotage = Relationship sabotage

When people, like Rachel, are in close relationships their Emotional Money Baggage and Money Patterns can wreak havoc. The anger that Rachel rightly feels about her unjust, abusive treatment from both her father and mother has been turned in on herself and her family. Her resulting shopaholic behaviour is actually self-sabotage. Spending her inheritance hurts not her father, who is now dead, but herself, her husband and her children in real time. Yet she is caught in an addictive trap and like a little mouse is going round and round on an addictive treadmill. (For more on this, see my book *Overcoming Addiction: Positive Steps for Breaking Free of Addiction and Building Self-Esteem* (Piatkus, 1994).)

Revenge

Current academic research supports the idea that some people spend addictively as a kind of revenge. This can include neglected wives who spend absent husbands' money. Dr Richard Elliott of St Anne's College, Oxford, Sue Eccles of the University of Bradford and Kevin Gournay of the University of London have published their findings on 'Addictive shopping in the UK' (University of Oxford, 1996). They believe that 1–2 per cent of the population are shopaholics and the figure is set to rise. Dr Elliott writes in the above paper:

A picture has started to emerge of consumers (predominantly female) who buy for motives not directly related to the actual possession of goods, in fact many of the purchases remain wrapped up and hidden in cupboards. They persistently repeat the behaviour despite its leading to severe financial and social consequences such as huge levels of personal debt and marital breakdown.

Dr Elliott and the others believe that shopaholics spend:

- to escape from painful feelings, like depression;
- to make themselves feel better (repair mood);
- because they believe buying things will make them happier;
- because they feel 'generally unsatisfied with life', to create meaning for their lives.

In particular, they spend:

- to take revenge on a partner or husband.

Dr Elliott writes: 'Some consumers see themselves as victims of betrayal in a relationship' and thus spending money they haven't got is a way of 'getting back at their partner'. In Dr Elliott's research sample:

- 63 per cent of shopaholics felt others would be horrified if they knew of their spending habits;
- 61 per cent often bought things when they couldn't afford them;
- 65 per cent often bought something in order to make themselves feel better.

In the later research done by Dr Elliott, Sue Eccles and Kevin Gournay, they concluded shopaholics:

- 'were profoundly unhappy individuals trying to compensate for an enormous burden of negative feelings';
- 'use the shopping experience as a form of self-expression and as an important element in the construction and maintenance of their self-identities';

but more importantly:

- 'as a means of having some control over a part of their own lives and having, or feeling they have, some control over their partner'.

Partners who feel either they can't express their feelings to their partner or that their partner has somehow let them down tend to use shopaholism as a means of revenge. However, as we have seen, it can be very destructive in a relationship as it sabotages all that is good or possible. In a sense, one partner's anger and dissatisfaction can run riot if the other partner is not wise or strong enough to deal with them. Yet this still doesn't mean the relationship has to end – necessarily. If both partners are willing and able to face the emotional hidden agendas under their money power games and talk about them together, things can ultimately be resolved. This is a matter of one or both partners needing to build and stick to firm emotional boundaries.

Power games and money addiction checklist

This chapter has been about the darker side of your Money Relationship, where you (or your partner) can play out unconscious and often destructive money power games. This may seem alien to you, but perhaps you have read something which seems familiar or uncomfortable, perhaps about shopping and spending too much, or perhaps about wanting to be rescued by a financial saviour or feeling resentful about financial imbalances in your relationship.

Take a moment to ask yourself:

- Do I play money power games with my partner/spouse/ex? Can I recognise what they are?
- Does my partner/spouse/ex play money power games with me?
- Am I addicted to money in any way – gambling, shopping, spending what I haven't got?
- Are there secrets about money which I keep from my partner?
- Have I uncovered any secrets about money my partner is hiding from me?
- Are there any games we both play with each other about money that I would like to stop playing?
- What's my next step?

Part Two

Making a Money Match

4

Dating and Mating

Let your hook always be cast; in the pool where you least expect it, there will be fish.

Ovid

Dating

'Every time we met for a date he'd never have any money on him,' remembers Sarah, thirty-five, with a sigh, about ex-lover Julian. He was a good-looking secondary-school teacher whom she dated for a few months last year. 'The time that really stands out in my mind was when we were going to the cinema in central London. It had taken ages to find a parking place and the film was due to start and then he did his customary "Oh, I haven't got any money on me" speech.' After three months of Julian turning up on dates cashless and expecting Sarah to bail him out, she found herself feeling understandably irritated. They hit their first major Crunchpoint after several money Flashpoints. 'I really wanted to see the movie, and it was getting late, but something inside of me said 'This time I'm not going to say "I'll pay for the film and you can pay me back later." Something made me feel "No, you can bloody well go and get your money if you've been so idiotic to turn up, yet again, without cash".' The nearest cashpoint turned out to be streets away, 'So we had to get one of our cars and literally go looking for a cashpoint machine. I was seething, but I felt bloody-minded about it, because it was after a long line of similar experiences with him.' Needless to say, they missed the film. 'Money was always an issue every time we went out. I noticed he had a very low limit on his cheque card, so he would ask me to put the bill on my credit card. "I'll give you a cheque tomorrow," he'd say. Then a week, two weeks, a month would pass. I'd remind him and it would be "Oh, yes, I'm terribly sorry," but still the money never arrived. I began to feel very hurt and taken for granted.'

In fact, Julian's attitude to money soon put the kibosh on their tender romance as Sarah became increasingly upset and disappointed. 'I found it incredibly unsexy because I found it hard to respect him, I'm afraid. It put me in that rather maternal, bossy older sister role. I didn't want to feel like an older sister lending money to her naughty younger brother. I felt very angry because I felt controlled by him in a negative kind of way.' Sarah knew that he was divorced and having to pay maintenance to his ex-wife and two children, 'Of course, I sympathised with that, but I still think turning up for date after date with no money was more a lack of commitment than about his lack of earnings.'

Dating and Emotional Money Baggage

When you go on a date you necessarily lug your Emotional Money Baggage along with you, whether you realise it or not. People have much more relationship experience than in the days when they courted one or two people and then married for life. Dating has become an activity which can go on throughout life. Most dating couples will probably have lived with someone, been married or cohabited one or more times; they may also be lone parents, have their own or stepchildren and/or be paying maintenance to an ex-family.

As in Sarah's story above, Julian came loaded down by his Emotional Money Baggage: a divorcee, forking out maintenance, perhaps jaded about starting again or feeling that as Sarah earned more (which she did) she should therefore look after him somehow (a mixture of Hoarder/Golddigger Money Patterns). Hence his ambivalence about paying his way on dates. Of course, Sarah had her own Emotional Money Baggage, which was twenty years of serial dating, including one serious long-term relationship with an older man, who earned much more than her at the time and therefore paid for most things. Now she wanted a long-term relationship, and maybe a baby, with a man who was solvent, equal and keen to commit: Sarah was clearly a Planner.

Dating etiquette

Your Emotional Money Baggage is illustrated much more by what you do than what you say. When you are getting to know someone new you are necessarily trying to assess, usually as quickly as possible, whether you are going to be a good match or not. Of course, dating is a good way to find out, but it is often complicated by the fact that many of us go out of our way to create false impressions, hoping to wow our date. So it can take quite a few dates before a prospective partner's true financial colours start to emerge. As we saw in the previous chapter, it would be so much easier (if somewhat embarrassing) if we could simply hand each other a money CV or relationship statement with personal checklist of assets, earnings, cash flow, Emotional Money Baggage and Money Patterns clearly stated on it and negotiate dating etiquette upfront.

Generational differences

The rules about dating and money seemed so much simpler in the 'bad old days': the man was expected to pay when a couple were 'courting' (unless the woman was fabulously rich or an aristocrat, in which case he was an emasculated 'kept man').

Pam, an adult education lecturer in her thirties, recently dated a wealthy man in his sixties, and found that the issue of paying for things became highly sensitive territory. At first she says she loved the luxury of knowing he had money and could take her places she would never usually be able to afford to go on her meagre salary. 'I even enjoyed the door opening and other old-fashioned courtesies which men of my age (whom I usually dated) knew nothing about.' 'At the beginning it was great that he paid for everything, too: theatre tickets, drinks and meals each time we went out and then the taxi home. I felt spoilt and it became a sort of ritual. I'd get my wallet out when a bill arrived and a look of disgust would come over his face and he'd shoo it away, which made me put it back in my bag. Although it was nice for a while, I eventually got fed up with it. It sounds ridiculous, but every time he whisked the bill away with an "I'll get this", it made me feel like a five-year-old out with her dad. I began to feel powerless, almost infantalised. I was a professional woman teaching adults at college, in my own right, but he made me feel very small. I noticed this went hand in hand with him sort of talking down to me about things. I quite expected him to say "Don't bother your pretty little head about this".'

Pam decided to take action. Things had to change. She liked him well enough, but she was a woman not a child. They were at a Crunchpoint. 'On the next date I grabbed the restaurant bill saying "No, no, let me, it's my turn, you've been so generous" and flexed my credit card. He was very, very insulted. There was an awkward silence all the way home in the taxi. I pressed my £10 half of the fare into his hand and that's the last I saw of him. I guess he was deeply offended by my wanting to pay my way.'

Increased financial, educational and social equality for women has brought with it increased complexity in terms of working out who pays for what when a couple go out. Although women still don't earn the same as men, most women today are in full- or part-time work, even if married with children. Among younger men and women (say, under fifty) there is a general expectation that a woman will be able to pay her way (or at least a significant part of it).

Money and attraction

Most people probably wouldn't be explicit about money on a first date. Many of us have a (false) belief that love can only grow in an idealised relationship (the old romantic ideal) where dirty words like money don't exist. Not so. Money will be there in your initial attraction to someone, on your first date, and in your fantasies about them because, necessarily, we all live in the real, material world. You might be attracted to someone with Eco-Warrior or Ostrich Money Patterns because they seem unworldly and uninterested in making money itself – this is nonetheless a value judgment about the role of money in their lives. Equally, you may be fascinated by a thrusting, successful businessman or woman with Gambler or Planner Money Patterns simply because they reek of material wealth and the ability to take risks.

Fantasy vs. reality

You need to be honest with yourself about what you are really looking for in someone (a mutual partner or sugar daddy/mummy?) and what you are sincerely attracted to in them; we often fall in love with an *idea* of who a person is (saviour, hero, Ms/Mr Right) rather than the more mundane reality. This is illustrated in Dr Maryon Tysoe's amusing book, *Dates From Hell* (Headline, 1994), in which both men and women recount their horrific first-date experiences. A recurring theme is the difference between the fantasy and anticipation built up before the date and the crushingly disappointing reality during and after, especially in relation to money. Roxanne, twenty-one, writes: 'I felt I was falling in love again after such a long time, and that finally Mr Right had come my way. Happiness made me feel dizzy. I pressed his hand and he responded to me. Even without words, we seemed to understand each other completely.' 'I've got to tell you something,' he said with a charming smile. 'I've had girls before you . . .' In her fervour, Roxanne imagines he is asking for some kind of sexual favour: 'I imagined all the spicy details of our love-making that a man like him, so stylish, so original could desire . . . Probably something like a champagne bath and underwear in purple silk . . . Or maybe a date when I'd wear nothing but stockings under my coat and we'd have sex on the top floor of a double-decker as it drove through the neon-lit streets.'

'You think you could cope with it?' he wondered.

'Whatever it is, it turns me on,' I whispered to him.

'OK then,' he said, 'my rent and phone bill, you know . . . can you pay them for this month and the next one?'

Blind dates and first dates

Blind dates and first dates with people you've been set up with by a mutual friend, or have met for five minutes in a drunken stupor at a party, or have found through a lonely hearts advert, carry the highest risk of a possible money mismatch. The less you know someone the greater the scope for misunderstanding. This is because we approach new acquaintances with a whole barrel-load of assumptions, often purely based on looks, accents and 'signs' of what they do for a living and their level of wealth. We simply don't know who they are (and they don't know who we are) so the field is wide open for delusion and confusion.

Great expectations

Approaching a first date with someone unknown we usually make a big effort to impress them by dressing well, tending to our appearance and projecting an image we hope will seduce. As for understanding who they are, often:

- *We make assumptions.* We look for clues and then guess at the person's 'worth'. We'll also be sniffing out each other's Money Patterns on a subconscious level (and it can also provide amusing fuel for dating post-mortems with best friends). A Golddigger will be particularly adept at sussing out wealth as their goal will be to extract as much as possible; or a Worrier may be horrified having spent an evening with a reckless Gambler.
- *We have expectations.* You might be dating 'for fun' which includes trips to Paris and hot sex in classy hotels; or you may be hunting for a prospective partner for marriage and children. You might well approach a new date eager with the hope that 'this is the one'.
- *We have emotional hidden agendas.* We each want something specific from a date which we may or may not make clear to our partner for the evening and day. If you are wealthy you may well hide the fact in the hope that the person you're dating will like you rather than your healthy bank balance; equally if you are a low-earner, you may try and overimpress, so that your new partner thinks well of you. You'll also probably be hoping that your new partner is at least solvent, possibly even well-off (or at least financially equal to yourself).

Sue and Damien's story: dealing with class differences
A problem may arise if you both come from significantly different classes or worlds with different lifestyles, or when the age gap is

wide; one of you may set standards which leads the other to feel they are out of their depth.

'The first time we went out he bought a bottle of champagne,' remembers Sue, twenty-seven, a nurse from a working-class background, who dated Damien, forty-five, an upper-middle-class, divorced company director. 'I thought "Oh, how exciting". But he was right out of my league, financially speaking. I also felt he was very posh and above my station in life. However, the next time we went out I bought a bottle of champagne on my credit card because I thought that's what he was used to.' A Worrier, Sue got very anxious about money when Damien (a typical Gambler) told her his previous girlfriend had been a big earner in advertising. He used to have a competition with her about who could buy the bigger, more expensive present. 'I felt I had to match him pound for pound to keep my independence,' explains Sue, wryly, 'but it was such a bloody strain. He'd take me to a really fancy restaurant and the bill would be astronomical. I'd cook him a nice meal next time, but I could tell he was disappointed.' After a while she began to think 'Just because you've got money you can't buy me, mate'. It also became difficult when Damien wanted to do something expensive, like go to Paris, Rome or Amsterdam for the weekend once or twice a month. 'Either he'd have to pay for us both or we didn't go – and neither of us liked that. I'd rather have had a day out in Brighton or gone for a picnic in the park, but that was too downmarket for him.' The relationship Crunchpoint was reached fairly soon because of their different levels of wealth and therefore lifestyles and expectations. 'The last straw was him giving me diamond earrings at Christmas when I gave him a CD. I felt awful. I couldn't keep up with him and he was disappointed in my lack of extravagance. I feel much more comfortable now going out with someone who's happy with a pizza and a bottle of plonk – at least I can pay my way without being humiliated or going bankrupt.'

David and Pratibha's story: dealing with cultural differences

Another significant dating issue is how money is used and viewed in different cultures. David, thirty-seven, a primary-school teacher sees himself as somewhat of a 'New Man'. He says he believes in women's equality and that men should do housework and childcare. A new teacher recently started at his school and he fell passionately in love with her. 'It took me ages to ask her out on a date, but eventually I plucked up the courage and I was over the moon when she agreed.' His date, Pratibha, came from a Muslim family and although she was 'modern' in the sense that she was earning her living, she still lived at home and her relationship with David had to be kept totally secret from her parents, who would never have approved of her going out with a white non-Muslim man. 'Even though she was rebelling against her family she never, ever paid for anything when we went out,' says David, somewhat bitterly. 'We both earned the same, but she simply expected me to pay all the time. I found this very difficult to swallow and found myself in the extraordinary position of having to explain why I thought men and women should pay equally.' David began to feel he wasn't a 'real man' in Pratibha's eyes. According to David, Pratibha had taken a step into the modern world of work, while her deep-seated cultural beliefs and values concerning women and men's roles (her Emotional Money Baggage) remained highly traditional and cultural-bound. Their many Flashpoints about money finally came to the Crunch. 'In the end her family found out and she suddenly ended the relationship,' remembers David sadly. 'I feel it was a shame, but long term we would have had a mountain to climb regarding our different cultures. Not impossible, but certainly challenging.'

Leroy and Shân's story: crossing the cultural divide

There are plenty of success stories, however, where couples have conquered the cultural divide regarding dating. Even though from completely different worlds, some people find they have more in common with each other than their own particular generation, class or cultural groups. Leroy, an Afro-Caribbean computer operator met Shân, a primary-school teacher, at a mutual friend's party in South Wales five years ago. On the surface they seemed to have nothing really in common: he was black, she was white; he was a technical whizz, she was a technophobe; his family, both in the UK and in Barbados, were Seventh Day Adventists, hers were devout Chapel. Yet, they 'clicked' as they chatted all night. He took her number and called the next day to fix their first date.

'It was an utter disaster,' remembers Shân, fondly, 'I was broke and suggested we just go for a drink. He was annoyed, as he was hungry. Then Leroy insisted on paying all evening, which I didn't like at all. So I bought a Chinese takeaway which we took back to my flat. He didn't like me paying for it and we virtually fought about money that first evening. When he left without so much as a cuddle, I thought "Well, that's it, won't see him again".' They'd got off on the wrong foot. Both were making wild assumptions about the other's expectations regarding money. Leroy was wanting to show Shân that he was a black man who had enough money to pay his way – especially with a white woman; Shân was wanting to show she was independent enough not to be 'taken out' by a man – black or white. It was a clash of the Titans on the independence front. Luckily, Leroy liked Shan enough to call her again and Shân thought he was intelligent and sexy, so she agreed to meet.

'Our second date was better as we were able to talk about what had happened,' says Shân. 'We were both not wanting the other to think we were poor or wanting to be looked after.' They found out they had both had fairly strict and materially poor upbringings against which they'd both rebelled. 'There was nothing but rules about absolutely everything at home,' remembers Shân, 'and Leroy had experienced much the same. Neither of us went to church any more and were fairly critical about things like that.' They both laughed with sheer relief once they'd ironed out their assumptions and agreed they'd split expenditure down the middle from then on. They've been together ever since and now live together and have a beautiful three-year-old child.

Gay and lesbian dating

Dating etiquette among gay and lesbian couples is something less easily defined, if equally fraught, on the money front. Where the usual sexist stereotypes don't exist (man pays, woman is paid for), gay men and lesbians are forced to negotiate their relationship rules along more complex lines. This can obviously be refreshing as everything is up for grabs. Some gay and lesbian couples reflect the more traditional heterosexual stereotypes, where one partner who is more dominant and/or solvent than the other tends to do most of the paying. Nonetheless there is usually more fluidity than in heterosexual relationships about who pays for what and how.

Dorann and Sandy's story: where money equals love

Money rows can get just as heated as Dorann explains about her relationship with her retired lover Sandy. 'She's got much more money than I have as she's got a good pension and I'm struggling as a self-employed painter, but she can be very mean. She splashes out on her herself a lot, but is penny-pinching with others – including me – which really pisses me off. We went to the pub for lunch recently, and I paid. Then we got a Chinese takeaway in the evening and I paid again. I said "Hey it's your turn to pay" and she just said "Is it?" Then she completely forgot about it and I got fed up reminding her.' There are no clear-cut, gender-orientated 'rules' for Dorann and Sandy, which means money becomes highly symbolic of love, care and freedom. 'I really do equate money with love,' says Dorann candidly, 'at other times Sandy can be wonderfully generous and I love her for it. When I was leaving my husband for her she gave me a video box on my birthday with £410 in it, £10 for every year of my life and said "This is for you if you need it". I have to say this compared very favourably with the £10 Gap socks my ex told me to go and buy for myself.'

Caroline and Paul's story: dating friends

Dorann and Sandy had fallen in love at first sight and it had been a complicated, painful and expensive process for them to negotiate being together, with both having to leave a respective live-in partner and spouse. The financial cost and continuing struggle was almost a sign of their commitment to their new-found love. However, if a friend or colleague turns into a date over time (sometimes a very long time), then negotiating money can be somewhat easier. Not only have you known each other for some time and have seen each other in all sorts of revealing and unimpressive situations (as in the film *When Harry Met Sally*), there is a knowledge of each other and an ease of communication which can make it possible to negotiate the most sensitive of issues: money.

This is true of Caroline and Paul, who have known each other since their teens. Caroline went to school with Paul's sister, and so they have literally all grown up together. Even so, on a class level, Paul and Caroline come from different backgrounds. Being from an upper-middle-class, fairly wealthy home (his father was an engineer, his mother didn't work), Paul went to public school; Caroline's parents are more mixed, her mother being a working-class part-time secretary, her father a middle-class, technical-college lecturer. She went to a state school. Paul went away to university and Caroline went to business college, so they only met once a year at Christmas back home with their families.

'Looking back I suppose there'd always been an attraction,' says Caroline with a grin, 'but he was my friend's older brother, so I blanked it.' Then they both found themselves working in London and Caroline was looking for a new flat: 'He rang me up and said he was moving out of his flat, maybe I'd like to see it. So we went out to dinner, and that was it.' Paul admits he'd always been attracted to her, 'But when your sister is sixteen and you're eighteen, it's not the done thing. Our lives diverged, but when we met again later, I was surprised she was interested in me.' Clearly besotted, they talk candidly and openly about how they handle money together. 'Because we're such old friends I feel I can say anything to him,' says Caroline warmly. This includes the ticklish issue of money. 'Money on those early dates wasn't really an issue for us, but at least we feel we can talk about it, if we need to.'

Negotiating the dating money minefield

Clearly, dating is a money minefield. However, there are a number of ways you can try to manage your dating etiquette to maximise your success with a relatively unknown, or even better-known, partner. Although it may seem forced or awkward, it's crucial to try to make things as clear as you can from the start about how you'd like things to be. Your mind may be clouded by romantic feelings, your need to impress or downright shyness, but you don't have to let them get in the way. This is especially important if you want to get off on the right foot with a potential new partner. So:

- *Forget trying to impress them about your wealth.* You don't have to look a million dollars or splash money around; nor do you have to count every penny to defend yourself from being taken for a ride. Rule of thumb: relax and be yourself.
- *Be assertive, not aggressive.* Don't say 'I'm damn well paying for myself, OK?' to keep your hard-won independence. Rather be

lightly confident by acknowledging the awkwardness of the situation and saying what you want: 'Look, I know this is a bit embarrassing, and we hardly know each other, but can we talk about how we're paying for things tonight?'

- *Be constructive.* If you haven't got much money suggest you do something simple, like go for a walk or a drink, not a four-course gourmet meal.
- *Listen and negotiate.* If you make your proposal, listen to what your date has to say back. Try not to be dogmatic, argumentative or a doormat. If your date says 'fine' to your proposal and offers no comment, then accept it at face value. Don't start double-guessing what they really mean or didn't say. Equally, if they come up with a counter-proposal, give it some thought. Don't let embarrassment about talking about the dreaded M-word mean either you clam up totally and agree with a nod, or fight to the death for your principles.
- *Be flexible.* Try and deal with money on your date with a flexible and relaxed 'let's see how it goes' attitude. If you have rigid ideas about who should pay for what you will spoil your date and stop things developing 'organically'. After all, this is only a first date, and if you enjoy it then who knows where it will lead? If you don't either feel ripped off or sold into sexual slavery, then the possibility of meeting again is increased.
- *Be patient.* Because first dates are so fraught with expectation and tension, try to give each other the benefit of the doubt if the first time out is a bit of a disaster. As you get to know each other you will relax and be able to talk more easily about difficult things, including money. You don't have to reveal all on the first date, but neither do you have to build up a mysterious smokescreen or an impossibly romantic image.
- *Identify your own Emotional Money Baggage.* It's so easy to project onto a new partner all your bad (and good) experiences from the past. People tend to react and overreact – they had a mean first husband, so they never trust another man; they had a shopaholic last girlfriend, so they are very mistrustful of women. Try and see your new date for who they are as a unique individual, no matter who they remind you of in your past. Give them time to reveal their true selves to you, but try not to test them out at every turn.
- *Identify your date's Money Patterns.* Although you don't know your

date well yet, watch their behaviour. Do they leap to produce their wallet at every juncture or is there a pause while they wait for you to offer? On subsequent dates (if there are any), have they just missed the bank, left their wallet at home, forgotten to book tickets and it's down to you to fork out? Or do they get shirty if you so much as pay for an ice lolly, feeling you're casting aspersions on their ability to pay? Listen to how they talk about money, what they say about other people and their money, how they describe friends' and ex's money and what they say about their family background, and you'll begin to build a clear picture of their main Money Pattern.

- *Evolve what's right for your particular relationship.* No two relationships are the same, even if they seem similar. If your first date evolves into more dates and then into an ongoing relationship, there will be time to work out together what suits you both on the money front. The first few dates won't give you the whole picture about each other: the Spender may be trying to impress, but you'll soon come to understand that they are always horribly in debt and have to deal with the consequences of that; or the Worrier will always be saying 'We can't afford it' if you want to splash out on a gourmet dinner, opera tickets or a trip to Florence.

Negotiating money groundrules for dating

Set money groundrules, preferably right from the start, even before you meet up the first time, perhaps on the phone, or at least when you buy the first round of drinks or are walking to the cinema. Be confident and friendly in your approach. No big preamble or justifications needed. You could propose the following:

1 *Going Dutch – paying 50/50.* This is the simplest way of negotiating a first date without getting too embroiled. Both of you can pay half of each bill or take it in turns to get in drinks or tickets, regardless of what you earn. You can say, 'Look, hope you don't mind, but I'd prefer to split costs – it keeps things simple.' For a woman, paying her way is empowering; she can feel in charge because the boundaries are clear. For a man, he can feel relief that he is not supposed to fork out for everything – after all, he may well be earning less than his date. It also keeps things clear

sexually, as neither the man nor the woman feel they are being bought or used.

2   *Take it in turns to pay.* Whoever instigates the first date pays for it. If you ask someone out for dinner, there is an assumption you will pay as the inviter. If you want this, you can say 'It's my treat'. Or if you don't want this to set a precedent, you can say 'I'll pay this time'. Then on the next date, the other person can pay. But there are risks involved in this strategy. First, it assumes optimistically there will be another date; second, unless you say 'Let's take turns' at some point, your date may expect you to pay each time. Relationship patterns can get set very early on and the first date is crucial in setting the tone. Also, if you are the instigator and you've forked out for an expensive meal you may feel resentful if the relationship goes nowhere. This strategy gets more complicated in working out who pays for what as the stakes rise and you move from dating to going out longer-term, with weekends away and longer holidays.

3   *The one with most money pays more or all.* This is obvious if one of you isn't a wage-earner and the other is in full- or part-time employment. However, don't make assumptions that a working person has more money than you, because they may well be providing for an ex-wife and three children, looking after an aged parent, saving every penny to travel the world or may have huge debts. Stay flexible about this, so that if circumstances change, the proportion each of you pays can change.

4   *As two earners with different levels of pay.* It's quite complex, but not impossible, to negotiate as two earners where one simply earns less due to the type of profession or being part-time. But watch out for feelings of resentment, as the one who pays more may come to feel aggrieved or taken for granted over time; equally, the one being subsidised can feel humiliated or beholden. This can work if 'payment in kind' is acceptable in terms of the less well-off person cooking meals, doing some decorating or fixing a car as an alternative to paying for going out. However, some women are still wary of being 'bought' for sex; a similar 'toy-boy' dynamic can occur for younger men who go out with older, monied women.

Handling feelings about negotiating

It's easy to feel very awkward about negotiating straightforwardly over money. This is because we often fear what the other person will feel about us or that they will judge us. One woman said of her new boyfriend, 'Every time we go out on a date we both get our wallets out to pay, but I say "Oh, it's OK, I'll get it", and he puts his wallet away. I don't want him to think I expect him to pay and I don't want to feel beholden to him.' However, she feels resentful afterwards: 'I find myself thinking about how much he owes me, sort of mentally totting it up, but I feel too silly to ask him for some money, because it was my fault in the first place.' She clearly feels embarrassed to be backtracking with hindsight.

It's important to remember that dealing with money, especially with someone you hardly know and whom you want to impress, will obviously bring up all sorts of strong emotions:

- fear (of being thought mean or a pushover);
- embarrassment (at mentioning the M-word and seeming to be too money-minded);
- awkwardness (at agreeing to something, then wishing you hadn't; or feeling awkward about the actual negotiating – as if it shouldn't matter);
- irritation (that you paid last time and now it's the other person's turn – although they don't seem to be taking the hint);
- resentment (that overall you've paid for more and you don't earn more – or you don't think you do);
- anger (it's not fair, you feel ripped off, abused, used, and so on).

You need to:

- expect feelings to be aroused by the subject of money;
- try to detach your feelings from the money issue at stake;
- prevent the feelings aroused about money from fuelling a fight over something else, like sex or a personal habit (like snoring or burping);
- try and address a difficulty as it happens rather than store it up for later. An accumulation of resentments tends to lead to a nuclear

explosion or an icy withdrawal. It's always better to deal with something as it happens and then it is past and you can move on;
- expect feelings to be strong about money and you won't be caught off guard;
- remember that just because you're dating you can't expect things to be all sweetness and light about money. Some people avoid conflict about something so real because they feel it sullies romance. In fact, working out the money stakes can make things much more sexy and real – intimacy is the root of true love after all.

When dating becomes mating

Some people enjoy dating for dating's sake: they like going out a few times with a new partner, but are not keen to establish a long-term, serious relationship. For others, dating necessarily leads to mating. It obviously depends where someone is in their life as to what their attitude to dating will be. Coming out of a long-term relationship or after a partner's death, someone might well be wary of getting in too deep. Whereas a woman in her thirties, even forties, may be longing to find a man to have a baby with. Almost mysteriously, couples move from dating into 'going out' over a certain period of time, maybe six months to a year. There are markers along the way, maybe saying 'I love you', or going away for a weekend or on holiday, or even starting to live together. Some couples move from dating to mating in a matter of hours, days or weeks, for others it can take years. There are so many factors involved – individual psychology, age, aspirations, character, circumstances, hidden desires – it is impossible to say exactly how this process evolves. It truly reflects the nature of the two individuals.

Choosing a mate

Whatever a couple decide to do, the issue of money will remain central to their ongoing relationship, whether they are fully conscious of this or not. Choosing a mate not only involves being socially and sexually compatible, it also involves feeling comfortable in the crucial area of finance. As we have seen, because the rules about male/female relationships have become more fluid and confusing, due to women's increased independence, couples need to be more conscious than ever concerning the taboo area of money. When choosing a mate you need to ask yourself some serious and straightforward questions about money in your relationship. There will be all sorts of things which are already niggling or concerning you; there may be other things which you welcome.

Because two people come together as two distinct individuals, it is crucial to become more aware of what are your own expectations concerning money. It is only by doing this that you will be able to pre-empt rows about money. After all, arguing is only a clumsy way of couples trying to put their views across to each other in order to be understood. You are disappointed, they are frustrated; you are angry, they are evasive. So you clash. Accumulated relationship Flashpoints turn into relationship Crunchpoints, perhaps leading to a split. It's therefore essential to make conscious, as far as you can, what is really unconscious about your individual Emotional Money Baggage. This will help you make a smoother and more satisfying transition from dating to mating and into a long-term relationship. However, we only really start contemplating these more serious issues once the relationship itself becomes more serious. If you have fallen in love with each other, or are contemplating living together or marrying, then the stakes are higher and money suddenly becomes much more important as an issue between you.

Making a money commitment

Caroline and Paul, whom we met earlier, are facing this next step, and all the dilemmas it raises over money, right now. Both in their twenties, and both working full-time (he's a computer software engineer, she's a retail buyer), they both earn roughly the same (£25,000 p.a.). During our candid interview, their individual (and therefore joint) money situation became clearer to them as we talked. Both admitted to having a range of credit cards (two each, up to the limit) and both have substantial debt. They are typical of two newly beloved Spenders living happily together; Caroline having streaks of Planner and Worrier, with Paul being more of an Ostrich mixed with Gambler. 'We're terrible with money,' they both laugh good-naturedly, 'we go out a helluva lot for meals and drinks with friends, plus weekends away here and abroad. We think nothing of putting it on our plastic.' They both admit paying around £200–300 a month purely on interest repayments.

When we add it all up they have £20,000 of debt between them (including Paul's £9,000 car loan); there is a moment's stunned silence. They have said during the interview that the next step in their relationship will probably be moving house, then marriage and children. Caroline looks worried. 'God, it's scary when you add it all up, isn't it?' Paul looks less perturbed, 'Yeah, I know a friend who wakes up every night and has cold sweats about it, but I'm more laid back, live for today and forget about tomorrow.' Caroline looks irritated by this comment: 'But we can't be as carefree as we have been, can we?' No comment from Paul. 'Actually I have made a spreadsheet and I religiously fed in data each month, trying to make a monthly budget for us, but I showed it to Paul and he wasn't that interested.' 'Yes, well, I don't know how compliant I would be to being managed,' pipes up Paul, 'I might rebel, especially if she was trying to limit me while buying Prada sandals.' Caroline ignores this and continues: 'So we ended up saying "bugger it, let's go out for a drink".' They both laugh, good humour restored.

However, the moment of tension about money hasn't passed entirely. Caroline is clearly thinking something will have to change if they are to move from dating to mating, on a long-term basis. 'Maybe we should get on and get a mortgage to consolidate our debts,' she suggests, 'then we could start again.' 'I guess, I'd find getting a mortgage sufficiently scary to tighten up,' admits Paul, 'but it does feel like a big grown-up step to take. Once you decide to become an official couple with a mortgage and house and all that, it all seems a bit intense.' 'Well,' says Caroline, adopting the sensible position, 'what else are we going to do? We can't really go on as we are.' They are both silent, sipping red wine on their rented sofa, deep in individual thought. Caroline breaks the silence, 'Well, I guess we've colluded with each other thus far, but if we're serious about living together and getting married, then things will have to change.'

Dating and mating checklist

If you are dating (or contemplating dating) at present:

- Is there anything you would change about how you handle money issues when you go out on a date?
- Are you holding back from sorting out something which is making you feel resentful with your date about money?
- Do you believe in 50/50 (going Dutch) or taking it in turns or treating each other? What does your date think or want?
- Could you be clearer about what you want and expect regarding money when you go on a date? Be specific.
- Would/do you want to mate your current date?
- Would money be an issue between you or is it sorted?
- Is there any unfinished business coming from your Emotional Money Baggage which is affecting your dates?
- Do you know which kind of Money Pattern would be most compatible with yours? If not, go back to chapter 2 and think about it. After all, your current, and future, happiness may depend on it.

5

Living Together

This above all: to thine own self be true,
And it must follow, as the night the day,
Thou canst not then be false to any man.

William Shakespeare

When a couple start considering mating, rather than just dating, the stakes get higher financially speaking. And when the stakes are raised, so are emotions, expectations and tempers. Couples often find themselves beginning to bicker precisely at the point they decide to live together because they have to confront issues about money which previously they have been able to avoid. Putting your relationship on a more fixed footing means deciding precisely how you will share, manage and pay for living together: money can then become a symbolic battleground.

Cohabitation trends

Sorting out money before and during living together is important as increasing numbers of couples are cohabiting. According to the Office of National Statistics, in 1996 1.6 million couples lived together and this is set to rise to 3 million by 2021. Two-thirds of people who live together never marry and a third are divorced. Also people who live together are belonging to older age groups today and by 2021 it is estimated that more people over thirty-five will be cohabiting than under thirty-five. Living together has usually been viewed as something young people do in their twenties before they 'settle down'. However, it looks as if living together will become simply a normal way of life to people of all ages, as the twenty-first century progresses.

Commitment

One main reason people cite for not marrying is fear of commitment. If you have fears about your relationship not being 'the one', or are frightened of committing long term because of fearing to make a mistake, or feeling trapped, or repeating the past, you or your partner may find yourselves baulking over making big purchases, signing agreements or making other financial commitments together. Deepening your commitment is like going down a flight of steps: with dating at the top of the steps, each step down is a further step towards intimacy, trust, permanency, buying flats or houses, joint ownership of other material goods, or eventually marrying and having children. As you descend the steps you get in deeper and deeper, entwining your lives more intimately and permanently, with your names on legal documents, loans, joint accounts and hire purchase or credit agreements. This can be exciting, and it can make you grow as a person – and, of course, as a couple. However, it can also be very scary, especially if you come from an unhappy background where people bickered constantly, couldn't communicate and finally separated or divorced.

Vee and Darren's story: fear of commitment
Vee, twenty-three, and her partner Darren, twenty-four, began living in a scruffy rented flat for six months when they first moved to Bristol. They'd been students at Manchester University together, then Darren had moved to Bristol for a job in a specialist music store, and Vee, a playgroup worker, followed. Both knew their first flat was a temporary let because they were finding their way in a new city, as well as with each other. However, without confiding in Darren, Vee began to have doubts about their relationship. She was frightened of making a big commitment to him because she didn't

know whether they loved each other enough. Was she too young and inexperienced to be making a long-term commitment? She was at a personal Crunchpoint – as was their relationship – even though she felt afraid of confiding her real fears to Darren. As a consequence, Vee became obsessed with wanting to move with him into a bigger flat in a better part of the city. She told herself that better housing would perhaps solve her commitment problem.

Then the money fights began. 'We'd never rowed about money up until this point,' Vee explains, 'in fact, we'd never rowed about anything. But I wanted to move, desperately, and began looking at properties. We started working out we'd have to buy a washing machine, a cooker and all sorts of domestic appliances.' Darren flipped. 'He couldn't understand why I was so intent on moving and he didn't want to spend his money on a microwave,' says Vee ruefully, 'he said he didn't want us to turn into his mum and dad. He'd rather spend his wages on CDs, ciggies and beer.' When Vee found a nicer flat eventually, Darren wasn't really interested in moving in because it was more expensive, so she moved out on her own as the relationship fell apart. 'I think our rows about money and buying things together was really all about us trying to make a deeper commitment – and failing,' says Vee with hindsight.

Agony Aunt for the *Sunday Mirror*, Virginia Ironside, agrees:

> I believe that when a couple is arguing about money in this way it is nearly always that they are fighting about something far deeper within the relationship. Money represents commitment, which is why I always recommend couples don't give up their individual flats if they can afford to keep them on while they go and try living together. At least keep some other bolt-hole open so you can retreat when the going gets tough.

As a relationship gets more serious, so does the issue of money. While you're dating you can rub along, ignoring, accepting or tolerating each other's different values or money habits. Even if you've got vastly different incomes, assets and attitudes, you can simply agree to pay 50/50 or take it in turns to pay while dating (see chapter 4 for more discussion of options) because neither of you really wants to get too embroiled. However, once you contemplate becoming a permanent 'item' money will suddenly seem to matter more.

Commitmentphobia

People fear commitment because they fear getting in too deep. They fear repeating the past (or their parents' past mistakes), are anxious about becoming too intimate and therefore being known too well (and being found out). They might even be unsure as to whether they even love their partner or prospective spouse enough or even at all. Some people fear committing to one person because they wonder if Mr or Ms Right is still out there somewhere and they don't want to limit their choices or experience. Commitmentphobia is a term used in popular psychology books to describe this common fear of commitment. Some people run from signing legal documents, even rental agreements, with each other because they fear being engulfed by the relationship or by the other person. We hear a great deal about men being commitmentphobic today (see Zelda West-Meads' book *How To Make Your Man Commit: And What To Do If He Won't* (Hodder & Stoughton, 1999). However, women can be equally frightened of getting in too deep. Resistance to becoming embroiled *financially* can be one of the first signs that the relationship is not working at root.

Money management styles

Exactly how couples manage their money between them has been a bit of a mystery until quite recently. Jan Pahl, a Senior Research Fellow at the University of Kent, has done some groundbreakingly original research into how couples organise their finances. Her two books on the subject, *Money & Marriage* (Macmillan, 1989) and *Invisible Money* (The Policy Press, 1999), publish the results of her fascinating study of what has until now been both hidden and taboo areas in couples' lives. Jan Pahl wanted to re-examine 'the assumption that the household is an economic unit within which resources are shared equitably'. Her research was prompted by her discovery of the fact that women in battered women's refuges reported they were better off financially once they had escaped their violent partners and husbands, rather than worse off (as might have been expected). 'It was clear that some of the [partners and] husbands had had substantial incomes, but had kept so much for their own use that their [partners and] wives and children lived in grim poverty.'

It is not possible to explain the myriad results of Jan Pahl's research here – I would direct the reader to her very accessible books. However, there are some general conclusions which are of interest for the purpose of this book:

- The assumption that when a couple set up home together money is simply pooled and shared is an outdated notion. Even in traditional marriages (husband earning, wife at home), there has seldom been 50/50 sharing, because the man has often kept the lion's share of money for himself and dished out a lesser amount of 'housekeeping'.
- How couples organise their money today is highly complicated and unique to their own particular relationship – there are as many permutations of money management as there are couples.
- Women's liberation has increased women's participation in the workforce (over 40 per cent of married women work), but it doesn't necessarily mean they are better off at home. This is because women take time off for childbearing and rearing and men still earn 20 per cent more than women overall. Plus, men's social habits such as drinking, gambling and playing sports can take money out of the family unit.
- Control of money mainly happens where the money enters the household (so if the man earns more, he controls more).
- In terms of management styles, the higher up the social class system you go, the more men are in control of money – there's simply more at stake.
- Women still tend to be in charge of the everyday management of money, particularly for household things like food, clothing, children, etc.
- Working mothers tend to see their money as paying for their children's needs.
- The increased use of electronic money (cash tills, Switch cards, Visa, PC banking) is largely disadvantaging women, whose access to credit and computers is more limited than mens'.

Jenny and Nathan's story: deciding to buy a house and live together

When a couple decide to live together they are joining not only their hearts, minds and bodies, but also their Emotional Money Baggage and Money Patterns. Jenny, thirty, has been going out with Nathan, also thirty, for the past nine months. They are utterly in love and spend most evenings or weekends at her place (because it's more comfortable than his and has a well-stocked fridge/freezer). They both work full-time: he's a manager of a men's clothing store and she's a magazine sub-editor. 'I earn a bit more than Nathan, but I'm very careful with money,' explains Jenny. 'Although we come from similar working-class backgrounds, my parents were really good at sorting money out. They literally used to count it out on the kitchen table and they taught me to always save.' Nathan's family is completely different: 'My folks just say "live today, tomorrow we die". My dad likes the good life, so his wages are always spent before my mum gets her hands on them. I have to admit I'm just the same.'

We're sitting round Jenny's kitchen table in a beautifully decorated one-bedroom flat in South London as I gingerly raise the thorny issue of living together and money. 'Well, I've been thinking about this a lot,' Jenny begins (Nathan raises his eyes to the ceiling in mock boredom, then grins) and I think we should be saving for our mortgage deposit.' 'Save? You've got to be joking,' chips in Nathan, 'on my salary it's virtually impossible to save anything. We'll have to get a 100 per cent mortgage.' 'But if we do that, we'll be paying enormous amounts each month – which I'll end up paying most of,' flashes Jenny. The heat is rising in the kitchen and the oven isn't even on. Here's a money Flashpoint and it's pretty clear they've been through this argument a few times before. 'Anyway, we've got solicitors' fees and furniture and decorating to pay for, too. How are we going to do that if we don't save?' Nathan looks skywards again. There's a tense silence. 'I don't see why we can't ask our parents to help out,' he says defiantly. At this Jenny flashes, 'Well, I do. My mum and dad haven't got any spare cash, neither have yours. And anyway,' she adds snappily, 'we both work, so it's a bit of a cheek, isn't it?'

When Nathan goes to the loo, Jenny whispers conspiratorially: 'Actually I've saved about £8,000 while I've been working but I haven't told Nathan about it. It's my special, secret nest egg, so I could manage a deposit on my own. But, I want us to agree that we'll start saving before I tell him.' Isn't that being a bit underhand, I ask? Surely if you're going to marry you need to be completely open and honest at this stage? 'Ye-es, I can see your point,' agrees Jenny, and she pauses to think, 'but you see, Nathan needs to learn some good money habits and he didn't learn them from his parents, so I guess I'm the teacher. Anyway, I think it's not a good idea to give everything away in one go.'

When Nathan returns we carry on talking about the pros and cons of living together. Both parties have cooled down and they say they both feel it's essential to see how they really get on financially as making a commitment to buying a property and moving in together is a big thing for them both. Do they fight about money at present? 'We-ell,' begins Jenny, looking meaningfully at Nathan, who looks away unperturbed, 'there have been niggles recently – like the one just now. I'm still paying out for the rent, lighting, heating, Council Tax and all that . . .' 'Yeah, but I pay for the shopping and meals out,' says Nathan in defensive tones. 'Ye-es, . . . but you have to admit I pay more overall,' Jenny snaps, beginning to get shirty again. 'Well, I think it evens out over time,' says Nathan. 'Well, I don't, especially as you spend more on yourself than I do,' snipes Jenny. They're at another Flashpoint: both feel aggrieved. If this pattern continues as they try to buy a house together and move in without resolving their differences about money, they could soon be reaching a relationship Crunchpoint.

What is being exposed here is the difference between their individual Emotional Money Baggage and particular Money Patterns. Jenny was raised to be prudent and to save; Nathan to spend and squander. She is clearly a Planner (with a big Hoarder streak); he's more of an Ostrich (with a streak of Spender). I wonder at her somewhat high-handed teacherly approach and whether this will put him in a childlike pupil role: something which could backfire later on. Healthy relationships need to be mutual in power terms, rather than allowing one partner to dominate the other. Jenny and Nathan will have to work hard to bridge the abyss between their respective money viewpoints if they are going to live happily ever after together. Buying a house will increase the level of commitment both emotionally and financially – the question is can their relationship take the strain?

Paying for life together

When a couple decide to cohabit they have to make some crucial decisions about how they are going to pay for their life together. Whether both partners are working full- or part-time, if one or both is unemployed, or one is not earning through being a house-husband or wife, there seems to be three main management styles couples adopt:

1 'His' and 'Hers' – totally separate money.
2 'His', 'Hers' and 'Ours' – separate money, but with a joint money account.
3 'Ours' – totally joint money.

We will look at these three money management styles in more detail here, highlighting their respective advantages and disadvantages.

1 'His' and 'Hers' – totally separate money: Ginny and Dan's story

Ginny, thirty-five, a senior hairstylist, and Dan, thirty-three, a freelance caterer, have lived together for five years. They don't have any children and say they don't want any. Ginny earns £15,000 p.a. and Dan's earnings fluctuate anywhere between £8,000 and £20,000 p.a. 'We have always had totally separate bank accounts,' explains Ginny, 'mainly because I hate the idea of him knowing what I'm spending on. My dad was a total control freak and my mother never had any money of her own, so I feel it's essential to keep my independence.' Ginny admits she's a bit of a Spender, with Worrier and Gambler patterned streaks. 'I like to feel my money's my own. I'd hate to feel tied down to direct debits and standing orders, even though I know they're sensible.'

Dan's family was very sober and restrained (his father was a Methodist lay preacher) and he is able to be quite controlled and frugal. He would like them to have a joint account, but because his money comes in in dribs and drabs he knows he couldn't sustain regular payments into one. 'It's really feast or famine,' explains Dan. 'If I work for a film production company I'll suddenly have masses of money coming in, then I might have three winter months with hardly any work, except for the Christmas party rush. It makes planning money very difficult.' Dan's more prudent than Ginny, and saves regularly for his tax and pension. Predominantly a Hoarder, he's got a Planner patterned streak. However, Ginny's spending drives him mad. 'I know she gets loads of tips, sometimes it runs into hundreds of pounds, and I want her to save it all. But she says "I've earned it, so I'll spend it", and she'll blow it all on a good night out or some designer clothes.' Then bills arrive and there's always a wrangle about who pays them (there's no set pattern – it's whoever has some money at the time pays that month or quarter).

This is management by chaos, usually at the last minute. They never have money meetings as Ginny gets too upset talking about money and Dan loses his temper. Ginny and Dan rent a flat together and, as yet, have no plans to buy. Ginny baulks at the level of commitment and self-restraint it would take; Dan fears his fluctuating income would make them both dependent on Ginny to pay for things, like a mortgage, which she really doesn't want to do. Ginny doesn't have a pension, which Dan thinks she should have. So what are their money fights about? 'Mainly my spending,' admits Ginny candidly. 'Dan wants us to sit down and make a plan, but I hate talking about money. I think money's just a means to an end – you earn it, you spend it.' Ginny has credit card debts, although Dan refuses to use one, unless it's in an utter emergency. If they take a holiday (usually they can only manage one or two one-week holidays a year), they buy their own air or train tickets and take it in turns to pay for meals. What about the future? Ginny is resistant to buying a house, settling down, taking on the further financial commitments of a joint nature. Whereas Dan would like some security in life. 'I'm not sure how we are going to sort this one,' says Ginny, 'as I will always need to have my own money even if we stay together until we're really old. I don't want some man giving me pocket money, that's for sure.' 'I would like to buy a house,' says Dan, 'so maybe I'll do that and charge Ginny rent and half the utilities. I can't ever see us having a joint account and mortgage, though.'

Advantages
Keeping things separate means each person keeps their independence financially and emotionally. Both retain freedom to spend their money exactly as they wish.

Disadvantages

They may be avoiding facing something about trust and intimacy in their relationship. Ginny's Emotional Money Baggage about her father's attitude is making her have a rigid fear of trusting men – Dan in particular. And Dan's Emotional Money Baggage-based frugality is almost pushing Ginny towards greater spending extremes (if he spent more, she might well find herself spending less, almost perversely). A lot of time and energy can go into wrangling over monthly or quarterly bills which could be handled through direct debits or budget accounts. If either lost their job or suddenly earned more, there is no easy way for them to negotiate handling the change if they haven't learned to talk about money constructively.

2 'His', 'Hers' and 'Ours' – totally separate money with a joint money account: Julia and Naz's story

Julia, twenty-nine, works full-time for an insurance company, and Naz, thirty, is a quantity surveyor. They have lived together in a rented house for eighteen months and have no children (although they would like them). Both agree theirs is a 'trial marriage' as both their families are putting pressure on them to tie the knot (Naz's family is Turkish Cypriot, Julia's is Irish Catholic). 'We have separate accounts, which our salaries go into,' explains Julia, 'and then we have a joint account in both of our names. Each month we put the same amount into the joint account which pays for bills and holidays. We've recently opened a savings account which is supposed to be for our mortgage deposit. Again we put the same amount into this each month.'

It all sounds straightforward, except for the fact that Naz earns £5,000 more than Julia and therefore has more spending money. He likes buying expensive suits and stereo equipment, which upsets Julia. 'She's more down to earth than me about money', admits Naz, 'and I do like going out on a Saturday and buying loads of CDs and clothes.' In fact, Julia finds it hard to spend on herself and also feels she has to compensate for Naz's extravagance by cutting back. 'I worry what will happen when we finally buy a house and have a child,' she says. Julia's a Planner, but with a big Worrier streak. 'I know Naz likes betting as well.' Naz nods in agreement: 'I used to put masses on the dogs, but I've cut back to about £50 on a Saturday.

It's my weekend extravagance.' More of a Gambler, with a Spender streak, Naz says he worries about whether he'll ever be sensible enough to be a parent. It actually annoys Naz that Julia doesn't spend more on herself. 'It was her idea to have a joint account and I'm glad we've got the basics covered. But I would like her to spoil herself occasionally.' Naz tends to foot the bill for meals out and weekends away, which they both accept. But Julia would like him to save more. 'I'm not sure I ever will,' he says with a rakish grin.

Advantages
By having a joint account they are covering their basic household expenses, plus they both have individual money to spend. They are saving towards their future together, which is good training for married life, especially with a child.

Disadvantages
As one partner earns more, the lesser earner is disadvantaged by having less spending power. They could equalise their incomes more by the greater earner spending more on joint expenditure – except for the fact that Naz is a Gambler and likes to spend. This may become a problem for them if and when Julia stops working while she has a baby.

3 'Ours' – totally joint money: Bren and Paul's story
Bren, forty-one, and Paul, fifty, have lived together for ten years (they never got round to marrying, they say), and they own a semi-detached house. The have two teenage children. 'All our accounts are joint and we both feel that that's how a partnership should be,' explains Bren. She works as a part-time secretary in a small firm and Paul is a builder. 'All our money, no matter how small, is pooled. We keep some cash at home for emergencies and simply dip into it when we need it and otherwise both our wages go into a joint account.' Sometimes Paul's wages are cash, sometimes a cheque, depending on the job, so monthly money fluctuates. Bren and Paul sit down at the kitchen table once every two weeks with a calculator and work out how to manage the money. 'I have to say Bren is the overall manager,' says Paul sheepishly, 'I'm happy to get my beer and fags money, while she works out the supermarket and household bills,' 'Yes, I like to be the one in charge,' grins Bren, 'it's what I do

at work anyway and I have access to a phone. So it's easier for me to do it than Paul on site.'

Nonetheless, if it comes to making any big financial decisions, like going on holiday or buying furniture or a car, they come to a joint agreement. 'We believe in saving,' says Bren, 'so we tend to save up and then spend on something important, like a sofa or Christmas presents or a family holiday.' However, even though they come to joint decisions, it tends to be Bren who shops around and executes their agreements. 'We now have a credit card account, but we always pay it off monthly. We hate being in debt, so I'm quite careful about what we spend. But I do have a real eye for a bit of a bargain.' Paul seems very happy with his lot. 'I don't need for much. Bren forks out for a pair of new boots or jeans for me when I need them and I always get clothes for my birthday. I don't really need much else.' The kids are another matter, and Bren and Paul say they both spend most of their disposable income on their kids' needs for designer clothes, CDs and computer gear. There's no resentment about who earns more or less, however. 'We feel it all balances out in the end,' says Bren contentedly.

Advantages

Totally joint money systems like Bren and Paul's show a great deal of trust. They are definitely a unit and work together as a family, for the family's benefit. By pooling their money, they can maximise their resources. It helps one or both partners budget for the present and future, and gives them both a sense of a security. There are also no hidden (nasty) surprises – as everything is above board. This system can work best when one partner – Bren in this case – is overall manager. It's always harder to accommodate two heads of the household, so this model tends to have the least strife.

Disadvantages

Neither party has their 'own' money, and Paul (the one not in control of the finances) could feel at a disadvantage. This might rankle if one of them wanted to go on a spending splurge, or wanted to do something special for the other. It's difficult to have surprise presents and events, when all the household money is openly accounted for. Plus, if partners disagree about spending priorities, it is difficult to do anything else than go along with what the one holding the purse strings wants. Women usually find themselves in this position, but it's not unusual these days for men to be the lesser earners. This can also lead to strife.

Johnny and Fiona: finding common financial ground

Because talking about money is such a taboo subject, many couples feel uncomfortable about raising the issue. When you are in love and want to live together, there is a common assumption that things will 'work themselves out'. However, if you are unable or unwilling to voice doubts and fears about money *before* you start living together, it's possible that very soon you will be arguing about who spent what, when and where. 'I thought Johnny and I were fantastically compatible before we started living together in my flat,' says Fiona, thirty-nine, a childminder, about her engineer boyfriend, 'but it was amazing how far apart we were on the money front.' The first weekend they were together at her place, Johnny said he would do the shopping. 'He came back with all sorts of weird and expensive things,' remembers Fiona, 'but he'd left out the basics like toothpaste, toilet roll, tea, butter and bread.' Johnny boasted that he'd only spent about £40, but when Fiona spent £80 next week he was furious. 'But I was having to buy all the basics that he'd left out – like tins of things, pasta, sauces, cleaning stuff, washing powder. He would buy a pack of smoked salmon and a couple of bottles of wine and think that was enough.'

Their money rows soon escalated and started clouding their relationship. 'We then decided to go to the supermarket together, but everything I put in the trolley he would take out and vice versa. We ended up having screaming matches in Sainsbury's, it was dreadful.' Fiona felt this situation could not go on. 'I was beginning to hate him. He was like my father, impractical, ridiculous, pigheaded. I thought, "Why didn't I see all this before? I certainly wouldn't have lived with him if I had".' However, they did love each other and after a blazing row over whether to buy avocados or not (Johnny thought they were an absolute essential, Fiona thought they were an expensive luxury), they agreed to talk. 'We went for a long walk in the countryside and tried hard to talk about the whole thing without too much emotion,' says Fiona. It turned out that Johnny had never ever lived with anyone before, hated cooking and usually lived on convenience foods and takeaways. He ate most of his meals at work or out and only ever kept a few luxuries in the fridge. Fiona had put his empty cupboards down to laziness or working too long hours before she lived with him. Johnny now admitted to her he knew absolutely nothing about cooking or housekeeping – and what's more wasn't really interested in it all. 'This was a revelation to me,' says Fiona, 'as I had already lived with two guys and had shared households with women. I love cooking and am quite careful with money, but I do want a good standard of living.' Fiona would never buy convenience foods, ate out seldom (only special occasions) and worried about the quality of what she purchased (mainly organic fruit and vegetables). 'I suppose I didn't realise how far apart we really were until we started living together. Buying groceries brought things to a head almost immediately.'

Johnny and Fiona's Emotional Money Baggage

What's more, as they talked they realised how their Emotional Money Baggage was hooking together. Fiona came from a fairly poor, working-class background, where her mother always bought the 'own-brand' labels, cheap cuts of meat and left-over veg and fruit. Whereas Johnny came from a well-heeled background, where his mother had groceries delivered. He had never actually gone round the shops with his parents or seen them shop together, so it was all a bit of a mystery. Luckily, they were able to negotiate with each other. 'We came to a solution fairly quickly. We'd spend £50 a week on basics and then Johnny could choose his luxuries and pay for it himself over the top. We'd eat in three or four nights a week when I would cook, and then he'd either buy takeaways or take me out. As he earns more, that's fine by me.'

Money talk

The crucial thing here is that couples need to have a money talk before they move in together to iron out money differences. Failing that, you should try to talk about money as soon as you can once you start living together. Patterns get set fairly quickly and it can be difficult, although not impossible, to change once routines have become established. Of course, each couple will do something which suits their own needs specifically as there is no 'right' way to talk about or organise money. However, it is *essential* to air issues around the subject of money otherwise there may well be a build-up of misunderstandings and resentments which can really damage a relationship if left untended.

Some basic negotiating tips

- Talk about how you will organise your money, *preferably* before you start living together (or as soon as you can after you've moved in with each other).
- Work out your money-management style: 'His' and 'Hers', or 'His', 'Hers' and 'Ours', or just 'Ours'.
- Face the realities of rent, mortgage, council tax, utilities, phone bills and food bills, and decide how you will pay for them, together and separately.
- Talk about how much you both earn – perhaps you can pay for things proportionately (the higher earner paying more).
- Do you want to save together? If so, how much, how often, for what and with whom?
- If you can (and if you feel it's appropriate), come clean about current debts, savings, alimony payments (received and payable) and other assets. This may only happen once the relationship has become well established and you feel you can truly trust each other.
- Don't make assumptions or hint and hope the hint is taken – spell things out. No matter how uncomfortable this may seem in time you will feel happier together because of it.
- Keep channels of communication open. Just because you said you'd organise things one way, it doesn't mean you can't change your mind if it doesn't work out or one of you doesn't like it. Try to be flexible and consistent at the same time.
- If you find yourself fighting about money as you move in and/or just after, remember that there will be a lot of fear, tension and anxiety about whether the relationship is going to work or not. Both of you will be hauling your Emotional Money Baggage (see chapter 1) with you, so perhaps it's a good time to talk about past relationships and what happened with them concerning money, in order to see how your current partner is different from them.
- Try and analyse your respective Money Patterns (see chapter 2) so that you can begin to see who you are as individuals trying to

live together. Don't expect your partner to be like you simply because you love each other. Remember Chalk-and-Cheese makes for a dynamic relationship, but there can be a lot of misunderstandings. Even if you are Mirror-Images of each other, you are still two distinct individuals. So try to draw back from your assumptions and see who the other person is and how they behave (see chapter 3).

- If you are arguing a lot about money, take time out to think separately about what it really symbolises for you. If the money fights continue, it may be a cover for deeper emotional difficulties. Money can become a focus when other things seem harder or impossible to talk about.

- Take heart – it is possible to move past where you are arguing about money, even if you seem to have got off to a bad start with each other. In time, with patience and communication and some positive experiences of working as a team, your relationship can grow and you should be able to learn to live together in a way that accommodates you both as two distinct individuals. People can change as long as they want to – and the rewards of living together harmoniously are manifold.

Cohabitation contracts

However a couple decide to organise their money – whether separately or jointly – there is still a need for trust, honesty and openness if a relationship is going to work long term. Some people feel that writing everything down in a cohabitation contract is the best way forward for couples to protect themselves concerning money when they live together. Most relationship experts agree it's a good idea to work this out before you move in together, although it's perfectly possible to negotiate a contract even if you've lived together for months, even years. It's important to note here that a cohabitation contract you scribble on an envelope has no legal status (although it may be used in evidence in court or by a solicitor as a document of intent). It is vital therefore that you get help from an appropriate solicitor while drawing up a document, so that it is correctly worded and legally viable (this may cost around £600 at time of writing).

Of course, as a couple contemplating moving in together or buying a property together, it can be very useful to create your own cohabitation contract as a way of setting down some basic, mutually agreed groundrules about money. The process of negotiation should help air any concerns about your individual financial situations, attitudes, practices and beliefs.

Writing your own cohabitation contract

Before you start
- You'll need paper, pens or access to a computer and a calculator.
- You need to allocate substantial time for the task – maybe a half or whole day at a weekend, or two or three evenings.
- It's best to have information like pay slips, bank statements, savings books, household utility bills to hand for reference.
- Have the meeting sober, as drinking alcohol can make you both over-emotional and unclear, sparking a row. Celebrate your hard work afterwards with a drink if appropriate.

First
- Set a time limit – no one likes meetings to go on for hours and if you fear money you might take ages getting down to detail. A time limit focuses the mind.
- Take a piece of paper each and write down:

  - why you want to live together;
  - what's exciting about the prospect;
  - what you love about each other;
  - what your wildest dreams/hopes are about living together;
  - what you fear the most;
  - what your 'bottom lines' are about living together.

Then swop papers and read each other's and see which items you have in common. Note them. Then see how different you are. This sets a good tone for the meeting and if there are any problems to iron out, you can identify and talk about them at this point.

- Next you need to agree basic principles as to how you are going to organise your money together:

- are you splitting all bills 50/50?
- are you splitting bills proportionate to who earns more – so if you earn £10,000 p.a. and your partner earns £30,000 p.a., you'd pay a third and they'd pay two-thirds?
- are you setting up a joint account for household bills or simply taking it in turns to pay as bills come in?
- bills include – write a list (rent/mortgage, shopping, electricity etc.);
- make a list of things which are excluded: such as personal debts (Visas, overdrafts on individual accounts), child maintenance, alimony, any personal welfare benefits, inheritances, winnings, savings etc.;
- if you are renting afresh together make sure you write down what agreement you have about who owes what for deposits, monthly rental, etc. and how it will be paid (by cheque on the 15th of the month, standing order, in cash, and to whom);
- if one of you already owns the property you're going to live in together, do you want rent, if so how much, when and how paid? Does rent include or exclude utilities, food bills, council tax, etc?
- if you want a joint savings account, write down how much each of you will put in and when and what it is to be used for (emergencies, holidays, etc.);
- if you have a pet and/or a child or children, write down who is responsible for paying for their expenses;
- if one or both of you have a car (or other transport) work out insurance and running costs. Do you want to share them or keep them separate? Do you want to be named on each other's insurance policies, which might mean an extra premium payment? If so, work out who will pay for it;
- if one or both of you have children from a previous relationship or marriage, write down who pays for their maintenance and treats. Is it to be jointly shared or kept separate? Equally, if one of you is paying the Child Support Agency, is it the responsibility of the ex-partner/spouse or both of you?
- make it crystal clear who is responsible for what – who's setting up which standing orders, etc.
- also make it clear how you will pay for things like parties or other social events.

Second

- If you have long-term goals of getting married, having children, buying a house, are you going to start saving now? If you are, you need to set up a joint savings account and agree how and when it will be spent.
- If you want to plan long term, do you want to explore setting up a will (or separate wills), pension schemes, life insurance (important if you have a child or children) and other insurance policies?
- This might sound premature (and off-putting because it could tempt fate or reflect a lack of commitment), but you could write down how you will divide up money and property if things go wrong and you split up. For instance, any material goods bought jointly for the flat or house (like sofas, beds, carpets) to be divided up on the basis of current market worth or sentimental value. If either of you put a lump sum down for a deposit or put more money into a joint mortgage, you might want to write down that you would reclaim this amount. Or you might simply want your investment to be absorbed into the whole purchase deal in order to split any profits 50/50 should the property be sold (or bought out) at a later date. Some people feel this latter way represents greater trust and faith in the relationship working long term.

Third

- Either hand-write or type the document. Make sure you both read it and are happy with it, then sign it and put it somewhere safe so either of you can refer to it if you feel things are unclear. Human memory is both fallible and selective and it's often possible to remember agreements in all sorts of distorted ways. If you're in the throes of a heated argument about who was responsible for paying the council tax bill, then get out your cohabitation contract and check it together.

A word of warning

- Cohabitation contracts do not replace or supersede any of the legal agreements you may have entered into with landlords, banks or building societies. If you have a mortgage, you will be bound by the rules of that mortgage agreement. Your cohabitation contract has no legal status and will not stand up in a court of law. It's really useful because it's a statement of *intent*, showing how you wish to divide things up between you financially. It is also a useful focus and may well help you talk about all the nitty-gritty money issues you might otherwise avoid.

- There is no a such a thing as a 'common-law wife' or 'common-law husband'. A man or woman living together have no such legal status, the common-law term is a myth. This is often tested when a woman, who has been living with a man for a long time, tries to claim she has property rights. It makes no difference whether you have been living together for two weeks or twenty years, you will be viewed as separate individuals by a court of law.

- A cohabitation contract doesn't remove the need for you both to negotiate with each other on a day-to-day, week-by-week, month-by-month or year-by-year basis. Situations and circumstances change. For example, one of you may get a promotion, lose your job, have a baby, take time out to study, become disabled or chronically sick, go travelling, or come into money (see chapter 8).

Working out what's best for you

All these things test the openness, honesty and commitment of your relationship. There is no right way of sorting things out financially: what works best for your relationship will be what works best for you as two unique individuals. Just because your parents, last partner or ex-spouse handled money in a certain way does not mean that is the correct way for your current relationship even though it feels absolutely right for you. This is where Emotional Money Baggage and Money Patterns take over and we stop thinking. All you can do as a couple is say to each other: Who are we together as two distinct individuals? What do we want (short-, medium or long-term goals)? What works for us? Agree your contract for now, but keep an open mind if things change. Don't be rigid with each other and resist change. And don't hide behind a cohabitation contract. Sometimes making everything concrete can replace the very necessary need for trust. Sometimes relationships aren't equal, or everything doesn't balance out, or people forget what they agreed. If you like, respect and love your partner, you don't need to be vigilant about being hurt or ripped off.

A cohabitation contract is only worth the paper it is written on if both parties really agree to it wholeheartedly. Don't force the issue if your partner isn't really not keen on having one. This may tell you about some basic incompatibilities you have. You may feel as a couple you prefer to muddle along, working things out as you go. Fine. Cohabitation contracts don't work for everyone. It will nonetheless be a good idea to agree on some basic groundrules about money – even if it's just a verbal agreement.

Spencer and Jane's story: cohabitation contract vs. trust

Spencer, thirty-five, and Jane, thirty-eight, had drawn up their cohabitation contract when they went from Spencer living in Jane's rented flat to buying a house after five years together. They worked the contract out over mugs of tea at the kitchen table and were eventually satisfied with an agreement which covered most aspects of their life together, especially money. Each year, on their anniversary, they would renew their agreement with each other. However, by year five Jane was beginning to feel their life was too narrow and boring. Spencer was happy working in a bank, but Jane wanted to change her career from primary-school teaching to the travel industry. 'I needed wider horizons, more travel, some adventure. Spencer was unhappy about the changes, especially when I said I didn't want to write down everything we spent any more as I found it totally tedious.' Their custom had been to make a note of every single penny each one spent, from 26p on a stamp to £20 train fares, in a notebook on Saturday mornings. Then they religiously added up their respective lists and balanced out expenditure, with money passing from the one who had spent less to the one who had spent more. Everything was always accounted for. They also agree ahead of time how much they would spend on birthday and Christmas presents, usually no more than £10 each.

'I began to feel I was in a financial straitjacket,' says Jane of their money system, 'of course, it was fair, but my God, was it boring. There was absolutely no spontaneity and worse, no real generosity. How could either of us surprise the other with a luxury gift if we both knew it was never more than ten quid total?' The problem was they had fallen into being extremely rigid about enforcing their repayment system and it was symptomatic of other rigidities and narrownesses in the relationship. Jane began to wonder if she really wanted a child with Spencer (which was the long-term plan), or even if she loved him at all. They began to fight over money, especially when Jane suggested they loosen up their accounting system. 'Spencer hit the roof. It was really the first time we'd had an all-out, shouting match.' Jane says she wanted things to ride more on trust, but Spencer thought this was outrageous and only felt safe if everything was neatly accounted for: he felt threatened by change. Jane's proposal to alter how they ran their household finances symbolised the changes happening on a deeper level. Unfortunately, this tension was the beginning of the end of their relationship.

Things fell apart when Jane finally changed jobs and met someone new at work. She fell in love and confessed to Spencer (after all this was part of their cohabitation contract) and they went to Relate for six counselling sessions to try to save their relationship. As their relationship was falling apart Jane stopped writing down her expenditure, to Spencer's fury. It was a kind of rebellion. 'Our Relate counsellor could not believe how rigid we'd been,' remembers Jane, 'she said we clearly didn't trust each other, and that was absolutely true.' Spencer's father had died when he was five and he had been utterly traumatised to the extent he'd ended up in hospital with pneumonia and nearly died. Trust was still a major issue for him because of this. And Jane had been sexually abused by her father as an eight-year-old, the public exposure and prosecution of which had led to her parents divorcing. Trusting (even liking) men was far from Jane's experience. Jane and Spencer had clung onto their cohabitation contract and rigid accounting rules as a buffer against potential abuse from each other. However, the lack of trust and deep-seated fear on both sides meant their relationship could never really thrive. A cohabitation contract could not keep them together once their love had died.

This is a fairly unusual case, and cohabitation contracts can work very well in providing general guidelines concerning living together. However, the moral of the last story is that the real live issues about money in any love relationship need sorting out as openly and as honestly as possible between partners. No cohabitation contract can replace trust and honesty – or love. The really tough job in healthy love relationships is being able to:

- negotiate as you go
- allow for change

- be flexible
- build emotional boundaries
- listen to each other
- allow privacy
- operate tough love where necessary
- be emotionally supportive
- be mutual
- respect each other
- not keep score
- forgive
- laugh (and cry) together at adversity.

Living together checklist

Living together always raises issues about money, so ask yourself these questions.

- If you are about to start living together, have you had a 'money talk'? If not, why not? If yes, are you happy with what you have agreed?
- If you are newly living together, do you feel things are divided equally between you or in a way that is fair? Is there anything you need to air with your partner about money?
- If you've been living together for longer than a year, do you feel money is sorted out between you? If not, is there anything you would like to change?
- Do you have a cohabitation contract? If so, is it working well? If not, would you like to have one?
- If you are fighting about money, do you understand what is provoking the arguments? Can you see how your Emotional Money Baggage and Money Patterns might be fitting together and/or grating on each other?
- Are either of you playing money power games or addicted to money in any way? If so, what will this mean for living together?
- What do you like about living together on the money front?
- What, if anything, would you like to change about how you deal with your finances together?

6

Getting Married

Neither be cynical about love; for in the face of all aridity and disenchantment it is as perennial as the grass.

Max Ehrmann

Money and marriage

Marriage used to be all about money, especially for the middle and upper classes and, of course, royalty. Up until the early twentieth century, marriages were organised by prestigious families according to class, wealth and social position. 'Making a good match' was really about making a good money match, with lands, treasure, property, servants and livestock being central to negotiations. Women were also 'priced', whatever their class background, not only as to what they were 'worth' financially, but also as to whether they were a good investment for child-breeding, beauty, age, working hard and keeping house. On occasion, women were even sold like slaves or livestock at markets. The nineteenth-century novelist Thomas Hardy witnessed one of these dehumanising events which inspired the beginning of *The Mayor of Casterbridge*. A drunken husband sells his wife for five guineas to a passing sailor, and the wife, who is originally shocked, throws her wedding ring down, crying 'I've lived with thee a couple of years, and had nothing but temper! Now I'm no more to 'ee; I'll try my luck elsewhere.' This almost sounds like a speech from a modern marital break up, although it was actually written in 1886.

Married women's property

Indeed, until the late nineteenth century, women could not even keep hold of their own money and property when they married. According to Jan Pahl, author of *Money and Marriage*, 'The husband who stood in the church and promised "with all my worldly goods I thee endow" was in truth taking possession of his wife's goods and all her future earnings.' This was because 'under the common law, marriage meant that husband and wife became one person, so that the legal existence of the woman was incorporated into that of her husband. This implied that any property which a woman possessed or was entitled to at the time of her marriage, and any property which she became entitled to after it, became her husband's to control.' In addition, 'A wife could only make a will with her husband's consent and if she died without making a will her personal property continued to be her husband's absolutely, to the exclusion of her children or other relatives.'

Legal changes

After radical campaigning by women's rights activists such as John Stuart Mill and Harriet Taylor during the mid to late nineteenth century, the law was finally changed in women's favour. The Married Women's Property Act of 1870 was a landmark law, enabling married women without marriage settlements (like dowries) to hold onto property in their own right. In 1882 there was further legislation, another Married Women's Property Act, which finally gave married women the same rights over property as men and unmarried women. Even so, women were still not entirely equal to men, legally speaking, and it took another law as recently as 1964 to enable savings from a housekeeping allowance given by a husband to a wife to belong equally to them both. Before this Act money belonged to the husband and the woman was deemed to be acting as his 'agent'. Today, the law still discriminates against women as Jan Pahl explains: 'Under the 1964 Act money given by a husband to a wife for household purposes does not become hers but remains jointly theirs, while if a wife gives a husband money for household purposes it becomes his and he can keep any savings from it.'

Women's Lib

During the twentieth century, from the early 1960s, there arose a new Women's Liberation Movement in both the US, UK and Europe which pinpointed marriage as a symbol of inequality for women. Feminists attacked marriage as being unfair and degrading to women, especially in relation to money. Radical books, like Germaine Greer's *The Female Eunuch*, Betty Friedan's *The Feminine Mystique* and Hannah Gavron's *The Captive Wife*, made women think more than twice about marrying – many rejected it completely. In the late 1950s women had become 'model wives' in a reaction to the unglamorous hard labour and stringent suffering of the Second World War. People were told by the then Prime Minister, Harold Macmillan, that they had 'never had it so good'. Songs with lyrics such as 'love and marriage/love and marriage/go together like a horse and carriage' represented the popular myth of marriage being the zenith of women's lives.

However, by the mid 1960s women were burning their padded bras, taking the Pill, throwing away their stilettos, screaming at the Beatles or the Rolling Stones and demanding greater equality not only in bed (having orgasms) but in the workplace (earning their own money). 'Y B A Wife' was an early 1970s feminist campaign which encouraged women not to marry. Even when the virginal Diana Spencer became betrothed to Prince Charles in 1981, there was a prophetic women's campaign with the slogan 'Don't Do It Di'. All of these campaigns focused not only on the sexual slavery and lack of independent status many women now felt marriage bestowed, but also the lack of financial freedom, and therefore power, that married women endured.

No more 'pin money'

During the 1970s and 1980s women fought for the right to be better educated, to work on an equal basis to men, to 'find themselves', to have enjoyable sex (few married women ever had orgasms) and to explore their sexuality (becoming lesbian and bisexual). All of this went hand in hand with having their own money. Because money meant power, women wanted it for themselves (even when overt materialism was renounced). Up until then if a married woman worked it was often called 'pin money' and not taken seriously. Single women were also paid less as they weren't deemed 'breadwinners' (lone motherhood was considered a shameful sin). Now women wanted to have careers, rather than jobs, with equal pay and pensions, just like men. To this end, the Equal Pay Act (1970) and Sex Discrimination Act (1975) were landmark laws in the liberation of women.

Living together

Couples began living together openly from the 1960s and 1970s, during the hippy 'flower power' era, and although it was called 'living in sin' and shocked the general public at the time, it has now become virtually commonplace (for more on this see chapter 5). Cohabitation is today even recommended by some enlightened religious leaders as a sensible precursor to marriage. The increasingly popular practice of living together meant that couples could stay together not because they had to legally, but because they wanted to. Of course, what was not understood at the time, and which is better understood now, was that when women had babies it was (and still is) extremely difficult for them to remain financially independent. And this in turn affected a couple's love relationship, financial security and, therefore, quality of life. (This is still a much-debated and written-about issue today and one which needs careful management in relationships, as will be discussed further in chapter 7.)

Men's Lib

In the late 1980s and 1990s many men began to embrace women's increasing financial equality as a benefit to themselves. The so-called 'Men's Movement' began to support women's equality because as women became more financially independent it actually removed the burden of being the sole breadwinner (and all that comes with it pyschologically speaking) from men's shoulders. Things have now come full circle in that, by the twenty-first century, men expect women to earn as much, if not more, than them *and* to have babies. Both men and women expect and want greater choice today, which has led to many women choosing to stay at home with their children, or work part-time, or work at home, or limit their careers; and some men have even decided to be 'househusbands' and stay home with the children. Also, it is expected that nearly a third of mothers will be lone parents by the year 2010 – and the figure is set to rise as the twenty-first century proceeds.

Twenty-first-century marriage

It's a twenty-first-century paradox: marriage has never been so popular, while marital breakdown has never been so great. Even though one in two marriages end in divorce, we are still keen to marry, so the remarriage rate is high, with people experiencing one, two, even three marriages during a lifetime. The old notion of marrying one partner for life has been replaced by the practice of serial monogamy – one serious relationship after another. Most couples live together for at least a short period before they marry today.

However, according to the relationship research organisation One Plus One, it seems couples have a better chance of staying together if they decide to marry quickly rather than get settled in their ways as cohabitees.

Simone and John's story: happier cohabiting than marrying

'I lived with John for ten years quite happily,' explains Simone, forty, a social worker. 'We had settled into a routine of work, shopping, cleaning, gardening, social life, and a two-week annual holiday. Then we decided to marry – I guess we felt we might as well.' They had a quiet wedding, which seemed appropriate after all that time together. 'We said we were going to try for children as I was thirty-eight, going on forty. John was keener than I was, but we tried anyway, to no avail. Anyway, amazingly, within a year our relationship was over. Somehow, once we married, it just all fell apart. Basically, the gaps in our relationship – and between us as two people – became apparent once we tried to take the next step together.'

Simone and John found themselves arguing more and more about everything, especially money. Then John fell in love with someone new, left Simone and was soon the father of a little girl. And Simone realised that she didn't really want children – she had just been trying to appease John and keep their dying relationship alive. It's quite a common phenomenon: the longer you live together, the less chance a marriage after, say, five, seven or ten years will probably work. This is often because there has been a lack of intimacy or a problem of commitment which only really surfaces once the decision to marry is made.

Getting married

As we saw in the previous two chapters, each step, from dating to mating, is a step towards greater commitment and financial entanglement. In the 'bad' old days, couples fell in love and married; or the woman got pregnant and the couple were forced to marry, or their parents organised a marriage based on class, money and social position. Today things are very different. Couples seldom 'save' for a long time to get married today: they either drift into living together through convenience or may even rent or buy a property together because it makes financial sense before marriage. The ceremony itself can be a mere legal formality taking place once the home has been set up or the children born ('illegitimacy' no longer being a social stigma).

As a result, engagement has waned. Today, getting engaged is almost seen as a 'quaint' romantic custom and mainly a reason to buy a ring. Engagements still have a symbolic worth for people who live and work far apart (such as those in the services) as a statement of intent to marry. And, of course, getting engaged is still a strong custom within specific religious and ethnic groups.

Pre-nuptial agreements

Like cohabitation contracts (see chapter 5), pre-nuptial agreements are an American idea imported to the UK, with little or no legal standing here. We read with fascination about rich celebrities like Michael Douglas and Ivana Trump hammering out their pre-nuptial agreements in glossy magazines like *Hello* and *OK!* This is because vast amounts of money and property are at stake and very little emotional honesty and trust is involved. Celebrities seem to need to protect themselves (and their fortunes) from unscrupulous gold-diggers by agreeing elaborate legal documents before each marriage. But what about the rest of us?

Mandy and Ricki's story: pre-nuptial hell

Mandy, thirty-three, an advertising executive, had fallen totally in love with a famous soap actor, thirty-five-year-old Ricki (not his real name), whom she'd met at a celebrities' charity event. They began living together in his parents' house within two months of meeting, with a view to marrying as soon as possible. 'We paid rent to his parents and I did pay half, usually by cash or cheque, although Ricki was a hell of a lot wealthier than I was. We also split the bills, although he paid more when we went out or on holiday.' Overall, Mandy and Ricki lived together for a year while buying their dream house and planning their wedding. 'He was (and still is) the love of my life and we were very, very happy. I'd been buying my own flat before we met, which was discarded once we agreed to buy a property together.' In her profession, Mandy was used to being thought of as well paid. But in comparison to Ricki, she felt poor. 'I wondered sometimes if he thought I was taking him for a ride, financially speaking. We were buying a house in a very fashionable area and it was much more than I ever could have afforded on my own. But we were in love and I thought we were just putting in whatever we had to make a go of it together and for ever.'

Mandy was utterly shocked, therefore, when she had a call from Ricki's solicitor, asking her to go to his office for a meeting. 'We were nearing completion on the house deal, the wedding was booked, my dress had been made, we'd bought carpets and sofas and had a kitchen installed. So I went to the meeting and was utterly gobsmacked that the solicitor was asking me to sign a pre-nuptial agreement, signing away my right to half of everything.' Mandy was utterly astonished. Not only was Ricki absent from the meeting, so couldn't explain himself to her, but he had never even raised the issue with her. 'He had put up much more money than me for the deposit, and had spent more than me on the building works, furnishings and decorating. But I thought we were in love and that it didn't matter.' The document asked for Ricki to be paid back £100,000 should the marriage fail and everything had to be sold: he wanted his investment back before everything was split 50/50. 'I couldn't believe it, I was utterly shocked that he didn't trust me or didn't feel our relationship would last. He was asking me to sign a document to stop me stitching him up. What's more he didn't even have the guts to put it to me face to face. I realised at that moment he didn't love me really – and that he probably couldn't love anyone.'

Mandy signed the document. She felt she didn't know what else to do. But the wedding never went ahead and she never moved into their dream house. 'I went home and said "I don't like you as a person, I don't respect how you are treating me at all".' To her astonishment, he didn't really answer her. 'I knew then it was over. Even though I loved him, I couldn't live with someone who couldn't trust me.' Money was a major issue between them, she then understood. 'I think it would have been different if I'd earned the same as him. He'd become perverted by fame and money. I felt all the joy and happiness go out of our relationship once I understood he put money before me. I felt like it was "his" house and I was just tagging along like a golddigger. That felt so terrible, that I left him soon after signing his bloody agreement.'

Mandy says she still loves Ricki, although she doesn't like him. He moved on to a new girlfriend fairly soon after she left. Mandy says she has learned never to fall into such a trap again. 'Next time I want everything spelling out upfront. If he wants a pre-nuptial agreement, then I'm out of there. It's either "trust me or nothing". To my mind, if a couple buy a house in marriage it's for ever. If it doesn't work out, then you simply either sell up and split the money or buy each other out. I found it cynical and insulting that Ricki wanted to guarantee his investment ahead of time. It showed no faith in our relationship or love at all.'

To some people it might seem very logical and sensible to spell things out legally ahead of marrying, especially with the divorce rate being so high. However, on a psychological level, it seems important for people to enter marriage with a positive attitude of hope and a determination to make things work. Because everyone comes into a relationship with their own respective Emotional Money Baggage and Money Patterns, it is not possible always to assume or double-guess how a partner will react to something like a pre-nuptial agreement. If you are thinking about drawing up such an agreement before you marry, it is essential to consult a specialist solicitor.

Wedding nerves and money fights

Couples can also suffer from wedding nerves, which are a typical cause of money fights. When couples marry one partner may want a full-blown event, with white dress, top hat and tails and masses of guests, while the other may want a small, informal affair. Children or stepchildren may be present as bridesmaids and pageboys; ex-partners and spouses may even attend. Equally, a couple may decide to have a 'quickie' register office wedding, with no fuss and a simple get-together of friends afterwards. Or, with the loosening up of marriage laws concerning wedding venues, a couple may choose to marry alone on an exotic isle or in the wilds of Scotland or on a boat at sea. However, once the decision to marry has been made there are many practicalities to face about paying for the wedding as you both become more and more entwined financially. As the 'big day' looms money fights can escalate because couples have very different views, beliefs, fears and expectations about how the event should be hand-led. Class and cultural differences can come to the fore and each partner may feel the other is making unreasonable demands. The relationship is under stress as there are external pressures (relatives' desires, beliefs and expectations) mixed with the internal pressures of changing your status from boyfriend and girlfriend or cohabitees to husband and wife.

Tips for reducing wedding nerves money fights
This book is obviously not a wedding manual, and I would direct the reader to magazines like *Wedding and Home* and *Bride*, and etiquette manuals available in most newsagents, for more detailed advice when organising a wedding. However, if you want to reduce money fights which may arise when you have decided to get married, it may be useful to do the following, whether you are simply going out or already living together.

- Work out individually what kind of wedding you want to have.
- Explain to your partner what you would like and why. Then listen to what they want.

- Try and cost out what such a wedding would be: you don't have to have all the trimmings if you don't want them. Face as much as you can about money ahead of time. Costs can escalate; 'if you think of a number, double it' is a good rule of thumb. When contacting venues (including 'honeymoon' suites in hotels) or services (like photographers, car hire, flower shops), find out 'hidden' costs like VAT and add them in to your overall estimate.
- Have the kind of wedding which reflects your relationship and which is true to you as two people. If your families are pushing you to have a grand affair and you both only want a quiet event, try and resist the pressure.
- Work out how you will pay for the wedding. At this point you need to think about:
  (a) whether you are paying for it yourselves and how (especially if this is a second or third wedding for either of you or you have lived with your prospective spouse for some time);
  (b) whether you expect money from 'her' parents and how much;
  (c) whether you expect money from 'his' parents and how much.

It used to be the custom that only the bride's parents paid, but today anything goes. Parents may contribute something towards their children's weddings whether male or female; equally, parents may feel it is inappropriate to contribute if their offspring are divorced or wealthier than they are. Similarly, couples may feel they want to pay for everything themselves to retain some independence and control. What is essential here is clear communication between all parties concerned: something which is difficult, although not impossible, to achieve when all the emotions surrounding a wedding are in play.

Couples need to keep in mind:

- feelings will run high before a wedding and money will often become the focus of unresolved family feuds or interpersonal strife;
- the more independent a couple is from their family the less friction over money there will probably be, simply because the couple retains the control;
- organise something within your means. You don't want to be in terrible debt for the first five or ten years of your married life because you had to have the perfect wedding. Remember life (and

Visa bills/loans) go on a long time after the actual wedding day;
- don't try to get it all right or be perfect – a wedding is a symbol of your love, not just an occasion to spend as much as possible. Remember less is often more;
- if you can't agree on expenditure or the kind of wedding you want – take time out and think again. You both need to compromise. Indeed, marriage is all about compromise, so organising the wedding together to your mutual satisfaction is a good place to start;
- if you are buying a property, try and do this either before or after the wedding. Doing both at the same time is a recipe for mega-stress and strain;
- if the woman is pregnant, try and have your wedding before the sixth month (and after three months) of the pregnancy or after the birth, as in the latter months she will be both big and tired. The less stress you have in later pregnancy, the happier the baby. If you want to get married late in pregnancy, then make it a small, quiet affair.

Money management in marriage

The wedding is over, the honeymoon (if you had one) is past and you have to settle down and get on with life together. If you've been living together beforehand you might find nothing has changed very much. But if you have started living together for the first time, moved house, had a child or got pregnant, life will have changed dramatically. As Jan Pahl writes in *Money and Marriage*, the 'control of household finances is a crucial factor in marital power and suggests that the way in which a couple handle its money is a significant indicator of their relationship'. Thus, if a couple have already been living together beforehand, they may continue with their money management system or they may revamp how they organise their money. If they are beginning to live together for the first time after marriage, they will need to discuss how they will deal with money management. In chapter 5, we looked at the three main ways couples tend to organise their finances: 'His' and 'Hers' (totally separate money); 'His', 'Hers' and 'Ours' (totally separate money with a joint money account); 'Ours' (totally joint money). Couples often live together under the first option and adopt the second option when they marry. The third, totally joint, way of organising money used to be automatic for couples marrying, but with married women working more today it has become less popular. Some couples feel very happy with pooling because it is a simple system, and it works particularly well if one person is the overall money manager.

Money issues married couples fight about

There are many everyday money issues which couples may argue about. Money fights seem to have increased in relationships because there are now two heads of a household instead of one. In other words, the woman in no longer subsumed under the man, she is a person and an earner in her own right, with her own ideas, beliefs and needs. Because of this, life is more complicated than it used to be and therefore couples will row if they are coming at their money situation from very different places. Within marriage there are certain issues which may well cause a relatively compatible couple to start fighting about money. These are:

- different spending priorities;
- debts/gambling/shopaholism;
- paying for stepchildren and ex-spouses.

Julie and Mark's story: different spending priorities

Julie and Mark e-mailed me in response to an article I had written in *New Woman* magazine in Australia about money and couples in conflict. I cite them here because they are a good example of how two sets of Emotional Money Baggage and Money Patterns can grate against each other destructively within marriage. They are both in their late twenties, having been married for five years (no children) and both work full-time. They have separated temporarily while seeing a counsellor as their money fights are dominating their life together. 'I think money will be the end of our marriage because we can't agree on a lifestyle,' writes Julie, sadly. 'My husband thinks I'm a "monetary harlot" because I like to spend. He has more money than anyone else our age we know, yet he lives in fear of having no money: he says I will ultimately ruin him. He makes me beg to go out anywhere or buy an item of clothing. I'm a spontaneous person which includes spending money. I think the essence of life is enjoyment, such as going out to dinner or away for a weekend. He won't spend money although he's got it. I call it "saving for death" as I don't believe he'll ever have enough money to make him feel secure enough – and then he'll die'.

Clearly, they have very different spending priorities: he has money, but won't spend it; she has debts, but likes to spend. A typical Hoarder vs. Spender dynamic. 'I admit I tend to shop when I'm down,' admits Julie, 'I'll spend maybe £50 or £100 once or twice a year on a shopping splurge. I'm not sure whether this is partly a rebellion at my husband or just the way I cope. But if I'm earning £300 a week, £150 every six months is not too terrible, surely?' Although Mark has a secure job in a bank which is well remunerated, he feels they must be very careful with money – or they will face penury. Consequently he is furious at her spending and refuses to splash out on their life together. According to Julie, 'He gets angry if we spend £10 on a pizza and he won't go to the pub unless it's Happy Hour when beer is £1 a pint – I don't even drink beer. I feel he could buy me flowers occasionally (he says flowers are a waste of money) and when I was overseas I called him (but he said international calls were too expensive and didn't call back). I'm now on antidepressants and he even complains that they cost £15 a month.'

Julie passed on my e-mail reply to her husband and he e-mailed back giving his side of the story. 'I have felt Julie is out of control with her spending,' he begins. 'When I find out we are more in debt than we agreed I hit the roof. She says she doesn't spend more because I will be upset (which I would be), but it makes me feel less trust and more upset when she doesn't tell me what she's spent. I feel betrayed over money even though we never seem to be short of it.' Nonetheless, he says he is really determined to make their relationship work. 'I desperately desire intimacy with Julie, but I do feel threatened by it. I want her to be happy because I love her, and I want to change my attitudes, but can a leopard change its spots?'

Julie and Mark's Emotional Money Baggage

Both Julie and Mark agreed to analyse their Emotional Money Baggage in the hope of understanding how they could come back together and continue their marriage (which they both want to because they say they both love each other). Mark was honest in owning up to the origins of his Hoarding patterns: 'My attitude to money probably comes from my parents' relationship. My dad died when I was sixteen and I can see he controlled mum completely. This led my mother to retaliate in anger and frustration against him, which led to their separation before his death. I always felt mum was irrational – she spent to get at dad and built up huge debts. I blamed her for dad's illness and death for years. However, I now can see there was a devastating drought on our farm which was poorly managed by my father and which contributed to his illness and subsequent death.'

Julie, on the other hand, comes from a family (she's one of four) where 'we did not have much money and often my dad was crying over the accounts, but we did have an abundance of affection and my parents sacrificed everything for the kids' education. My parents always gave generously as well – they gave a lot away when they earned better later on and they really enjoyed their money.' The conflict between Julie and Mark over spending priorities reflects the conflict in their Emotional Money Baggage. 'Part of me suspects he [Mark] is using me to take his anger out on his mother,' Julie explains. 'His mother is an emotional manipulator who threatens suicide to get her son to obey her.' Their attitudes to money are simply Chalk-and-Cheese. Julie continues: 'In my family money in the bank meant you hadn't paid a bill or something. I see money sitting in the bank and then ask if we can do something special to which I am told "no". I beg to go out to dinner and if he relents he afterwards curses it as a "waste" of money.'

Although Julie and Mark are still separated, they are trying hard to understand how they can move towards each other. Julie knows she needs to exert more self-control, stop getting into debt and stop asking for 'permission' from Mark. Doing the latter puts him in the dominant role, which is inappropriate for a modern married couple who both work. Equally, he has to stop blaming Julie, as if she were his mother and he were his father. The reality of the situation is they are far from poor and although it irritates Mark that Julie spends, she is actually quite under control as she can contain herself most of the time and keeps track of her money. Mark needs to loosen up, Julie needs to tighten up: it's possible for them to meet in the middle in time if they are willing to do the necessary emotional work separately and together.

Resolving different money priorities

If you are fighting about having different money priorities, then try the following for starters:

- Stand back from the situation and from your emotions and remember that you are two separate and distinct individuals, not the same person.
- Understand that you are both carrying Emotional Money Baggage which will be colouring your viewpoint. Try to disentangle the past from the present and see what belongs to the current situation.
- Negotiate: you both have valid ideas about spending priorities, so try and find a compromise. There is always a finite amount of money, so perhaps you can save some towards one priority, spend some on another, or agree to take it in turns. You can't both win, but you can work together towards a common goal.
- Identify, accept and understand your own and each other's Money Patterns. If one of you is spending, gambling or squandering money, then get help with the problem; if one of you is ignoring money, then pay attention to it; if one of you is hoarding to the point of meanness, try to loosen up. It will feel uncomfortable, but it may help heal the rift in your marriage brought about by a money Crunchpoint.
- If one of you is particularly good at handling or thinking about money, then build on that person's strengths. But don't assume that person can make all the decisions about spending priorities.
- Also don't assume the man knows best. Both partners have equally valid views about spending, whatever their gender. Respect each other as you negotiate. Understand that Flashpoints about spending are really a clash of your patterns, beliefs and ideas: no one is 'right' or 'wrong'.

Lana and Ben's story: gambling away the family finances

Lana and Ben have been married five years. She's twenty-two, he's thirty-two and they have a three-year-old daughter, Kiri. Lana used to work as a dental nurse, but hasn't worked since Kiri was born. Ben used to do shift work making car mats in a local factory, but gave up working nights because Lana needed support with Kiri.

They now live on income support in a council flat and don't have any credit cards or savings. Ben does some 'moonlighting', fixing cars for a friend (although he's not qualified) who runs a local garage for cash-in-hand. Lana is very good at making a little money go a long way. 'My parents didn't have any money,' she explains, 'I come from the East End [of London] and money was always tight. I always saw my parents struggling – dad worked in a factory and mum was a part-time receptionist. We never had nice things. I always had cheapee trainers and clothes. I'm still a bargain-hunter, even now.' Lana had four brothers and sisters and it was out of the question for the family to go abroad on holiday. 'My parents were always arguing about money, about which bills had been paid or where the next meal was coming from. I hated it.'

Ironically, although not unusually, Lana has ended up in a relationship which is repeating her parents' marriage. Lana's a Doormat when it comes to money and puts up with Ben's spending habits: he's a typical Gambler. 'He bets on horses, the dogs, anything that goes fast,' explains Lana wearily, 'I try to keep track of money when it comes in, but he helps himself to it and then it's gone. It's a constant source of rows, especially now we've got Kiri.' Typically, Lana goes to the Post Office to get the family's weekly money, which is £100 a week after rent. 'I go and get £200 for two weeks and hide it. We spend about £40 on food, £10 on electric, we get £25 each to spend. I spend most of mine on Kiri – going out to playgroups, swimming, bus fares, Kiri's clothes and sweets. He spends his on the dogs.'

What really upsets Lana is that if Ben wins he puts the money straight on the next bet. 'He told me he won £100 the other night on a £10 bet, but lost it straight away. I was really angry, but what can I do?' The money from the moonlighting Ben does also goes on bets. 'I wouldn't mind if he came home with food or furniture or we could save to buy our own place, but he just spends it because he thinks it's his.' Occasionally they go out for a drink or a meal when Lana's mum babysits, but holidays are out of the question. 'I feel like I'm living my mum's life all over again,' says Lana, sadly, 'we don't have no ice cream, chocolate, biscuits, cakes, fruit even. I buy food in the cheapee shops and never get clothes for myself. I feel like we're in a hole and we'll never get out.'

For Lana to stand up to Ben and say 'no' to his gambling would mean she would have to face his wrath. Her Doormat tendencies mean she'd rather keep her head down to keep the peace. However, as long as Ben's Gambling Money Pattern dominates, the money fights will continue and Kiri's future remains both limited and uncertain. The only way Lana could really change Ben's gambling behaviour would be by threatening to leave – and then actually leaving with Kiri. People addicted to spending money, be it gambling or shopaholism, usually can only change their behaviour once they realise the stakes have become unbearably high. Even then, somebody utterly wedded to their addictive behaviour (rather than their spouse) and who believes the old adage, 'What's yours is mine, what's mine's my own', may sacrifice their own and their family's happiness for the sake of their destructive Money Pattern.

Resolving debts/gambling/shopaholism

If one spouse is running riot with the family finances through unbridled gambling, debt or shopaholism the other spouse will have to develop firm boundaries if the relationship is going to last. If your spouse is out of control about spending in this way:

- confront the situation constructively. To let it ride will only increase the problem. You have to sit them down (at an appropriate time) and say 'We have a problem and we need to sort it out'. Try not to blame them, no matter how angry or abused you feel;
- set out what you think should happen – for instance, you become the overall money manager and give them 'pocket money'; or, you cut up your credit cards together; or, you make a booking with a Citizen's Advice debt counsellor together or contact the Consumer Credit Counselling Service for an appointment. Whatever you do, try to talk as honestly and openly as you can about money and your current situation. Make it clear that you are not prepared for the situation to continue, but you are willing to help in sorting it out – together;
- prepare for feelings: money is all about emotion. The spender will be feeling guilty, frightened, defensive, attacked and needy. Be prepared for fireworks when money is mentioned, but don't be put off by it. You will also be feeling frustrated, annoyed, irritated

and frightened yourself by opening up the subject. If you fear your partner may become violent if you challenge them about their spending, then take a good friend or family member into your confidence and confront your spouse with them present (but beware this may humiliate them, so it may make them react even more strongly);

- set limits: if spending is out of control, you have to set limits. You can set deadlines by which your spouse needs to start paying back or stop gambling. If these deadlines arrive and nothing is done you need to work out what sanctions you are going to impose. Don't threaten to leave and then stay. You have to do what you say you will do otherwise you will lose all credibility;

- try and continue to love the person while disliking their patterns of behaviour. Under the worst kinds of profligate patterns there is a nice person struggling to get out. Remember you loved each other when you married and you've got into trouble together – even if it is your spouse's spending which has gone awry;

- talk to a third party, like a Relate counsellor or relationship therapist before it's too late. Money problems are usually about something else deep down in the relationship. Past resentments, children, lack of sex, early misunderstandings, jealousy and envy can build up and make one partner punish the other through spending or gambling;

- make it a condition of your staying that your partner will go and get help themselves. If they don't, consider what you will do yourself – get help yourself, separate for a while, carry on stoically, etc.

If you are the gambler or spender:

- you owe it to your relationship and spouse to face what you are doing squarely and start doing something about it;

- get help: there is plenty out there like Gamcare and Gamblers Anonymous, plus my own book on *Overcoming Addiction* (see Help section at the back of this book);

- put your relationship first. It can last a lot longer than the immediate thrill of winning or spending. Think about your future without your spouse and children or house – a lonely, scary prospect if you don't face your addiction and understand the feelings keeping it going.

Stop colluding

Finally, it takes two to make a marriage where spending or gambling is dominant. Both partners will be colluding to some extent with each other. The only way forward is to try to disentangle your Money Patterns and understand each other's Emotional Money Baggage on the way to making a healthy Money Relationship. Both spouses need to do this actively and honestly otherwise the marriage will simply fail.

Paying for stepchildren/ex-spouses

Even though you go into a relationship with your eyes wide open, the reality of having to live with your partner's past in the shape of stepchildren or their ex-spouse's alimony payments can be very challenging. When this includes paying for children who are not yours, but who live with you or go to an expensive school, it can test a new relationship to the full. We will examine this subject in more depth in the next chapter. However, some general points can be made here, if you are fighting about stepchildren and ex-spouses and money.

- You need to be very clear what your separate roles and responsibilities are in relation to children and stepchildren before you marry. You need to agree who is going to be financially responsible for whom and understand together what it will mean for your marriage.
- If one of you is unhappy about paying towards alimony or for stepchildren's expenses, you need to get this out in the open and talk it through. It may well be that there are misunderstandings or feelings about paying money towards a past relationship which makes it hard for the new spouse to accept. Try and find a compromise, but keep the situation under review.
- Get advice or help from a good solicitor, the National Stepfamily Association, Child Support Agency and/or Citizens' Advice Bureau if you feel you cannot agree or do not know what your respective rights are.

Marriage and money checklist

If you are getting married or are already hitched and are fighting about money, take time to think about these questions:

- Do you feel the way you organise your money together is fair, sensible and suits you both?
- If not, how would you like to organise it differently?
- Do you fight about spending priorities? If so, can you see a way to agree them differently?
- Do you want to have a pre-nuptial agreement? If so, what would it include?
- Is one of you a spender or gambler or in debt? If so, what should you be doing about sorting it out, individually and together?
- Are you feeling confused or resentful about paying for stepchildren and ex-spouses (if there are any)? If so, could you renegotiate your agreement?

Part Three

Money Relationship Crunchpoints

7

Having a Baby

*It may be that some little root of the sacred tree still lives. Nourish it then,
that it may leaf and bloom and fill with singing birds.*

Black Elk

Having a baby can be the most wonderful thing in the whole world
for a loving, committed couple to experience together, whether
married or not. Of course, having a baby is a step into the unknown
– it always has been – but it can be a source of great stress and
tension as couples' lives are more pressurised today than ever before.
Money is, necessarily, a major consideration – in both partners' minds
– before, during and after pregnancy. According to One Plus One,
the relationship research organisation, it is largely accepted among
researchers that the first year of having a baby is one of major
emotional strain for relationships. If there have been cracks in the
relationship before the baby came along, the stress of having a
newborn child will open those cracks up into fissures, if not canyons,
due to lack of sleep, anxiety, work stress, lack of sex and time to get
close, and, of course, money worries. Gone, for the majority of the
population, are the wider family networks and free support systems
of the bad old days, when aunties, grannies, neighbours or friends
held the baby while women worked at home, in the fields and
factories.

Women's lost earnings

However, because women still have the children and do most of the childcare and domestic drudgery, it is fairly inevitable that they will have to take time off work during the early and latter stages of pregnancy and, probably, during the early weeks, months or maybe even years of childrearing. This means a substantial loss of earnings for a woman – and for a couple – as well as a loss of the woman's status and promotion opportunities in the workplace, particularly as most women with children work part-time. Of course, women today have far better maternity rights than their grandmothers and mothers, but state support is still fairly minimal in the UK when compared with other European or Scandinavian countries (especially Sweden and Finland).

Recent research at the London School of Economics estimates that a woman with low skills who gets pregnant in her teens or early twenties will lose out on nearly half a million pounds of earnings over her lifetime – assuming she is a stay-at-home mother or works part-time. Previous reports have shown that a woman with two children is likely to sacrifice 55 per cent of her earnings over a lifetime.

Cost of having children

The actual cost of having children today has escalated since the Second World War. The supermarket chain ASDA undertook a three-part survey called *What Price a Child* (vol. 1, from birth to 5; vol. 2, school years; vol. 3, from 16 to 21), which it published in 1996. Although the figures need updating (there has been no similar research since then), they do give an indication of what parents are up against, financially, when they embark on parenthood. Roughly, ASDA estimate 'some parents will spend over £50,000, the price of a small terraced house, on their first little darling even before it starts school'. Average spending during the first five years is estimated at £20,000. This covers what ASDA's researcher Jan Walsh calls 'direct costs', such as pregnancy, equipment, food, clothes, household expenses, education and entertainment. However, the £20,000 excludes 'indirect costs', such as childcare, which could add at least £18,000 to the basic figure. The research worked out it can cost anything from £934 (low-income households) to a staggering £2,276 (high-income households) to dress a child for the first five years of life.

These costs reflect the increase in consumerism in our culture as many parents-to-be are made to feel they 'must have' certain costly products and brands for their newborn. The cost of having a baby starts even before the baby is born, with pregnancy tests, improved diet and vitamins (folic acid) and maternity clothes, costing, according to ASDA, anything from £373 (low-income households) to £5,990 (high-income households) from conception to contractions (add on another £3,000 if the baby is born in a private hospital). Any couple embarking on parenthood might well have pause for thought if they looked at these figures squarely. The truth is most of us embark on parenthood oblivious of the real possible cost: if we did we'd probably never ever have children. Yet, the intuition that having a baby is going to change things for ever, and that there will be much less cash available for life as it used to be enjoyed, is a tension which affects a relationship from the moment a couple (knowingly) starts bonking for baby. Of course, in a planned pregnancy, the couple will have time to readjust emotionally to this fact. However, when a baby is an 'accident' it can stir deep emotions, for both parties, about the unexpected financial commitment it will necessarily create.

Trying for a baby

'Trying' for a baby can indeed be very trying. When it comes to pregnancy and childbirth it is very humbling to realise that not everything can be managed by sheer will or new technology. Getting pregnant (or not) will come down to luck, timing, fate, nature, God, or whatever you want to call it. You may have planned your pregnancy and career break down to the finest detail, taken your daily folic acid, made love during ovulation and still not got pregnant for two or five years – or at all. Equally, the woman might have stopped taking the Pill and be pregnant within a month, throwing any well-honed savings plans out of the window.

The relationship is usually under pressure from trying to conceive onwards and, unless the couple are incredibly rich and totally emotionally well adjusted and mature, there will inevitably be tensions.

Feelings run high

When a couple is trying for a baby, or get pregnant by accident, feelings will run high. There may be euphoria, but there will also be anxiety, fear and anger. Couples often find themselves arguing about all sorts of things and money can be a focus for their annoyance. From the moment of conception couples will be thinking about all the costs as they pore over baby magazines or as the woman craves caviar one minute, curry the next. You should expect your emotions to be heightened, even for the man who is not physically pregnant (some recent research has shown that men go through a kind of phantom pregnancy in relationships). Couples may well worry.

- Can we really afford a baby?
- Do we need to move flat/house or buy a property?
- Will we miscarry?
- What if we have a disabled/Downs baby?
- Will we be good enough parents?
- Will I retain my individual identity once I'm a mother/father (often more an issue for mothers)?
- How will a child affect our relationship?
- Will we still be close, love and have sex with each other in the same way (often more an issue for men)?
- How will we continue with our work, social lives, holidays, leisure activities?

Flashpoints and Crunchpoints

Your relationship, and therefore your Money Relationship, might have been working really well, but when the added pressure of trying for or having a baby occurs, the machinery creaks and couples snap at each other. She wants to buy the best of Baby Gap; he thinks second-hand gear will do: they argue. It's a typical Flashpoint. He assumes she will do all the childcare or organise and pay for it (she's the mother after all); while she assumes they will share it practically and financially as partners (they're equals after all). Another Flashpoint. What's more, he wants to put the child's name down for public school before it is even born (he has an inheritance); she believes state education is the best (they should use his money to create the baby's nursery or open their baby's bank account). Flashpoint number three. Plus, she assumes he will support her financially; he thinks she should get back to work as soon as possible and pay a childminder out of her earnings. Accumulated unresolved Flashpoints soon turn into a Money Relationship Crunchpoint.

Fear of dependency

The stress of trying for a baby over months (maybe years) and the need to save money can create fierce fights in relationships where dependency is an emotionally sensitive and unresolved issue. When a couple get pregnant, money rows can rock those who were previously peaceable because they:

- fear the dependency of the woman upon the man (even temporarily);
- fear the dependency of the child upon them both to survive;
- have different perspectives and spending priorities before, during and after the pregnancy.

Women's independence

Women used to be dependent on men in every way, unless they had private wealth, and even then they were often ruled by fathers who wanted to marry them off to increase their families' wealth and social standing. Then, in their marital families, they were ruled by husbands who helped themselves to their wives' wealth. Today, most couples enter a relationship with both partners being independent. There is an expectation, on both sides of a relationship, that the man and woman will earn their own money and be responsible for their own physical, emotional, intellectual and spiritual needs. Although income levels will vary, from income support to executive salaries or unearned inheritances, a couple nonetheless has to negotiate the new-found dependency of the woman on the man when she becomes pregnant. For the first time since they have known each other, the woman needs to lean, is perhaps more needy, both physically and emotionally. This does not mean she is demeaned in any way, nor does it mean she will give up her identity, her career, or her own life.

But there are physiological and psychological changes which can occur without either party really being prepared for them.

Patricia and Stephen's story: learning to depend

'I've always been a career woman,' explains Patricia, forty-four, a freelance trainer, 'and I fell in love, probably for the first time, at forty-two, with a younger man, Stephen (thirty-four). We had a passionate affair and I knew, suddenly, desperately, I wanted a child with him.' Patricia and Stephen started living together immediately in her house and she was soon pregnant. 'The weirdest thing was I suddenly felt I wanted to put my feet up and depend on him. Neither of us were prepared for this happening. I earned twice as much as him – he's a teacher – I could command two weeks of his salary in a day or two. But I just wanted to curl up and focus on my baby.' They were in for a rough time as neither had anticipated how Patricia would feel. 'I was nearly sterilised in my twenties as I was so anti-babies; in my thirties I put everything into my career and by forty I was joking about the menopause and breeding cats being next. Then I met Stephen and, literally, across a crowded room everything changed. Now I feel like I'm being run by my hormones, which sounds ridiculous, as I don't even believe in them, really.'

Patricia has been a staunch feminist all her adult life, believing nurture is more crucial than nature, but now she feels like a cavewoman; she wants Stephen to take over the financial responsibilities, at least until her baby is safely born. 'If you'd told me two years ago that I would feel like this I would have laughed in your face. My friends can't believe this is me. I just want to do yoga, some gardening, eat well and sleep as much as possible. This baby means the world to me and suddenly I feel I'm in the grip of something much bigger than me, much bigger than my bloody job and making money, which seems totally irrelevant at present.' Patricia, who has been self-employed for fifteen years, has been prudent in that she has a pension and some savings, although they are not enough to live on for long. 'I feel pretty lucky, but Stephen is going to have to support us for a while and I don't know how that is going to affect our relationship. So far I've been the one with money; now all that will change. I can't take too long off work, but my God I'm going to enjoy this baby after waiting all this bloody time.' Like many couples,

Patricia and Stephen are wondering how her increased dependency will impact on their love relationship.

How the Money Relationship can be affected

- The increased financial dependence on the man may make him feel pressurised. He may fear he can't earn enough, or that he has to take on the typical male 'breadwinner' role. This may make him feel resentful or frightened, especially when he is used to his partner pulling her weight financially, or even commanding a better salary or wage than himself.
- Her financial dependence on him may change how they feel about each other. If he feels resentful or anxious, he might feel less sexually capable and less turned on by his partner; similarly, if she feels beholden or demeaned, she might feel less sexually desirable or less interested in him sexually.
- When/if the woman has to ask for money (if she has no independent money of her own), she may feel humiliated and he may feel annoyed. It shifts the relationship dynamic and many women say they feel awkward asking the man and would rather eke out their child and maternity benefits which they feel is their 'own' money. Some women can feel infantalised by having to 'ask' their partner for cash – a bit like asking your dad for pocket money.
- When/if the man goes out and spends money on himself without considering the woman's and/or baby's needs this can cause friction. Some men compensate themselves for feeling over-burdened by spending a lot at the pub, or on the dogs, or CDs. They feel it is their due as they have 'a wife and family to support' for the first time.
- The couple no longer has time or the possibility to enjoy social life with each other as equals (romantic dinners, weekends away), unless they have relatives nearby and/or access to cheap baby-sitting. The increased dependency on each other in merely practical terms can make them begin to wonder if they have a romantic relationship any more, thus bickering can increase;
- The increase in fear and anxiety, or mere discomfort, at the woman being more dependent can cause the couple to argue more. Both men and women can feel trapped by the change in their circumstances (in a good relationship couples can feel closer and more

'in love' at this time as mutual interdependence strengthens their bond).

- The current situation suddenly reminds them of their past family experiences or past relationships. Emotional Money Baggage can begin to play a large role in stimulating fights. Two independent people suddenly find themselves in a situation which reminds them of their stifled or struggling parents – something they have striven all their lives not to repeat – and the blue touchpaper is lit. 'I think I was always fiercely independent because I saw my mother being so dependent and trodden on by my father,' admits Patricia. 'I vowed I would never depend on a man, and yet, now I'm pregnant, that's exactly what I want and need to do. God, it's so confusing.'

Tips for handling fear of dependency

If the balance of power shifts in your relationship, causing the woman's increased dependence, and it causes rows:

- *remember it is a temporary shift*: babies grow up fast and the woman will probably be able to go back to work part- or full-time within a few months, or at least a year or two (according to what the couple choose to do about childcare, of course);
- *you are still the same people*: remember what you fell in love with each other about and then remind each other;
- *you are not your parents*: even if it *seems* like you have turned into them, you haven't. Emotional Money Baggage can make us feel we are living out the same script: it can feel like an exact repetition, especially when you say to each other in frustration 'God, you're just like your mother/father', or 'Help, I'm turning into my mother/father'. However, it's not the same, it just *reminds* you of the past. Try and separate out in your mind and emotions what belongs to back then and what belongs to now;
- *biology is there for a reason*: women are conditioned genetically, to some extent, to protect their offspring. The desire to hunker down and take it more easy is a positive sign;
- *'confinement' passes*: once the baby becomes more independent, the woman will have a chance to become her old independent self again;
- *approach change as a challenge*: try not to be threatened by it. Having

a baby can be marvellous if both partners can embrace the challenges and somehow adapt their lives to meet them. Resisting the challenges (or ignoring them) just creates more grief long term;

- *remember relationships are not static things*: having a baby will change your relationship, but probably for the better if you can approach the whole business with a positive viewpoint. It's bound to be tough, but it will be worth it in the end;
- *negative Money Relationships can become more positive*: with time, patience, honesty and love (see chapter 10 on Building Your Money Relationship).

Planning for a baby

Planning means looking at your Money Relationship objectively, as if it is a separate entity, and seeing how it is working, how it will need to improve or change, once a baby is part of your life together. You can improve your Money Relationship ahead of having a baby by talking openly and honestly.

- *Talk about your individual fantasies about life with a baby.* Tell each other how you imagine it will be – the good points, the bad points – and see what you have in common.
- *Visit friends with babies.* Talk to them about how they manage their money. Some may be reticent, some may be happy to share their experience with you (remember money is still a taboo subject), but most will probably have helpful tips and practical advice on managing money.
- *Talk money.* Be open with each other about how much money you have apart from earnings or benefits. Does either of you have savings, for example, which could be drawn on for financial support when the woman stops working? Would you want to change your money management system from, say, 'His' separate money and 'Her' separate money to 'Our' joint money, or have a mixed system with a joint account?
- *Own up.* If you have debts, or a gambling or shopaholic habit, now is the time to own up. Once a child is on the scene it will be much harder to pay off credit cards and debts. If one of you has

shopaholic tendencies, you might even find yourself spending more because of the stress of being pregnant or having a newborn. Get help if you need it.

- *Talk feelings.* How would you feel if the woman depended on the man financially? How would you feel spending your savings or not having treats (holidays, a new house or car, designer clothes, expensive meals out)?
- *How long would you want to take off work?* If one of you is going to be the main breadwinner, how long will the other stop working for? Will they be full- or part-time?
- *What kind of childcare do you want?* Do you want to split the responsibility, so you both work part-time and do childcare equally? Or are you keen that one of you works full-time (the higher earner, not necessarily the man, these days), and the other is a housewife or househusband? Or do you both want to continue working, maybe part-time, while using a childminder or nanny/nanny-share, a nursery or playgroup? You need to talk about what you believe in and also what you could afford and cost it out as much as you can.
- *Do your research.* Call your local authority to find out about childcare in your neighbourhood, talk to your employer about what they offer (maternity/paternity rights, crèche facilities), phone specialist organisations, like the National Childbirth Trust who can send information about your locality, talk to your GP surgery's midwife, chat to neighbours, friends and colleagues about what they do/where they go, and look at local shop and library noticeboards where childminders advertise.

Money Relationship Crunchpoints

Even if you have planned your baby, nothing really prepares you for the reality. And there is often a difference between men's and women's reactions − perhaps because the man experiences the pregnancy at one remove. One woman told me her partner had been utterly euphoric when she said she was pregnant − they had been wildly in love for three years − and they decided to move into her flat together. Even through the pregnancy, he was pleased and excited, yet the minute the baby was born, he was off. Their relationship hit a Crunchpoint: the reality of having a baby hit him – and them as a couple – and he was not prepared to deal with it at all. He felt jealous, emotionally excluded and started an affair with another woman almost immediately. Sadly, it was the end of their love and the beginning of another lone parent's struggle to make ends meet (he refuses to pay maintenance). Even couples who have known each other a long time and feel they are very compatible can be tested when a baby arrives.

Joanne and Charlie's story: reaching a Money Relationship Crunchpoint after having a baby

Although Joanne and Charlie have been very much in love and happily married since their teens, having had a child they are now arguing non-stop about money. Their relationship is at a serious make-or-break Crunchpoint. Joanne, twenty-five, has packed a bag and left Charlie, thirty, temporarily, taking their two-year-old son Thomas with her. 'Since we had Thomas we haven't stopped arguing about money,' admits Joanne tearfully, 'we've been at each other's throats the whole time.' Joanne breaks down in tears and sobs quietly. I wait for her to start talking again. 'We were very happy before Thomas. Of course, we never had much money, but it didn't really matter because we had each other.' She pauses to blow her nose. 'Since Thomas was born we've fought about money all the time and it's reached a point where I can't stand it any more.'

Both Joanne and Charlie work: she's a part-time dental nurse and he's a bookkeeper for an insurance broker. 'He enjoys dealing with money and I suppose I let him get on with it,' confesses Joanne. 'I used to be an auxiliary nurse, working all kinds of shifts, but after Thomas arrived I decided to try and get a part-time day job. I suppose I earn about £250 a month and I know Charlie earns much more than me, but we never really discuss it, anyway he'd never even tell me if I asked him direct.' They took out a £48,000 mortgage, based on Charlie's larger salary, and bought a small house three years ago. 'Charlie arranged everything about the house. Although I had my own bank account, all my money went into the joint account for bills, so I never had any money of my own. We've always had to scrimp and scrape since Thomas, so I never felt we had any money at all.'

The problems seem to have started during pregnancy. Joanne was very sick during the first three months and was working for a dentist who dismissed her unfairly. 'I couldn't keep anything down at all and I went on holiday for a week. When I came back they had someone else in there doing my job. I was absolutely furious. I went to Citizens' Advice, but I hadn't worked long enough – or enough hours or something – so I couldn't take a case. Suddenly I didn't have a job and I was completely dependent on Charlie. We both hated it.' Joanne tried to get other jobs and then worked for an agency, but continued ill health throughout her pregnancy made it difficult for her to work more than one or two days a week, if that. 'Charlie got really resentful about me spending any money even though he spent anything he wanted to without telling me. We began to row about money seriously then. I felt guilty about depending on him, but what else could I do?'

Joanne began to get scared about how it would be once Thomas arrived. 'Charlie comes from a strict Mormon family, which is very male-dominated. Up until I got pregnant it didn't really bother me at all. I know he loves me, he's very reliable and good with money, so I thought he was a good catch.' Joanne didn't realise there was a bigger 'catch' involved: she had to be completely obedient in exchange for him managing their money. 'I didn't really want to marry him, I was happy living together, but his family thought we were "living in sin", so his father offered us money to marry and I thought "Wow, why not?" I suppose I was young, I was nineteen then, and I didn't really understand what I was letting myself in for. I knew he'd stay by me, and I thought he'd make an ideal parent and I wanted kids.'

What Joanne didn't reckon on was the increasingly claustrophobic monetary straitjacket she'd have to accept as his wife. To some extent, Joanne colluded with Charlie's desire to control: she has Doormat patterns (with Ostrich patterned streaks) to his Planner (with big Hoarder/Spender patterned streaks). 'I didn't look at bank statements, either mine or ours, I left it all to him. He took on the money manager role and I let him do it, stupidly. Then he kept telling me we hadn't got any money at all, and I believed him. He'd give me weekly spending money of about £30 cash. Anything I spent was on clothes for Thomas or going swimming with Thomas or something. I had nothing for myself. Recently I've felt I was working for nothing and I've lost my identity really.' The truth was that

Charlie was hoarding their money and spending a lot on himself. 'He's been writing cheques willy-nilly while keeping me in the dark. He's turned out to be completely selfish, which is a total shock, as I thought he wanted to sacrifice everything for a baby, like me.'

The money rows escalated when Joanne tried to take back control over her money and her life. She wanted to change the rules they were living by. 'I suddenly wanted to be more independent when I found out what was really going on. It came to a head last Christmas in a mega row about going out somewhere. He said he was going out alone and I thought he'd be spending loads on drink, dinner and his mates. I said I wanted to come, too, and that mum could have Thomas, but he said no I couldn't come. I was furious that I wasn't invited at all as he always said we didn't have enough money to go out socially together. I thought he must have a woman tucked away.' Joanne gatecrashed the evening and, indeed, there was a young woman from Charlie's office who draped herself over him most of the evening. 'That was it really, I suppose. We'd stopped having sex ages ago and I thought "Right, I'm going to have my wages to myself from now on".'

After that night, and yet more rows, Joanne took charge of her money, to Charlie's utter fury. She now pays her wages into her own bank account and then contributes a proportion of her wages towards household bills and Thomas' upkeep. In desperation, Joanne persuaded Charlie to go to Relate for one counselling session. 'I was amazed that what came out was how jealous he was of my relationship with Thomas. He felt excluded and was angry that I loved Thomas so much. I said "He's our child, don't you love him, too?"' Charlie did love his son, but he was compensating himself for what he felt was emotional neglect now they were a threesome. Because Charlie felt so out of control at home, he was trying to control their money, for his own ends. 'I couldn't believe he would deprive his own son of money and spend on himself instead,' says Joanne bitterly. 'It was the last straw when he took up smoking. He was paying for ciggies – over £3 a day – when Thomas and I had to walk rather than catch a bus. That was it.'

Joanne and Charlie's Emotional Money Baggage

In retrospect, and as she grieves, Joanne says she now understands how different their Emotional Money Baggage is about money. She can also see why they fitted together so well for so long. 'His family were really into making money, whereas my family never had any. I didn't know much about Mormons, which I do now. They just want to control everything, hoard money, make women obey. I suppose that suited me when I was young because I was quite insecure.' In fact, Joanne's father had abandoned her mother when she was three. 'Mum worked and worked and worked. She was a seamstress, working such long hours for nothing really. We never had holidays, we never had nice things – always second-hand clothes. I started working when I was at school, childminding and that. When I came home from school she was never there, so I went to my gran's.' Joanne was used to being neglected and her Emotional Money Baggage was based on this as well as fear: 'I was scared of money and I felt it was hard to come by. So I suppose I leant hard on Charlie thinking he was "the man".' Their Money Relationship reflected this relationship imbalance: he dominated, she submitted, but only until she felt the price was too high. 'I was so young, gullible and naive,' says Joanne, 'much more than I am now. Now I'm a lone mum, just like my mum was, although I feel I've finally woken up to myself and asked "Who am I?" '

This lack of self-esteem and self-awareness reflects Joanne's lack of power in the marital relationship. She found herself agreeing, unwittingly, to a traditional marriage which removed all responsibility and control from her as a wife and a mother.

In Joanne and Charlie's case there were two main issues at stake: Joanne's unwitting dependency on Charlie, which increased when Thomas came along, and Charlie's jealousy of Joanne's close relationship with Thomas, which made him more selfish with his money. At first they agreed upon the 'rules' of their relationship: Charlie dominating and controlling and Joanne being submissive and controlled by him about money. But once she understood their Money Relationship rules were unfair and negative, Joanne needed to 'grow up' and be more responsible. However, trying to change the internal rules of their Money Relationship into more mutual and positive ones soon brought them to a relationship Crunchpoint – which is currently still unresolved.

Putting a price on the baby's head: assisted pregnancy

There are other issues which affect couples' relationships, and therefore Money Relationships, when they are trying for a baby. Increasing numbers of couples are suffering from infertility problems. Having a baby can entail much stress, effort and expenditure. Infertility can be caused by increased male sterility (sperm counts are down in the population as a whole, due to stress and/or pollution), women having babies later in life (thirty-five plus, even forty plus), or other physiological or environmental factors. The fertility industry has been booming since the 1980s, with couples turning increasingly to new technology to help them conceive. The advent of test-tube babies in the 1970s radically changed our ideas about conception, and the range of options for couples who want or need assisted pregnancy has increased enormously since then. However, it is a notoriously expensive business, which can easily eat up a couple's savings and prompt huge loans. Some couples sell their house, car and other assets to raise cash for a baby, which creates more emotional pressure and money rows, and there is no guarantee of success. It literally puts a price on the baby's head – and on the relationship.

IVF (in vitro fertilisation)

Treatments such as in vitro fertilisation (IVF) – where eggs (usually three) and sperm are fused outside of the woman's body and then placed in her womb, hopefully to implant and make a baby – can cost upwards of £3,000 a time. Couples often commit to at least three treatments to give themselves a real chance to conceive.

Tania and Marek's story: savings blown on IVF

Tania, thirty-two, and her husband Marek, thirty-one, decided to use IVF as they had been 'trying' for a baby unsuccessfully for five years. Both had had a battery of tests – to check his sperm count, her ovulation and eggs, their blood counts, genetic make-up and so on. Tania worked in a bank as a counter clerk, a job which she found fairly stressful, so they decided she would take unpaid leave during their first trial. 'We couldn't really afford me to take time off work,'

Tania explains, 'but we so wanted a baby it seemed worth it at the time.' She went for treatment, which involved several visits to hospital, injections and plenty of good food and rest. Marek, a sound engineer, carried on with his work in a recording studio as usual, but was worried that they were using up all of their hard-earned savings. 'It put so much stress on that first treatment,' remembers Tania. 'We knew we'd saved up for a couple of years to pay for at least three treatments, but it was still hard to hand our money over.' Despite not working and resting as much as possible, the treatment failed. They were deeply disappointed, but resolved to try again. 'By now we had stopped going out for meals, we'd given up our hobbies and I suppose we were getting a bit stir-crazy with each other,' admits Tania. They started rowing about the money. 'We ended up crying our eyes out after a blazing row – I'd shouted at Marek for buying a Chinese takeaway, which was ridiculous. We realised that we both felt we were investing too much in the whole business. Luckily, we could comfort each other – which was great.'

Past this first Flashpoint, they tried a second and then a third time. During the last trial Tania got pregnant and the couple were utterly over the moon. 'We were delirious. We drank champagne and went out for dinner, something we hadn't done for ages and we were both grinning ear to ear,' remembers Tania. 'It was like we'd got our old relationship back. It was only then we realised how stressed out we'd both been. It had been bloody grim, I can tell you.' Sadly, she lost the baby at six weeks. Tania became depressed and Marek started drinking heavily. 'We had spent all our savings and had got nowhere,' says Tania wearily; 'we thought we might go to my family for money next, but I knew my dad would say "Why should it work if it hasn't worked so far?"' Both from working-class backgrounds (Marek is Polish), they were going against the grain spending in the way they had. Tania's Planner Money Patterns were rubbing up against Marek's Spender Money Patterns: a typical Chalk-and-Cheese liaison. He felt he had been curtailed for too long and wanted to break out. The rows escalated as Marek's drinking soon plunged them into credit card debt. Eventually he took time off work to dry out and, a year on, they are still trying to heal the rift. Tania went back to work part-time, but the relationship is struggling to regain its former equilibrium. 'He does go walkabout,' says Tania, 'he disappears for a couple of days, like he wants to let me know he has his independence. I don't ask him where he's been or what he's spent, because we'd only row. We don't save at the moment as there's nothing to spare. We won't try for a baby again – in fact, we haven't had sex for nearly a year now . . . so at this point I just don't know if our marriage will survive.' She says she wishes sometimes they'd never gone through the whole IVF business. 'I think it showed up cracks in our relationship, really. Marek's more selfish than me and he resents us having spent that money that way, although I don't. But we just can't agree with each other any more . . . about anything, really.'

Tania and Marek's story is a very sad one and, at time of writing, is unresolved. However, there are plenty of examples where assisted pregnancy through IVF has worked wonderfully well and a couple who never thought they would have a child is blessed with a baby, to their unbridled joy. Even so, the financial cost – as well as the emotional cost – is a factor which takes its toll, even when there's a real baby at the end. And, if treatment fails, couples face difficult decisions about trying further testing and new techniques, all of which can cost large amounts of money and which demand a vast amount of continuing emotional and physical courage, commitment and dedication.

Monica and Simon's story: IVF success . . . at a cost

Some couples do win through, however. Monica, forty-two, had her four-year-old, Rosa, with Simon, forty-five, through IVF, and although it cost in the region of £15,000 in treatment to get pregnant, they say they have no regrets. 'I think we got closer through the whole process,' explains Monica, a freelance management consultant. 'We had a plan and we stuck to it and learned we could really pull together as a team.' Although from well-heeled middle-class families, both Monica and Simon saved hard for five years and they also took out a second mortgage on their house. 'I suppose I thought "When I get to forty I'll give the whole damned business up and focus on my work". The minute I took my eye off the ball, as it were, wham, I got pregnant. We couldn't believe it. So many treatments had failed and we'd almost given up, and then suddenly I was pregnant.' Rosa was born after a completely trouble-free pregnancy, and Monica took a year off work and now works part-time from home.

During the last two years Monica and Simon have been deliberating about going for number two. 'We saved up again because we thought we didn't really fancy Rosa being an only child. You quickly forget all the hassle and only focus on how wonderful it is to be a mum, I suppose.' Three months ago Monica had her first IVF treatment for five years. Unfortunately, it failed. 'I felt throughout the whole thing, I just don't want to go through all this again. It was utterly nerve-wracking and Simon and I started fighting, which affected Rosa badly. It was the stress of the whole thing, physically speaking, but it was also about the money, as Rosa goes to nursery now and will soon be going to school. We'll have fees to pay and part of me now feels we ought to jolly well focus on her life, rather than spend money on more treatments which might lead nowhere at my age.'

Overall, Monica and Simon count themselves very lucky, not least that their Money Relationship could work well enough for them to go through something as traumatic as IVF, with all the associated expenditure, and come out still in love. Both ardent Planners, with Hoarder streaks, they have a real Mirror-Image relationship which means they think in the same way about money. Even so, their relationship came under immense pressure during the recent IVF treatment and their bickering about money shocked them both. 'It was so uncharacteristic of us that I thought "Hang on, neither of us is really that committed this time around".' They decided to drop the whole business and get on with life. Now Monica feels 'it was money well-spent', not only having Rosa in the first place, despite the sacrifice, but also finding out that a second child was not really necessary to make them happy as a family. We're lucky we were in a position to afford it as we know many people who'd like to do it, but who simply can't.'

Surrogacy

Couples who have exhausted all natural and unnatural means of having a baby and are desperate may well resort to hiring a surrogate mother who will have their baby for them. This has been possible since Kim Cotton was the UK's first surrogate mother in 1986 and set up COTS, an organisation which helps couples find surrogate mothers. The Surrogacy Arrangements Act (1986) outlawed commercial surrogacy. Nonetheless, over three hundred babies have been born to surrogate mothers since then. Couples may choose surrogacy over adoption or fostering as the baby will have the genes at least of one parent, the father. However, surrogacy remains controversial, not only due to the ethical and emotional aspect of the surrogate mother giving away her baby to the prospective parents, but also due to the cost. A surrogate baby can cost anything from £10,000 to £15,000 per pregnancy (although recent legal changes are aimed at limiting payments to expenses only). Even so large sums of money are usually exchanged between parents and surrogate mother. The money has often caused problems not only for the prospective parents, in terms of being able to raise the thousands demanded, but also for the surrogate mother, who may want to keep 'her' child even though it has been commissioned and paid for by the prospective parents. This means a surrogate mother may feel she can't afford to keep the baby even though she has a legal right to do so. It's quite common for working-class women, who already have their own children and/or who are lone parents themselves, to be paid by wealthy middle-class people to give them a surrogate baby. With increasing infertility and affluence, and with couples establishing new relationships or second marriages later in life, surrogacy may be something which couples may increasingly choose for having one or more babies in the future.

Maintaining children

The term 'afford' is one which every parent considers seriously not only when having their first-born, but also when maintaining subsequent children. In the ASDA three-volume report, *What Price a Child*, which covers the cost to parents of a child's life from conception to age twenty-one, the staggering total (at 1996 prices) amounts to an average of £100,513.83. Even taking into account the recycling of clothes and other gear, subsequent children will obviously still cost parents much more than one child. Factors such as using private versus state education will clearly affect how much parents fork out over time. And whether this creates friction between parents will depend on how much they are in agreement about the extent and nature of expenditure, as well as their ability to afford it. Parents need to think carefully about having more than one child – work out as far as you can how you will pay for holidays, clothes, extras like cinema and dance classes, and whether you will need to move house in order to house more children.

Fostering/adoption

This book cannot cover the ins and outs of fostering and adoption. However, should you be considering these options as a couple you should think extremely carefully about the financial considerations, as well as all the emotional and practical ones, in advance of taking on a child. Talk to your local authority's social services department and specialist fostering and adoption agencies (such as the British Agencies for Adoption and Fostering – see Help section) and get a breakdown of expected costs (immediate and ongoing). If there is financial help available, make sure you apply for it. The worst possible scenario would be for a fostered or adopted child to be at the centre of money rows for a couple, or even worse, to be blamed for costing them more than had been originally anticipated.

Stepchildren

Although there is no space to go into the complex issue of step-children in great detail here, it is nonetheless important to mention the issue when considering why couples fight about money. Negotiating exactly who pays for what can be extremely complicated and a source of much friction.

Dawn and Martin's story: successfully integrating their two households

Dawn, a mother of three in her late forties, remarried ten years ago when her children were all at secondary school. Her new husband, Martin, also had three children from his previous marriage. His children stayed with their mother and visited at weekends and in school holidays, while Dawn's children lived at home in the week and visited their natural father at weekends and in the holidays. 'It was all very complicated to work out at first,' she remembers, 'but I think our bottom line was that we were in love, we'd disrupted our lives and our children's lives terribly, but we had to make a go of it.'

Martin was generous towards Dawn's children – he was working full-time and she was working part-time; and Dawn was generous towards his. 'I think because our divorces had been fairly amicable it was possible to talk things through not only with our ex-partners but with each other. It was tough at times, but I think being able to sort things out straightforwardly really helped.'

Both Dawn and Martin came from working-class upwardly mobile families and both had Planner Money Patterns which fitted a Mirror-Image relationship perfectly. 'We had a few money niggles at the beginning, but it soon settled down. Luckily for us money never really became an issue. It would have been hell if it had.' This reinforces the message in Tobe Aleksander's book, *His. Hers. Theirs: A Financial Handbook for Stepfamilies*: 'If you are thinking of becoming a stepfamily, talk, talk and talk again before you commit yourselves. A basis of trust and understanding is vital. That means understanding one's own attitude to money which is often conditioned by past experience. Try to look ahead calmly and without emotion.'

Handling Emotional Money Baggage

Attitudes to money being 'conditioned by past experience' is another way of saying understand your Emotional Money Baggage. When couples are fighting about money while trying to have, or having a baby, exploring fertility treatments or surrogacy, deciding to foster or adopt, maintaining more than one child and stepchildren can make emotions run high. Fights over money may well be symbolic of deeper interpersonal power struggles. However, it does not necessarily mean that all is lost. Couples who love each other, like Dawn and Martin above, can succeed as there is a commitment to make their relationships and situations work. This might mean facing your own entrenched Money Patterns and working out how to accommodate them with your new partner and their children. It also means paying attention to your Money Relationship – which will be unique to your situation – and working out what will make it flourish.

Sue and Dean's positive Money Relationship

When Sue, forty, and Dean, forty-six, started going out in their twenties (they met at university), they were fiercely independent and didn't agree about money at all. They lived together for a while, split up, and had new relationships. Sue had a baby with her new partner, but the relationship did not work out. She met Dean again after two years of being alone and they realised they were still in love. Dean (who had also lived with someone else in the interim) said he wanted to marry Sue and make a go of it together. Sue was thrilled and agreed, but on one condition: 'It sounds awful now, but I said he'd have to sort himself out financially. Luckily, he agreed.' Sue said she would teach him her way of managing money and Dean was only too glad to learn. His reward was life with Sue, and her baby daughter, whom he loved.

Sue has Planner Money Patterns to Darren's Ostrich Money Patterns: so they are typically Chalk-and-Cheese. 'He used to drive me mad never having any money, always being in debt or not knowing what was in his bank account,' says Sue with a laugh. She always managed her money well, had money for her child and for other necessities and felt Dean was not long-term partnership material – unless he changed. Now, Sue and Dean have been happily married for eleven years and have two boys of their own (ten and seven). Working as primary-school teachers they both work long hours, but are hugely committed to all three children and family life, and they enjoy a good social life.

The essence of Sue and Dean's marriage is honesty, openness and trust. After the initial falling out and getting back together on new terms, they have a good working partnership. Dean learned about Sue's money management system, but has adapted it to suit his own and the family's needs over the years. 'I still have my weaknesses,' he explains, 'but I'm much better than I used to be – I guess I've grown up through having the responsibility of paying for kids.' Sue explains how their system works: 'Both salaries go into one account, everything is paid for (mortgage, utilities, Visa bills, savings), and then we give ourselves equal spending money, including money for the children's costs'. Over the years their Money Relationship has become a positive one. Sue still does the paperwork, but Dean prides himself on doing the research (particularly on the Internet) and they find they are mostly able to agree on paying for the essentials and spending priorities because they can communicate well with each other. They have their disagreements, but these are short-lived because, at root, Sue and Dean not only love each other, but respect and can listen to each other's points of view. 'Although we got off to a rocky start, having children has made us have to tackle money properly together,' says Dean.

Having a baby checklist

- Have you and your partner talked through the money issues connected to having a baby?
- How would your Money Patterns and Emotional Money Baggage work together if you had a child?
- Do you have any feelings about being more dependent on each other financially during pregnancy, childbirth and beyond?
- If you needed fertility treatment or wanted to use a surrogate mother, how would you raise the money? Would you think it was 'worth it'?
- If you or your partner have a child or children by a previous partner/spouse, how are you going to handle the finances? Who will be responsible for what?
- If your Money Relationship is embattled, can you see any way in which you or your partner can change? Is there a particular Money Pattern which causes friction? If so, what can you do about it?

8

Life Crises and Life Changes

Instead of seeing the rug being pulled from under us, we can learn to dance on a shifting carpet.

Thomas Crum

It's a fact of modern life that any love relationship which lasts a relatively long amount of time (say three years or more) will inevitably be hit by the occasional crisis. Whether married or not, a couple is inevitably challenged when their relationship experiences the swings and roundabouts of everyday stress and strain, either from within (through one or both of them making a radical decision, like wanting to give up work or go off and live as a castaway), or from without (through external forces, such as accidents, redundancy, even death). And when a relationship is under pressure from a crisis – whether internally or externally provoked – the Money Relationship will also be stretched to its limit, creating a Money Relationship Crunchpoint. Whether a couple can ride and survive a Money Relationship Crunchpoint will depend on the strength and nature of their relationship, their ability to communicate and negotiate, as well as how much they have already learned to handle each other's Emotional Money Baggage and Money Patterns.

Handling life crises and life changes

The give and take, ups and downs, good times and bad times are always part of love relationships. It's inevitable that when a major change, or crisis, comes along, a relationship will be tested severely. Inevitably, as the months and years go by, and couples learn more about each other, they usually learn to understand and accommodate each other's foibles and peccadilloes. He might never buy her a Valentine's card and bunch of flowers, but he is generous about helping her out with her Visa bill when it matters; she might want to redecorate the house every summer (which he thinks is unnecessary expense), but she also encourages him to go out and spend on golf clubs and eighteenth-hole drinks to relieve his work stress.

Just how a couple handles their relationship's swings and roundabouts will reflect whether they are able to work as a team and be drawn closer together in extreme circumstances, or whether they are driven apart because they are unable to support each other in times of pressure and stress. Money can become highly symbolic in these times of chaos as people can begin to use it to compensate themselves for the emotional pain they are feeling, or it might even become a psychological football kicked between them. Fights about money can escalate during uncertain times because, in a sense, money represents security and solace. Fear will be surfacing as a couple rides any particular swing or roundabout, and this fear might well manifest itself in increasingly frequent Flashpoints, such as: 'We can't afford it, so how do you think we'll survive?' or 'It's not fair – how the hell did you/we/I get us into this mess?'

Changes in life goals

When a relationship begins a couple will usually discuss their respective life goals in general terms: 'I want to travel the world,' he says; whereas she says 'I want to make lots of money and then have six children.' These life goals may be pipe dreams, or they may be something the person is absolutely dedicated to fulfilling. However, life goals necessarily become more significant as the relationship itself deepens from dating to mating and beyond. How much your goals coincide will affect your ability to commit to your relationship.

If you want to live in Australia and your partner wants to be near their ageing mother in Epping Forest, you may have a problem of agreeing joint life goals. If you really hate babies, and your partner wants a football team of kiddies, how will you agree what your life is about together? Life goals obviously depend on age and circumstance. Clearly, the life goals of a twenty-year-old will be significantly different from a fifty-year-old, although it doesn't necessarily mean the latter's goals are just about sitting by the fireside in slippers: it might be bungee jumping in the Andes or going to art school. Whereas the twenty-year-old might just want to get a steady job and have money to spend after years on the dole. Life goals may well change as an individual grows emotionally, intellectually, even spiritually.

Couples have an effect on each other: they change and mould each other through the power of love. Most of us have not had enough affection, validation, unconditional love and acceptance and we therefore look to our closest relationships to fill that gap. If two people come together with vastly different life goals, as in a Chalk-and-Cheese relationship, they will have to reach an accommodation with each other. And sometimes the power of love is all that it takes to bring about a great change.

The relentless pace of modern life has made many people question what they are doing with their lives. Making money and buying all sort of luxuries comes at a cost. Not just the cost of the things themselves, but at a cost on relationships and quality of life.

Downshifting

As stress has become a number-one killer in the late twentieth and early twenty-first centuries (especially through associated illnesses, such as heart disease, cancer, addiction and chronic illness), many people have questioned the need to maintain (or attempt to maintain) an affluent Ab Fab lifestyle. In the 1970s and 1980s when unemployment was high, people were desperate to work. Now, when unemployment is relatively low, the British work longer hours than any other European country. This has led to many couples feeling tied to a relentless work treadmill, which has a detrimental knock-on effect on the quality of their lives. Professor Cary Cooper and Suzan Lewis write in *The Workplace Revolution: Managing Today's*

Dual-Career Families that 'a demanding career may involve long hours of work, and the additional demands of domestic life and childcare can cause people to feel overloaded. There may also be conflict between the demands of career and family roles as work schedules are often incompatible with family life.' People are increasingly experiencing 'work overload' which can lead to occupational stress and workaholism.

As a consequence, there has been a trend over the past fifteen years towards downshifting. Having tasted life 'having it all', some big spenders are now simply much happier settling for less. Changes such as these – cutting your hours from full- to part-time, deciding to follow a spiritual or artistic path, leaving town for country, or 'following your bliss' – are fine if both partners are in agreement. However, it is far more complicated to satisfy the needs and desires of both partners (and take into account the needs of any children or stepchildren, elderly family members, etc.), whose life goals may well point in completely opposite directions. Whose life goals come first? Who decides? And how does it affect a relationship if one partner suddenly wants to downshift while the other wants to maintain a high-achieving lifestyle? As happens often, truth is stranger than fiction as Angie and Derek's story clearly illustrates.

Angie and Derek's story: moving the life goal posts

Angie, forty-one, and Derek, forty-three, have been married for fifteen years. They have one son, Andy, who's now ten and rapidly heading for secondary school and puberty. Angie and Derek are a hard-working couple, dedicated to their gorgeous detached house and garden in the country, their respective jobs (she's a freelance journalist, he's a secondary-school teacher), and to generally having a good life socialising with friends at the weekends. 'When we moved here it was an amazing risk because our mortgage almost doubled overnight,' remembers Angie of their move from a small, London terrace ten years ago. 'But we looked at the finances and managed to get a 100 per cent mortgage as we thought the house would be a good investment. We're both good at DIY, so we've spent hours and hours doing the place up evenings and weekends.' The job is still not finished, although their house, facing stretches of undulating South Downs, is homely and crammed with 1930s Art Deco furniture and *objets d'art*.

Until recently Angie thought Derek was completely happy with their situation. She knew he found teaching stressful and demanding and that he'd been doing the job for twenty years and had itchy feet, but she had no idea what was really going on behind the scenes. Angie works mainly for women's magazines, writing house and garden features. She has to work long hours travelling and writing, which includes precious evenings and weekends. 'It goes with the territory and although my son doesn't like it, he says he understands. His bedroom is next to my office, so when he comes home from school I can usually monitor him, while still carrying on my work.' However, their domestic arrangements were recently rocked by two things. First, they had to repair the roof, which cost a staggering £15,000. They could claim part of it on their house insurance, but they were still left paying a bill of £10,000. 'Our outgoings are astronomical as it is,' explains Angie, 'because I suppose we have a good lifestyle. But I believe in working hard to play hard, so I don't really mind.' However, what she did mind was that – without her knowledge – Derek had resigned his job three months previously. He had some of his own savings which he was secretly using to pay his part of the household finances (they operate a 'His' and 'Hers' separate money system). When his money finally ran out, he had to reveal the awful truth to an absolutely astonished Angie.

'What the hell do you think you're doing?' was her first response. It was late Sunday evening and Andy was safely tucked up in bed. Derek had been going off to work every day through the Easter and Summer terms, having resigned. Life had been seemingly normal, or so Angie thought, during the long summer holiday. As it was now the end of the August bank holiday weekend Derek realised that he couldn't keep up his pretence throughout the Autumn term. Even so, Derek was unable – or unwilling – to explain. All he could say was 'he'd had enough and wanted time to himself'. According to Angie (Derek refused to be interviewed as they are still fighting about what has happened), he was simply sick of working such long hours for so few rewards. 'But how could you do this to me – to us as a family – without telling me or at least consulting me?' Angie had screamed at him. 'How are we going to manage the money?' Silence. 'Why didn't you talk about it before you actually resigned.' 'I couldn't' was all Derek could say before leaving the room. Of course, at the centre of Angie's anger was fear: how were they going to survive on her freelance income? How would they ever replenish Derek's savings? What work would he do and how much would it pay? How would they maintain their mortgage, pay their roof bill, continue their lifestyle, buy Andy's expensive new trainers?

A few days later Derek was able to attempt to explain his actions. 'He told me he'd simply had enough,' seethes Angie, 'he'd been going into the same school for fifteen years and he couldn't face another term. The Head had reminded staff that any applications for transfer had to be in by Easter and he'd found himself writing a resignation letter in the lunch break.' What has hurt Angie the most is not the fact that Derek felt trapped by work and wanted to downshift in some way, but that he didn't trust her enough to talk to her about it all. 'I suppose if he'd asked me I would have said we couldn't afford it, and so he did it sneakily instead,' she adds honestly.

After many bitter rows about his decision and the monetary implications, Derek went out and reluctantly found new part-time teaching and lecturing work. The irony is he now works even longer hours for less pay than he did as a full-time school teacher. He's lost his pension rights and he's out of the house teaching four nights a week instead of two. 'I do all the childcare, all the housework, all the cooking, we never see each other and we don't have sex,' spits out Angie, furiously. 'As for money – we just don't have any and I'm still mad at him for doing what he's done. The only difference is I can see he's really trying hard to make amends now.' Derek tried to move his life goal posts as an individual without involving his wife in the decision. This showed a massive breakdown in communication and trust not only in their relationship, but in their Money Relationship. Perhaps he felt she would simply block his new life goals and make it impossible for him to change course? Angie is a definite Planner, but Derek is much more of a Doormat: she calls the shots in the main and his behaviour reveals how powerless he feels in the relationship; hence their Money Relationship is at a Crunchpoint.

Tips for handling life goal changes
These sorts of relationship swings and roundabouts can be managed, however, if couples can try to do the following.

- *Be open and honest with yourselves and each other.* Communication is essential for success. If you don't trust (or try to trust) your partner then your relationship is in trouble anyway;

- *Air the financial knock-on effects* – so that both partners can see clearly what it is they are agreeing to and why from the outset;
- *Look at the bigger picture.* If one of you is desperately unhappy in the current situation, how could things be improved within the existing circumstances? If so, what needs to change overall?
- *Recruit the support of your partner.* Don't make them into the enemy to be fought. Your partner may take time to come round to your way of thinking, but if they see you really mean business and you sincerely believe in your new plan, you can persuade them that your new life together would be better. They may turn out to be your biggest cheerleader after all;
- *Listen to each other.* Even if you don't like what you hear, your partner has a right to a fair hearing. Try to listen without reacting. Take time to think. Their need to change their life goals may ultimately enhance your own relationship and family life;
- *Reassess your Money Relationship.* In Angie and Derek's case, he, as a Doormat, let her call the shots as a Planner. He needed to take a more upfront, proactive role about money, thus reassuring Angie he would pull his weight financially. Equally, she needed to let go of her control, and let Derek do things much more his way. Perhaps they could decide to develop an 'Ours' joint money system, while keeping 'His' and 'Hers' money for individual use?

Jamie and Darleen's story: a positive example of changing life goals

Of course, there are some couples who manage to accommodate each other's change of life goals. Jamie, thirty, and Darleen, thirty-six, live together in a jointly owned flat. Jamie was working for a large computer company as a software engineer, while Darleen was a full-time nurse, working days. Jamie felt increasingly fed up with his job and knew in his heart and soul that he didn't want to continue in computing. He wanted to retrain as a shiatsu therapist and then go to large companies, offering 'stress-busting' neck and back mass-ages to workers at their desks. 'I had a friend who was into healing and personal growth and I went to a yoga and meditation course, which opened my eyes to another way of being,' explains Jamie. 'I was utterly fed up with working in a sterile business environment, all neon lights and deadlines, airless offices and stress. I just didn't want to end up like my dad – knackered and retired off at sixty.'

In fact, Jamie's father had had a massive heart attack at fifty-five, which had scared the family enormously. Jamie and his mother had struggled to keep the family going, while his father went through months of convalescence. This Emotional Money Baggage was clearly behind Jamie's deep desire to 'downshift'. Luckily Jamie felt he could talk to Darleen about his wildest dreams. 'I took her out for a meal and talked and talked about what I wanted to do,' he remembers. 'She looked shocked at first because we have quite a big mortgage and a nice lifestyle. But her main response was to hold my hand, look me lovingly in the eyes and say, "Jamie if you want to do it, you will do it. We'll find a way to manage".' Jamie was over the moon at Darleen's response as it meant he could really start planning a career move. However, Darleen had some conditions to make. 'I had known for a long time that Jamie was fed up at work – you could see it,' she says thoughtfully. 'He was a fish out of water, really. He'd rush home as soon as he could, change into casual clothes and meditate. It was like he was one person at work, another at home, and he couldn't stand the divide any more.' But she also knew they had to face up to their financial responsibilities. 'I said I would support him financially during his training, but that he had to start earning a bit afterwards and then start paying his way a year after that, otherwise it was no go.'

In fact, Jamie applied for a 'start-up' loan from his local authority and, having resigned, he did a two-year full-time training. Towards the end of his second year he began earning by giving his friends and ex-colleagues shiatsu massages. Finally, his dream of becoming a stress-buster in big business came true a year later. He had to buy some special equipment and have business cards printed, but he soon made contacts and started work. He doesn't earn as much as he did in computing, but makes enough to pull his weight at home. He's also far, far happier than before. Their Money Relationship was able to sustain the change in his life goals because Jamie and Darleen:

- were able to talk about the change in detail and air all the fears, problems and ideas ahead of time;
- were able to work out and agree a plan which accommodated both of their needs: his need to downshift and her need for security. Darleen needed to know there would be money coming

in at some point in the future, and it was helpful to Jamie that she took his ideas seriously and gave him something to work towards;

- had mutual love and respect for each other: he respected her enough to trust her and be open about his dreams and fears; she respected his abilities and desires and gave him space to have a go at achieving them;
- faced reality and made decisions accordingly. They wanted to keep their mortgage payments up, so Jamie pursued a retraining grant and they cut their personal spending (no new clothes, meals out or holidays) for the first year. Together they worked towards his goal for the sake of the relationship as a whole;
- made a deal: they agreed that Darleen would support Jamie on this occasion, but that she would have her turn later on, with him supporting her, should she want to retrain.

Changes in circumstance

Our Money Relationships can also be challenged by changes in circumstance, such as becoming unemployed, going from working full- to part-time, starting a business, becoming self-employed, being made redundant or retiring. The uncertainty of modern life today means couples have to be prepared for handling these sorts of changes. No longer do we have a job for life – most of us will work for several employers over a lifetime. We may not even go to a place of work in the future, as homeworking and self-employment become increasingly popular. Couples have to learn to be flexible both individually and together, to respond to changes of circumstance positively in order to make the best of the situation for themselves and their family (if they have one), if they want to survive in the twenty-first century. However, a threatened or actual change of circumstance can put a relationship under stress. And when this occurs, the Money Relationship can rapidly reach a Crunchpoint.

Ivor and Janey's story: sudden redundancy
Ivor, forty-nine, and Janey, fifty-two, had been living in relative luxury for fifteen years when Ivor suddenly lost his job. He worked for a merchant bank in the City, commuting each day from their roomy, Victorian house (a restored rectory) in the Cotswolds. Janey, trained

in fabric design, runs her own small shop, making elaborately embroidered handmade jackets, shirts, skirts and bags. They have no children as Janey had experienced three tragic miscarriages in her thirties, which rendered her infertile. Instead, they have two large labradors and three cats who lounge about happily in their sunny home. 'It's awful but I have to admit I had absolutely no idea that anything like redundancy was imminent,' says Janey obliquely. 'I suppose I wanted to believe that Ivor was fantastic with money. I'm not very good with it, although I get by,' she says gesturing at the Aladdin's cave of her tiny shop; 'I like creating things, I'm no banker.' Indeed, Janey's turnover is quite small. As an artist she sees her shop as an extension of her creative work. She's a self-confessed Worrier about money, with Ostrich patterned streaks. 'I find money very frightening and I suppose I always felt very secure with Ivor because he seemed to know what he was doing. Now I'm not so sure.'

It seems that Ivor had worked for the same bank since school. Educated to GCE level (before GCSEs), he worked his way up from being a humble clerk to being a corporate insurance broker. He had a facility for figures, but as he came from a working-class background he felt he didn't really fit in with the university-educated upper- and middle-class 'City types'. Ivor had got a long way on sheer hard work and street savvy, but he had never been really popular. His downfall, it seems, was computerisation. Ivor says he found it very hard to grasp computer systems and soon found himself struggling as new technology took over. The company took on new, younger, computer-friendly staff who smirked at his love of working things out on paper or in his head. Soon Ivor began to drink heavily to deal with his terror of being found out.

In the local pub, Ivor flinches and looks like a beaten man when I ask him about the redundancy. There's a long silence. 'It was awful,' he whispers, drawing deep on his third cigarette, 'the threat of redundancy was around for over a year and I kept ignoring the signs. There was talk of an American take-over, then talk of restructuring. I thought I was secure, sort of part of the furniture. I believed in company loyalty – which I thought worked both ways – and had no idea I'd really be up for the chop.' The trouble was Ivor could neither confide in Janey, nor really face the situation for himself. 'She hates talking about money,' says Ivor slowly, 'we always end up rowing if I mention the subject, so we've sort of fallen into me managing everything. The mortgage, household bills, everything's in my name. She says she doesn't really want to know. Janey's kept house, done the gardening and run her little sewing shop, but that's been it.'

Ivor's drinking accelerated and productivity deteriorated even though he worked longer and longer hours. 'I was like a drowning man clinging to driftwood,' he exclaims quietly. As the pressure mounted he and Janey hardly saw each other, except at weekends. He was avoiding her. Increasingly, he rolled in off the last train home, extremely drunk, only to rush out hideously hungover to catch the 6.02 every morning to work. 'The threat of redundancy was worst. I kept thinking "poor old so and so, he'll go" and so was utterly amazed when the managing director carpeted me without warning.'

It was classic. Ivor had 'the call' at 11 a.m. one Wednesday morning. At 11.15 precisely he was shown the door by a burly security guard, having been stripped of his identity card and having had five minutes to empty his desk. Massively humiliated and bewildered he headed for the pub and got utterly drunk. 'After fifteen years of loyal service I was treated like the tea boy,' says Ivor bitterly. 'All I really had was debts and a nice house mortgaged up to the hilt. I had no idea how I was going to tell Janey.' Indeed, after his binge, Ivor spent the rest of the week at home recovering and only managed to break the news at the weekend to an astonished Janey. 'She went white, then she cried, then rushed out of the room,' Ivor remembers. 'We didn't talk for four whole days afterwards.' All this happened only six months ago and since then Ivor and Janey have really done nothing but argue. Janey has point-blank refused to talk about the situation, which has enraged Ivor. She says she can't forgive him for ruining their life. Being pragmatic, Ivor says they need to sell the house, but Janey won't countenance this solution. 'Why should I lose my lovely house because Ivor's become a bloody washed-up boozer?'

Ivor's sudden redundancy has exposed the weaknesses in their relationship and, hence, Money Relationship. Up until his sacking, Ivor had taken on the old paternal role of looking after the money. Now their relationship would have to shift to meet the demands of the present to survive. Things would have to equalise more, financially, even though Janey says she is not prepared to change anything at all right now. Thus their relationship has reached a

Crunchpoint as debts have mounted through Ivor's drinking and short-sightedness and Janey's unwillingness to co-operate and/or take responsibility. They are still at loggerheads at the time of writing.

Tips for handling changes of circumstance

When couples reach a stalemate, as in Ivor and Janey's case above, it is usually because one or both parties is furious with the other. Rigidity is a sign of fear as well as anger. With counselling at this point, they might both be able to see how each other's Emotional Money Baggage and Money Patterns fit together. They are both Ostriches, digging their heads into the sand, hoping the world will go away. Even so, Ivor had taken on the 'daddy' role to Janey's 'child'. The only way forward would be for them to understand and identify these roles and make a decision to change them – together. If couples are faced with sudden changes of circumstance, it's a good idea to try the following.

- *Allow time for the news to sink in.* Everyone's emotions work differently. It may take a few days or weeks, for the couple to work out what they feel about the situation as individuals.
- *Try not to blame each other.* A relationship has a life of its own and if it is a collusion between two people, then both are playing their part. It takes two to tango, as the saying goes. Blaming is a powerless activity and goes nowhere in relationship terms.
- *Take responsibility for your own part.* Think about what you can do to help the situation get better.
- *Be prepared to change.* This might involve how you live, what you spend, what you do, where you go. Clinging on to how things were is a recipe for disaster.
- *Talk and listen.* You both need to talk about what has happened, how you feel about it, what it means. This takes time and can be very painful, but is worth striving for. Take it in turns to talk and listen. This may take days or weeks and there will be plenty of feelings surfacing.
- *Let your feelings out – safely.* Don't hit each other, or take revenge or withdraw emotionally. Try and show how you feel, and listen to how the other feels. This can make you closer in time. You may need a third party to help in this process, like a relationship

counsellor or best friend or trusted family member, who can act as a conduit and umpire.

- *Be practical and act.* It's no good continuing to hope against hope that things magically return to where or how they were. They won't. All you can do is be practical about the present and the future will take care of itself accordingly.

Vi and Barry: a positive example of changing circumstance

Vi, fifty, and Barry, sixty-three, have been married for twenty-five years. They have four children and both have worked all their married life. Vi worked as a canteen cook in the local primary school once all the children were in school themselves, while Barry always worked in the local garage as a mechanic. Both from working-class families, they lived outside Nottingham in neighbouring streets in the same village. It was a close-knit working-class mining community (now defunct with the mine's closure) and they grew up together. 'We met at thirteen at a local hop,' explains Vi with a grin, 'and it was love at first sight I suppose.' Barry chuckles, warmly, 'Ayup, we've been together ever since.' Vi and Barry now live in an immaculately maintained council house. Pictures of children and grandchildren adorn every nook and cranny. They clearly don't have masses of money, but the doorbell keeps ringing as neighbours call in for cuppas and the phone keeps going as friends and children make contact.

'We never had much money,' explains Vi, 'I worked in a chip shop after leaving school. Then I got a job in the canteen and after the kids I went back to it part-time. Barry's always worked hard, all weathers, but the money hasn't been brilliant.' Indeed, they started life living with his 'in-laws' for a couple of years. 'That was really tough as it was so cramped, but we needed to save so we could start a family.' They were on the local authority housing list and eventually got their own place. There were a couple of sad times, too. Vi had a miscarriage before her first daughter was born, which devastated the couple. Then there was a cot death between child two and three. 'These times were very black and after the cot death I felt so depressed, but Barry was a tower of strength and we pulled through somehow.'

In fact, team work is really the watchword of their relationship.

This was finally tested to the hilt when Barry had a major heart attack at fifty-eight and had to retire – without a pension. 'After forty years in the job I went home with just my wages,' he says rubbing his head; 'it was dreadful. I was good mates with my boss, but I'd never thought really about pensions and such. We'd only ever had just enough to scrape by as it was.' Indeed, Vi and Barry used to pile up their wages on the kitchen table and divide everything up into appropriate envelopes. They never used a bank account – until recently. However, when Barry lost his job Vi was spurred into action. She was fed up with the canteen work and wanted to branch out. Vi had been fascinated by her son's computer and she went on a retraining course at the local college and soon landed a full-time administrative job in a large local business. 'I was earning more money in a week than I'd brought home in a month,' explains Vi proudly. Barry found it a bit difficult to swallow at first, not least when he had to get to grips with the housework, washing and cooking. 'I felt a right prat I could tell you,' he says good humouredly, 'I hadn't been in a supermarket for twenty-five years, let alone loaded up a washing machine, but now I was doing the lot.'

Vi and Barry worked out a monthly budget, including a savings plan for holidays and other expenses, which gave Barry time off playing golf and Vi time to do more computer training (she bought herself an Apple Mac, just for fun). Their children could not believe the new regime, as the youngest was still at home studying for A Levels, Barry was a full-time househusband. 'My mates teased me of course, buying me a pinny and a mop,' he admits, 'but I was really beginning to enjoy myself.' Vi brought home the bacon and Barry cooked it. 'I thought, well, I can follow a mechanics manual and fix a car, so I can ruddy well follow a recipe.' His chicken curry and apple pie are now renowned in the family. Now Vi has been promoted to section leader their income has gone up nicely and they are planning a holiday in Florida, their first abroad in ten years. 'I have to watch my health, but housework is gentle exercise and I'm eating better than I ever have,' says Barry. 'And it suits me to be going out to work after all these years at home,' says Vi.

It is quite an achievement to change the internal rules of a relationship after many years of being together, but Vi and Barry have managed it. Both with predominant Planner Money Patterns (Vi's more of a Hoarder, Barry's a self-confessed Worrier), they have been able to negotiate through troubled waters because they can communicate openly and clearly and then adjust themselves and their lives accordingly. By responding flexibly to a change of circumstance, they have enabled their relationship and Money Relationship to have a new lease of life past the Crunchpoint of Barry's heart attack. 'I can honestly say I have never loved Barry so much or have been so happy,' says Vi. 'Go on, you're just saying that to get the last piece of carrot cake,' quips Barry. They both laugh heartily.

Changes in health

There are also life changes caused by events such as road and train accidents, even bomb attacks or other, albeit rare, disasters. People can also suffer nervous breakdowns and chronic illness which, in turn, can stress their love relationships severely. Understandably, most of us live our lives thinking 'it will never happen to me' although we read obsessively about tragedy every day in our newspapers. Yet, if and when tragedy strikes, we are often not prepared for the impact it may have on our relationship. Usually this is through loss of earnings, but also a change in health may mean having to downshift from full- to part-time work, changing career or giving up work altogether. If you become economically inactive having been independent and self-sufficient, this will necessarily affect your self-esteem and also how other people view you, including your partner or spouse. If you have dependants, like children, it becomes even more complicated as you may need to hire help in the shape of a nanny, au pair or other kind of paid domestic help which, of course, costs money. Some couples find the change in health of one partner incredibly difficult to deal with, creating a relationship crisis and thus a Money Relationship Crunchpoint.

Peter and Sonia's story: how his accident tested their love
Peter, twenty-seven, and Sonia, twenty-five, had been living together for three years when he had his tragic accident. Peter talks about BA and AA – Before Accident and After Accident – in an attempt to inject humour into what has become a fairly grim situation. Peter and Sonia had met originally on a scuba diving course in Australia. Back in Britain their romance flourished between cities and

eventually Peter went to live with Sonia in Oxford, where she was an English language teacher. He was into fitness in a big way, going to the gym every day and surfing and diving as often as possible. These fairly expensive hobbies were supported by his small business – he restored old furniture which he sold either to antique shops or to private individuals. His work entailed a lot of humping of heavy furniture, carpentry and fine handiwork. But he loved his work as it gave him freedom to indulge his outdoor pursuits to the hilt. 'I felt I'd met my match in Sonia,' says Peter nostalgically, 'we both cared about the environment, were vegetarian and wanted to travel. We made a plan to do the grand tour together, perhaps cycling round the world.' Madly in love, they spent their time harmoniously, making love, walking in the Oxfordshire countryside, or cycling in the neighbouring hills, while saving for their big trip. 'We both had portable skills and we thought if we got to Australia we might just end up staying.' Neither particularly wanted children – at least at this stage of their lives.

Peter and Sonia had a fairly Mirror-Image relationship: both were 'Eco-Warriors' and they felt comfortable with each other shopping carefully, making sure their food was organic and their clothes were free of leather or fur. Sonia had a Spender patterned streak, however, and Peter was uncomfortable when she sometimes splurged on something he thought was 'unneccesary' or 'frivolous'. 'She loves jewellery and aromatherapy oils and stuff,' he says wryly, 'and she could go out and squander £30 or £40 at a weekend. I'd be angry and we'd row about it.' They'd end up living on rice and lentils, almost punitively, for the next week. Peter admits he took things a bit far at times. With a large Hoarder streak, he liked the idea of being utterly self-sufficient in a minimalist kind of way, 'which is just as well given what happened,' he says with hindsight.

Tragedy struck when they went on an idyllic holiday to the Caribbean, having saved hard for a whole year. Peter had a horrendous accident: he'd been surfing in Barbados, off the wild east coast, when he had misjudged a mega wave which sent him crashing onto submerged rocks. Peter was instantly paralysed from the neck down, having severed his spinal cord and completely smashed three cervical vertebrae. Luckily he was saved by a horrified Sonia, who plunged into the foaming surf, dragged him up the beach with another surfer and piled him into their hire car (they found out subsequently they shouldn't have moved him, which affected their legal claim for compensation). Valuable time was lost reaching the small local hospital across the island, and by the time Peter was airlifted back to Britain, it was becoming clear that his injuries were both serious and permanent.

Suddenly their relationship was at a major Crunchpoint and Sonia felt she was unable to help Peter with his new situation. Things were fine as long as Peter was active, but the new disabled Peter was not what she could cope with. This also badly affected their Money Relationship. 'It was downhill almost from the start', says Peter stoically; 'I thought we were mated for life, kind of soul mates, but I think Sonia was horrified and overwhelmed. She couldn't cope with my physical disability or financial dependency so she started spending like a maniac, I suppose, to compensate herself, in a way.' Sonia went on shopping sprees. She took out credit cards, she spent on all sorts of frivolities while Peter was in rehabilitation. 'I guess she felt she could only be with the old me, not the new me.' 'Her love evaporated overnight and she soon moved out, leaving me without any means of an income and a large joint Mastercard bill. I couldn't believe it, it was like she was angry with me for my accident and was punishing me instead.'

Peter and Sonia's Money Relationship could only work as long as they were totally joined at the hip as Mirror-Image Eco-Warriors. Sonia was unable to face the change in Peter's physical state which, although extremely challenging, could have brought them closer together rather than split them asunder had their love been strong enough.

Drew and Fiona's story: overcoming disability together

For some couples, this kind of challenge can serve as a uniting force. Drew, thirty-nine, and Fiona, forty, had been married for ten years when Fiona had her accident. Both from Edinburgh, they had gone 'down south' when Drew's acting career had taken off in TV. Fiona, a solicitor, had found herself a job in a radical practice in London and for a while their lives were fulfilling their wildest dreams. Somehow, along the way, they had made a decision not to have children. Drew felt acting was too precarious a career to build a family on and Fiona worked long, anti-social hours and travelled a great deal. However, neither bargained for how their lives would change the day Fiona was smashed into by a hit-and-run driver as she walked round a corner on the pavement. 'I really don't remember much about it,' says Fiona thoughtfully, 'it's all a blur. I can remember having bought a sandwich just before – tuna mayonnaise bap, silly what you remember, isn't it – but I was just putting it in my bag and thinking I'd better get a wiggle on because I'd be late for an office meeting, when, wham . . . that was it.' In fact, a teenage joy-rider had stolen his father's BMW and it had mounted the pavement as the car slewed out of control on the corner. Fiona was pinned under the front wheels, up against a wall, and the driver also had multiple fractures. Fiona was 'lucky' in that her spinal injuries and multiple fractures did not leave her permanently paralysed. However, after six months in hospital and two months' intensive rehabilitation and outpatient physiotherapy, she was still unable to return to work.

'It was a very difficult time,' she remembers sadly: 'I adored my career, got a real buzz out of preparing cases and whizzing in and out of court or round the country, but all of a sudden I was a homebody. I just didn't want to go out.' Long after her physical injuries had started to heal, Fiona found her psychological injuries were still raw and bleeding. 'She was incredibly nervous,' says Drew tenderly, 'we couldn't go out in the car – she had to sit in the back and she screamed every time someone passed us. She had night-mares, night sweats, she cried all the time. I was at a total loss as to what to do.' Being an actor, Drew was not afraid of strong feelings, but he felt Fiona's reaction was somehow too extreme. 'I was totally terrified of everything,' explains Fiona, 'I thought cars, buses, even bicycles, were going to mount the pavement to get me. I even had dreams about cars crashing into my house and "getting me" in bed. It was hell on earth.'

Unable to work at all, Fiona was on permanent sick leave. Drew's lucrative run on TV had come to an end and he was having difficulty getting new work. Although they had some joint savings, they soon went. Inevitably, they started to bicker about money. Then the fights got worse. 'About nine months after the accident,' says Drew, 'I felt I'd had enough. Fiona was a totally different character, a nervous wreck, and we had no money left. All I could see was misery and destitution ahead of us. I was depressed I couldn't get a new contract, but I also knew Fiona needed my support at home. She had changed out of all recognition – it was a horrible time.' At first Fiona had hidden her symptoms as much as she could from her colleagues, as she didn't want to lose her position in a very competitive firm, but she was visited regularly at home by one colleague in particular, who had been her closest friend and confidante on the staff. Dierdre was a specialist in personal injury claims and she was handling Fiona's case against the driver for her. It was Dierdre who planted the idea of how Drew and Fiona could begin to 'solve' their problems. 'I knew there was something terribly wrong with Fiona,' explains Dierdre, 'it suddenly dawned on me she was suffering from Post-Traumatic Shock Syndrome (PTSS). It was obvious, but because it was Fiona, who was usually so terribly capable and resilient, I hadn't really twigged.' Dierdre persuaded Fiona to go for some counselling, along with Drew, who was reluctant at first. 'Fiona and I were preparing her case, I thought that her relationship would be over soon if something didn't change soon,' says Dierdre pragmatically, 'so I put to them a survival plan.' The idea was that Drew (who was bored 'resting' anyway), agreed to put his TV acting career on hold for a year while Fiona had some PTSS therapy. He would become the main breadwinner and give her space to come to terms with the accident. Neither Drew nor Fiona warmed to the idea straight away, but they did see a therapist together and after three sessions, Drew came home and announced he had a new job. He was teaching acting, singing and dancing at a local private school to cover a teacher on maternity leave. Fiona visibly relaxed and for the next nine months she had regular therapy (twice a week), got herself fit and prepared for her case. Fiona had never been particularly domesticated, but she now enjoyed preparing meals and doing light housework. Meanwhile, Drew found he was actually enjoying teaching and that it was better than waiting around for the perfect part in a soap to appear.

With Dierdre's help, Fiona took a case and eventually won some damages. Although her original job had now been lost, she applied for a part-time job in a different practice and decided to become a post-trauma specialist. 'I decided to continue with my part-time teaching,' explains Drew, 'as it suited me well. The school offered me a permanent job-share with the teacher who'd been on maternity leave as she now wanted to work part-time. It's been perfect, as I'm still "waiting" for a break, but am earning meanwhile. I can always resign if the big one comes along.'

Three years after their 'disaster' Drew and Fiona's relationship is in a very different place. Fiona still has psychological repercussions from her accident – she has nightmares and night sweats whenever there's a national disaster like a fire or plane crash – but she feels far happier with their relationship, which has equalised much more over time. 'I realise I feel happier now I'm off the career treadmill that I was on before. I've learned to really trust Drew and I know we can work together when the chips are down. He's been fantastic to me and I love him for it.' 'We've come through a lot together,' Drew adds, 'I've learned you never know what's round the corner in life. I had no idea we could survive this kind of dreadful upheaval – but we did – and we now count every day we have together as an extra bonus.' When Fiona finally got her compensation, which was around £125,000, she split it three ways, between Dierdre, Drew and herself.

Tips for handling change of health

It can be extremely destabilising for a relationship when one partner suddenly becomes physically or emotionally dependent or unfit. Pressure will be exerted on the relationship by the unhealthy partner needing more care, money spent on treatment and/or counselling, and they may become economically inactive, even totally dependent. This kind of situation is particularly difficult to handle if either partner comes from a background where a parent was ill or disabled in any way, when Emotional Money Baggage may come to the fore.

So what can couples do to minimise the effects of this kind of change?

- *Face reality*. You both need to assess the situation as clearly as you can and face, as soon as you are able, what it will involve and mean.
- *Get information*. If one of you has a particular physical and emotional disability or condition, find out all you can about it. There is plenty of specialist help available, through voluntary organisations, support groups, your GP, books, etc.
- *Get help*. Isolation is one of the main things that drives partners to a Crunchpoint. Involve other people in your life together – family, friends, colleagues, helpers. Don't try to cope with everything yourselves.
- *Get emotional help*. There is no shame in getting counselling or

having therapy when you are facing a major life change. Couples can go to see someone together, or separately; talking honestly and openly to a third party can really help if you are under stress with each other.

- *Think laterally.* Life will have to change to adapt to your new circumstances. Think about all possible ways that you can change things – and have fun doing it.
- *Get financial help.* Physical and emotional problems are often costly in terms of lost working hours, increased treatment, finding and paying for specialist care. Find out what you can get through your local authority and through specialist voluntary sector agencies (like the Royal National Institute for the Blind if you have lost your sight).
- *Get legal help.* Check out your legal rights (talk to Citizens' Advice, the Disability Alliance, etc.). You may need to take a law case to make a claim for compensation. Contact a good solicitor to see what you need to do next.
- *Expect things to change.* One of the reasons relationships fall apart under this kind of stress is that one or both partners can't cope with things changing. Change is inevitable, so you need to accept it in order to make the best of it.
- *Plan your finances.* Clearly if one of you becomes economically inactive for a while or long term, this will put strains on your Money Relationship. Try to plan how you will use your limited resources and how you can raise money. Find out what retraining facilities and grants there are in local colleges, careers advice offices, manpower agencies, or the local Job Centre.

Swings and roundabouts

There are all sorts of other swings and roundabouts which can challenge relationships, both internally and externally, and which are too numerous to mention in detail here. Life will always throw up unexpected crises and change, and whether a couple can ride and survive a Money Relationship Crunchpoint will depend on the strength of their relationship, their ability to communicate and negotiate, as well as how much they have already learned to handle each other's Emotional Money Baggage and Money Patterns.

The couples who turn these Crunchpoints into something positive are those who are able to put their relationship first and roll with the punches. Those of us who adopt a throwaway attitude to our lovers and spouses ('If I don't like this one, I can get another, there's plenty more fish in the sea'), tend to end up throwing away one set of problems only to replace them with another. Of course, some relationship difficulties become intransigent and it might well be time to give up if you have been stuck at a Money Relationship Crunchpoint for too long. However, with some love, thoughtfulness, self-respect, respect for the other, honesty and flexibility, it is possible to turn what seem to be dire circumstances into life-enhancing ones. It's a matter of making a decision and plan of action, both individually and together, and then working out how to put it into practice. This is not easy, but it is the core of why some people can surpass their Money Relationship Crunchpoints, while others are defeated by them. It's not just a matter of love conquering all, rather it's a matter of love plus smart thinking plus team work conquering your relationship's swings and roundabouts.

Life crises and life changes checklist

- Have you been through a major life crisis (like change of life goals, circumstance or health) with your current (or past) partner or spouse? If so, what?
- How did these changes affect your finances?
- How were/are your relationship and Money Relationship affected?
- What feelings came up/come up with each other when you try to discuss these changes in your relationship?
- What exactly did you fight about if you had money rows?
- What have you learned about handling these kinds of life changes?
- What has it told you about your current relationship and how you and your partner/spouse work together?
- What would you do differently next time something happened like this?

9

Splitting Up, Divorcing and Starting Again

Yet when all's done you'll keep the emerald
I placed upon your finger in the street;
And I will keep the patches that you sewed
On my old battledress tonight, my sweet.

Alun Lewis, 'Goodbye'

It is one of the ironies of life that when you form a love relationship, money is often the last thing on your mind (unless you're a real Golddigger), and a difficult subject to talk about because it's so taboo. Yet if and when you split up, money will probably be the very first thing that concerns you both and is essential to talk about, especially if you live together or are married. This is because money is all about survival: if you've put your all into your relationship or marriage because you believed it would last for ever, there is a great deal of fear in facing how you will survive as a single person, maybe with children to support, having spent all your love as well as your savings.

The Emotional Meaning of Money

Money becomes highly symbolic if relationships go wrong because it becomes a focal point for anger, fear, frustration, greed, resentment, jealousy, envy, possessiveness and worth. Money becomes loaded with emotional meaning when a relationship is on the ropes. If a woman is cheated on by her husband, or a man is cuckolded by his wife, the wounded party may vow to 'take their ex to the cleaners'. The desire for revenge is often turned into financial punishment as the wounded party wants to vent their pain by destroying their ex financially ('hit him where it hurts, in his wallet'). Aggrieved partners can also become embattled over dividing up their worldly goods because the pain of facing the end of their once-wonderful love affair is too great to bear. The wrangling over possessions can obsess those who feel emotionally hard done by. Indeed, some people destroy each others' property in taking revenge, which can make the whole business of splitting up or divorcing into a sad and bloody farce, reducing two sophisticated adults to two bad-tempered toddlers wrestling in a playpen over a favourite toy ('It's mine', 'No, it's mine'). Revenge stories abound: one girlfriend, enraged by her boyfriend's infidelity, carefully cut the motifs out of all of her boyfriend's T-shirts, cut all of his jeans and suit trousers off at the knees and left his telephone calling a New York number for the weekend while he was away. An article I wrote in *Woman's Realm* (9. 1. 96) entitled 'When you earn more than him', a real-life story of Cathy and Robin Chater, reported how Robin, being an envious husband, burnt £8,000 worth of his wife's clothes as a protest against her success as a breadwinner, public figure, mother and attractive woman. Needless to say, they divorced.

Money Relationship Crunchpoints

There seems to be two main ways that money operates destructively in relationships which are on the ropes. First, when a relationship is in trouble on the money front, and it reaches a Money Relationship Crunchpoint, this can lead to fierce money fights which in turn can lead to a couple splitting up, separating or finally divorcing. Money fights can be exhausting when they are repetitive: they erode trust, love, patience and empathy as the couple slug it out over who spent what in the supermarket or who has more cash to fritter away on themselves. Sometimes a couple will split because the revelations about one partner or spouse's monetary behaviour undermine the entire nature of the relationship.

Karen and Paul: Money Relationship Crunchpoint led to a split

Karen, twenty-nine, is a self-confessed shopaholic. 'I just have to spend to feel better,' she admits, 'I can't seem to get through a day without buying something and I always spend too much.' Karen takes home around £600 a month after tax (she works in a leisure centre sports shop and gets commission on sales), but she can spend up to a £1,000 a month on clothes, cosmetics, shoes and jewellery. 'I get this urge and I have to go out and buy something, anything.' 'My boyfriend didn't know the half of it because I was very secretive, at least, until I went a bit too far.' Karen had lived with Paul, thirty, a computer software engineer, in his flat in south London for a year. They had had a whirlwind romance and she had moved out of her shared house to live with him within a month of their meeting. 'It was totally love at first sight,' remembers Karen sadly, 'it was fantastic sex, romantic weekends away, it was wonderful right from the start.' Paul, who earned at least four times as much as Karen, worked long hours and had to travel in the UK and in Europe, often being away for a few weeks at a time. 'I suppose I got a bit lonely,' explains Karen, 'I'm not very good at being on my own.'

She began to spend to make herself feel better. 'CDs, clothes, meals out, drinks with friends, cinema, takeaways, taxis, weekends away with mates in Paris and Amsterdam, it all mounted up.' Having reached her limit on one credit card, she simply took out another. Then another. 'I had five store cards, that was dangerous.' She also had three bank accounts with overdraft limits on each which she reached fairly quickly. 'I was paying Paul rent, but he mainly paid for everything else. He did start questioning me about where I got all the money from for Jimmy Choo shoes and a Gucci handbag, but I just said "the sales" or it was an offer or something.' Karen did have a conscience, however. She would lie awake at night sweating with sheer terror about what she had bought that day, which was now lying inertly in bags at the back of her wardrobe. Like many shopaholics, Karen would take clothes back and get refunds, but not always for the whole amount as often she could only get a credit note.

Eventually, Paul uncovered what was going on and he absolutely hit the roof. He had asked her for a raise on the rent when his mortgage rate went up and she said she couldn't afford it. Karen was at the limit on all of her credit cards, store cards and overdraft accounts to the tune of £8,000. 'Paul looked at me coldly and said, "But I'm only asking for £15 more a month to cover the mortgage. Look at all the crap you buy all the time. It's hardly fair." ' Desperate and in tears, Karen blurted out the whole truth and Paul was utterly horrified. They had a blazing row, their first, which shook them both to their roots: they were at a Money Relationship Crunchpoint. 'Paul came out with all this stuff about how he was sick of me always coming home loaded with shopping bags. I screamed I was sick of being neglected and ignored, and didn't I have a right to have some fun?'

Their row grumbled on for a week and then, the following weekend, they had a serious sit-down talk. 'He simply said to me that it was "over", that he didn't know me really and he wanted me to leave,' says Karen, her eyes filling with tears. 'He said he couldn't live with someone who had lied to him so much and he didn't like who I was. I was utterly devastated.' The relationship was over. Paul, essentially a Planner, had no patience with Karen's Spender Money Patterns. 'I begged him to give me a second chance, to help me sort myself out, but he just refused.' She wanted them to start again, she said it was 'their' problem not just 'hers'. But Paul didn't agree. 'I can't help you,' was all he kept saying, 'it's over, and that's final.'

Karen and Paul's Emotional Money Baggage

With a bit more probing, it came out that Karen had had a very poor relationship with her father, who was an international business-man. 'All my childhood, dad was flying in and out of the country and our house, always very busy and preoccupied, but he used to bring home fab pressies for me and my mum.' In fact, her mother used to compensate for her own loneliness by spending on the house: 'She was always redecorating and buying furniture. She also went out on a shopping spree with my grandma every week, so I grew up thinking coming home loaded with bags was normal.' Karen got used to her father's absence, but it hurt. 'He was never there at carol concerts, school plays or parents' evenings. He wasn't really interested in me, which hurt like hell, but just used to give me a cheque or some money to spend on myself when he went away again.' Karen can now admit that she has quite a big Golddigger patterned streak, which attached itself to Paul. They had a classic Chalk-and-Cheese attraction: his solidity balancing her flightiness, or so they both thought. 'Yes, I have to admit I was attracted by his ability to earn. When we first met I was wowed by his car, his flat, his clothes. We were always eating out in smart restaurants and I felt looked after.' What Karen was looking for was a modern-day sugar daddy, or, in fact, a real daddy to compensate for the one she had never had. Golddigging tendencies are usually based on feelings of loss, inadequacy and grief. The anger at having been neglected or cheated turns into a desire to extract compensation for the past from partners in the present. It's also a way of making them responsible for your financial survival. Karen was looking to Paul to accept her unconditionally, like a child needing to lean on a benign parent, and was utterly amazed when Paul's love evaporated in the face of her addictive spending.

Couples hook together with their Money Patterns and, at first, Paul felt protective towards Karen. He liked being the one with the money, because it made him feel big and masculine. However, he felt he could not trust Karen once her spending was exposed. It made him feel small, humiliated, abused – feelings which he was striving to avoid through being a successful man of the world.

Splitting up leading to money fights

Some couples report that they never fight about money – until they split. They might niggle about the washing up, childcare, sex, or bicker over relatives or where to go on holiday, but money is not a topic for wrangling over – until the gloves are finally off. One man told me he and his live-in lover were fantastically compatible about money. They never argued about it, it was never really mentioned; there was an easy ebb and flow in their relationship and no one kept tabs on what was spent or by whom. However, when they split up (after three years), they fought like cat and dog over who owned the bed and who had bought the dishwasher. It was as if they had suppressed the subject of money throughout their relationship, because it was too vulgar, or because it represented something very basic about their individual needs and differences. Once they fell out of love, there was no need to protect each other any more against the more animal and needy – or even greedy – aspects of their natures. Dividing their possessions became a focus of their grief: as they split things up, literally, their unbridled pain spilt over.

Obviously, long-term relationships and marriages can fall apart for all sorts of reasons, other than money, but when a divorce is being negotiated, money can become a hugely emotional sticking point. Thus, a threatened or actual split or separation can lead to a Money Relationship Crunchpoint. This, in turn, can lead to fights about money, which can lead finally to splitting up or divorce.

Ruth and David's story: threatened divorce led to money fights

Ruth, thirty-five, and David, thirty-eight, had been married for fifteen years and have two sons, eight- and ten-years-old. David works for a law firm at senior partner level and Rachel is a secondary-school teacher. They live in a roomy house in Surrey and their boys go to a private school nearby. 'I thought we were happy,' says Rachel sadly, 'but I can see in retrospect we weren't really. We were doing the "right thing" by the boys, staying in a marriage which was gradually going stale over the years.' Both Ruth and David worked hard, although David seldom got home before the boys' bedtime and usually left before they got up in the morning. 'He was like a weekend dad, really,' says Ruth, 'and everything else fell to me to do – ferrying the kids about, cooking, cleaning, shopping, housework, arranging our social life, ironing – on top of working full-time.' Ruth says she felt exhausted most of the time by her domestic and work routines, but was striving to be a 'proper' wife, supporting her high-powered husband, mothering her sons, putting herself last 'for the sake of the family'.

Ruth was therefore utterly shocked when their marriage finally came to a Crunchpoint. She discovered David was having an affair with his secretary. 'It's such a cliché, but I found a Visa bill with an Interflora payment on it; it wasn't for me, or for either of our mothers, so I sort of twigged, instantly.' She confronted David and he confessed, saying he was in love and wanted to live with his secretary – their marriage was over. Devastated, Ruth stopped eating, although her treadmill life went on. Humiliated and shocked, she begged David to give his secretary up, begged him to start again after fifteen years together and for the sake of the children. But he refused. Eventually, after a lot of blood-letting, he revealed his affair had been going on for five years. Although Ruth was in agony, she still believed they could work it out – at first. However, after getting legal advice and seeing a Relate counsellor for four sessions alone, she reluctantly filed for divorce. It was only during the legal mediation – when the couple had to come clean about their financial situation in the presence of two solicitors – that the whole story came out, bringing them to a Money Relationship Crunchpoint.

'I had worked all of our marriage, even when I didn't want to,' explains Ruth; 'there were times, when the boys were under five, where I pleaded with David for me to work part-time or even give up work altogether. I was always exhausted and guilty, I felt I wasn't a proper mum to the boys or a proper teacher at work. I spent my time running between everyone and everything. But David always said "we can't afford it".' Ruth believed him – because he was her husband – and stoically carried on, even though she became thinner and thinner. Although she knew he earned well, she actually had no idea how much because it was 'private' to David. Yet, all her salary (which he knew exactly) went on the boys and their private education (which David insisted on, she would have preferred state education). However, during mediation both parties had to declare all of their earnings, assets and savings. Ruth's jaw dropped not only when – after a lot of persistent probing from the lawyers – she finally found out the astronomical salary David was on (plus perks, like a nice fat pension), but also that he had an *extremely large inheritance* which he had hidden from her throughout their fifteen years of married life. 'Not only was there much much more money in the pot throughout our marriage – so I needn't have worked all that time and neglected the boys,' spits Ruth, 'but also he was hiding his inheritance from me, hiding it like a naughty schoolboy, *for fifteen years.*'

Ruth was utterly amazed and her faith in her husband crumbled into dust. When challenged by both the lawyers and Ruth to explain his actions, David kept repeating that he didn't think the inheritance was 'relevant'. He claimed that, as it had come to him before his marriage, it was solely his. Luckily for Ruth the mediating solicitors thought his hidden nest egg was highly relevant and belonged to them both.

'My attitude changed at that point,' admits Ruth, 'I really didn't care about money up until then, but I felt so betrayed, so cheated on, so abused, not only through his having an affair, but also keeping me in the dark about the money all those years, forcing me to work when I was almost breaking down physically as well as mentally. I thought "Right, you bastard, half of this is for me and the boys".' Ruth insists that, had she herself had a similar inheritance, she would have thrown it into the family money pot all along as 'Ours'. 'I find it hard he was so deceitful for so long. Who on earth was I really living with? Who was the father of my children? I realised I didn't know him at all. This destroyed my self-confidence and worth, it also destroyed my faith in men and trust in my own judgment. I could have got over an affair – just – but his meanness and dishonesty over the money, no, that's been the hardest bit to get over. My money was "our" money, but "his" money was "his".' They are now divorced: David lives with his girlfriend (he has access to and pays a decent wedge of maintenance for the boys) and Ruth says she is happy living alone with them.

Ruth and David's Emotional Money Baggage

With hindsight Ruth says now that she was a real Doormat in terms of her Money Patterns. Because she loved her husband, and respected him, she believed in him totally and demanded little. 'I can see this stemmed from my childhood as my mother was very similar, always serving my father, who was a harsh military man, and demeaning herself for me and my brother, the family, duty and so on.' Ruth and David, both from well-heeled upper-middle-class backgrounds, thought they understood each other tacitly and that their Mirror-Image relationship worked well. In fact, David, whose father was in the Stock Exchange, was not only a Hoarder but had large Gambler patterned streaks, which meant he lost large sums playing with stocks and shares from time to time. David absorbed both his father's prudence and profligacy. This meant he was often in conflict, psychologically, and was used to having a 'secret' Jekyll-and-Hyde financial life which he kept far away from Ruth, wider family, friends and colleagues. Ruth describes his view of women as being pretty archaic, as he divides them up into wives, mothers and whores, with his secretary playing the classic doting bimbo to his wife's dutiful mother. 'I don't think I'll ever trust another man,' says Ruth bitterly, 'but also I've wised up about money myself now that I'm on my own.'

Modern dilemmas

Luckily, David and Ruth's fairly old-fashioned kind of marriage, with the pattern of man as breadwinner, woman as homemaker earning 'pin money', is on the way out. Indeed, the twenty-first century is already challenging couples more than ever concerning money as women are set to outstrip men on the earnings front by 2030. Over the past fifty years women have become a powerful force in the workplace and marketplace, and although a lot of women still need time off for childrearing and childcaring, they can be immensely flexible, hard-working, pragmatic, person-friendly employees, which can often make a canny employer retain their services over more single-faceted men. Also, women are having babies later. At the beginning of the twentieth century, the average age of having a first-born was twenty-one, whereas at the beginning of this century it is now thirty. As the century continues, and as technology increases choice, women – who are fitter than ever – may choose to have babies in their late thirties, even forties or fifties (say, by freezing embryos in their twenties and implanting them fertilised when trying for a baby), once career and financial security is fully established. No one is quite sure yet exactly how these trends will affect traditional heterosexual relationships as the man becomes increasingly redundant, not only as sperm-bearer and father, but also as the main breadwinner.

In addition, a significant number of women are choosing to stay single, not have children, use AID (artificial insemination) to have babies alone, and/or not even live with men or have sex with them at all. Singledom will be on the increase as the century continues and as we live longer into old age. As we have seen throughout this book, changes in working practices and employment security are reflected in our relationships, to some extent. Few people will have a job for life in the twenty-first century, as work becomes far more diffuse, with people working on short-term contracts, at home or in small business 'units'. All that's really needed for a lot of white-collar workers today is a fax, phone line and e-mail address. Some people don't even have a desk at work, as 'hot-desking', the practice of walking around an office with a portable phone and perching on any available space, has become increasingly popular.

Short-termism and serial monogamy

Similarly, this shift – towards uncertainty and short-termism – is also reflected in our relationships. Serial monogamy is the norm as people become sexually active earlier and live with one or two partners before marrying (if they marry at all). With one in two marriages breaking down, remarriage is on the increase. Nothing is safe, nothing is sacred, everthing is up for grabs. However, even though the world around us is changing exponentially, our psychology, and to some extent our biology, often lags behind. Even though women are wedded to the notion of having a career these days, rather than getting a job for 'pin money' as in their mothers' and grandmothers' days, the biological clock still ticks away, making many women reassess their life goals as they approach thirty. Equally, men may give lip-service to supporting a woman's right to work *and* to have children (if and when she wants to). Yet, when it happens to their own partner or spouse, and affects their lifestyle and perception of themselves, the reality can bite harder than they anticipate. Men and women are still struggling with the shift in their roles and money fights can ensue as a consequence.

Unreal expectations

The 1960s, 1970s and 1980s led a whole generation of men and women to believe they could have it all: love, sex, education, work, training, babies, freedom, creativity, travel, fun, drink, drugs – and of course, money – on equal terms. Women, in particular, were led to assume that being a 'superwoman' was not only possible, but necessary. Yet by the 1990s, many women became wiser about the practicalities of juggling everything and began to remove the ideological halter of trying to be superwoman. Unreal expectations have taken their toll, as many women are permanently exhausted, fighting against rigid employment practices, feeling guilty at leaving their children, striving to find cheap and decent childcare, competing at the workplace for promotion, pushing for improved financial rewards, while being domesticated at home and a sexy lover in bed. As one woman said to me, 'Yes, I can have it all – but not all at once.'

Financial inequality

On the money front women have not yet become equal to men across the board. Even at the beginning of the twenty-first century, women's earnings still lag behind men's (women earn 80 per cent of what men earn) and the government-funded Equal Opportunities Commission is only just launching its first real major campaign to fight for women's pay equality since its inception in 1975. And there are still only a few women right at the top in all walks of life. However, while equality has not yet been attained, it is nonetheless also true to say that women are more visible and acceptable in positions of power than ever before. And this shift is reflected in home life. Women expect more from life, they have greater choice about what they do and how they do it. They can work full- or part-time, or be full-time mothers (an increasingly popular trend as many mothers feel the stress of trying to 'have it all' during their children's early years is far too taxing). Women expect, therefore, to have their own income, and/or at least to have an equal say in the household finances if the man is still the main breadwinner.

When she earns more

As we have already seen, men's and women's roles are gradually changing, and for some couples this has created a modern dilemma which has put their relationship under stress. Quite often this dilemma is focused on money – who earns it, who has more and therefore who has more power. In some cases, where the woman earns more, it has brought about the relationship's demise, mainly because it has shifted the balance of power. It's often hard for the man to swallow the woman's success, particularly on the financial front.

Lynne and Piers' story: her high earnings led to divorce

Lynne, forty-one, and Piers, forty-five, had been married for ten years when he lost his job as a chartered accountant in a large insurance firm. They have two small children, a boy and a girl, under school age and live in a three-storey house in a slightly decadent, but leafy west London surburb. When I visit, Piers is in the pub, where he is most days (and nights) to Lynne's fury. She explains why she and Piers are now living separately under one roof. 'It all started when I got this job,' she explains, gesturing at a pile of papers perched precariously on the edge of their large kitchen table. I notice the computer is on, and papers are strewn everywhere on the floor and surrounding chairs. Throughout our talk the phone keeps ringing and children keep coming in for something to eat. Lynne has to balance herself between dealing with customers coolly on the phone and adjudicating between squabbles in the living room. I feel exhausted just watching her. 'Piers lost his job very suddenly in 1993. He was earning about £40,000 plus commission. It was totally unexpected and we had taken on a huge mortgage based on his salary. I'd also had three lots of IVF, which cost us all our savings, and I'd given up work when I had my first child. So I – or rather we – were totally dependent on Piers.' It was slump time, but Piers was buoyant and believed he would soon get work. He wined and dined many ex-colleagues, sent out his CV, but nothing came of it. 'At first I thought, "Oh, it won't take long", but it took nearly a year.' During this time the couple survived on credit cards, bank loans and overdrafts. Piers took a six-month contract which was fairly lucrative. Things got better and this time Lynne fell pregnant naturally, to her delight. Piers felt differently, however.

'He was furious about the second pregnancy,' explains Lynne, 'he said we couldn't afford it, but I felt it was marvellous. It had taken five years to have our first child, then wham, I was pregnant with the second one a year later. I thought it was an amazing gift from God.' Under stress, Piers started drinking heavily. His contract was not renewed. 'He was grumpy all through the second pregnancy and didn't pull his weight in the house or with our first baby,' remembers Lynne. 'I should have seen the warning signs.' After the second baby was born, Piers was unable to get another full-time job or even a short-term contract and he gradually retreated into booze. 'I got my mum to come and live in to help, but she's quite old, so when the three months were up she went back to her own house.'

By then Lynne and Piers were barely speaking. When they did talk, it was to fight over money, which was almost a daily occurrence. 'I felt so stressed out having two children and a husband who was permanently either drunk or sulking, I thought "Bloody hell, I've got to go and do something myself or we won't survive".' Lynne found a local childminder first of all, then she got a job. She had been a legal secretary before her IVF treatments, but she felt she needed to make good money – and fast. 'We were way behind on the mortgage repayments, our bills and debts were sky high and Piers was simply not coping.' Lynne saw an ad in a paper for a job selling educational books from home. She had to buy stock and sell it to individual customers. As it was children's books she felt she had plenty of mums and friends locally who might be prospective buyers. Lynne was a natural saleswoman. She was rapidly promoted and was soon training her friends up as her new sales team. Within a year she was earning £50,000, more than Piers had earned at his peak.

'He hates me for it,' says Lynne, 'he loathes and detests me and has retreated further and further into drink.' Ever an optimist, Lynne believed she could mend her marriage once the money flowed in. She has been methodically paying off overdrafts and building up mortgage repayments. 'I pay a bit towards each debt each month – it doesn't go far as I'm the only breadwinner – but we are getting there.' They have also been in a negative equity situation for five years, in that they would lose money if they sold their house, because it had been worth less than when they paid for it when the market was booming in the 1980s. 'We are still living under one roof, but it's hell,' says Lynne, 'I've been on tablets for stress recently, and I know it's getting to the kids who fight all the time, but Piers refuses to move out.' Piers does not want to lose his house and feels if he moves he will be destitute. 'All trust has gone between us now – and all love,' says Lynne, 'it's like living with a hateful teenage son. I feel like his nagging mum – it's awful. I think he's envious I can run the house, look after the kids and earn my living as well. All he can do is play pool and drink.' Although he had agreed to it previously, Piers avoided our interview. With house prices rising, Lynne hopes to buy Piers out as part of their divorce settlement. Characteristically pragmatic, Lynne has got organised by hiring an au pair who now serves as a cheaper childminder, cleaner and babysitter. She also says she'll take in lodgers if it means keeping hold of the house for herself and the children.

Lynne and Piers' Emotional Money Baggage

Lynne explained that Piers had been adopted as a baby and could feel rejected very easily. For him it was essential to be powerful and in control and once Lynne took over on both the money and home fronts he felt completely emasculated and marginalised. As for Lynne, 'I come from a fairly normal working-class background,' she explains, 'both my parents worked in lowly jobs – my mum was a shop worker, my dad worked in a dry cleaner's. The one thing I learned, however, was you had to roll up your sleeves when the chips were down.' In retrospect she feels she lost respect for Piers when he lost his job. 'I hated him hanging around feeling sorry for himself, I went off him sexually then, too.' Her sexual rejection of him, and the birth of their second child coincided, leaving Piers literally out in the cold. It's possible that his failure to get work was a kind of rebellion against what was expected of him. It's also possible that the more Lynne took over their life, the less room there was for Piers to manoeuvre. However, he hadn't bargained for Lynne turning into a big earner, which paralysed him even more. Love was lost – along with their mutual respect.

Adam Jukes, psychotherapist and author of *Why Men Hate Women* (Free Association Books, 1993), explains that 'men can become envious and jealous of women's successes'. 'Peer group pressure dictates that men should dominate women, and often a man's rank is determined by his relationship to his partner, as well as his earning power. In this situation, men can get aggressive as a way of trying to control women.' Indeed, their fights had become vitriolic, even physically violent when on one occasion Piers lashed out at Lynne drunkenly. This was the last straw and Lynne insisted he move out to a bedsit the next day. When relationships get to loggerheads like this, it can seem as if their problems are completely intractable.

Handling Money Relationship Crunchpoints

While Lynne and Piers' story has ended in divorce, this is not always inevitable when a couple come to a Money Relationship Crunchpoint.

If the feelings involved can be dealt with, and if both parties are willing to identify and handle their Emotional Money Baggage and Money Patterns because they want the relationship to work again, then there is hope. Both men and women have got to learn to live in a world which is full of monetary swings and roundabouts, which in turn affect the nature of their love relationships. To survive, enjoy life together and flourish, couples have to learn to:

- adapt to change;
- be able and willing to swop roles;
- let go of the past;
- be flexible;
- be realistic;
- adopt a positive attitude and viewpoint;
- manage any children together;
- handle their feelings – no matter how explosive or frightening;
- trust and respect each other;
- identify their respective strengths and weaknesses – and build on them;

and most of all:

- communicate as openly and as honestly as they can about their situation in order to reach mutually agreeable solutions;

while:

- keeping the situation constantly under review in order to make fresh decisions to meet the changing challenges of the situation.

Starting again

One of the biggest challenges facing men and women in the modern world is when they have to pick themselves up, dust themselves off after a major relationship split, and start all over again. It seems to be part of the human condition, that no matter how bruised and battered we may feel emotionally when love dies, and no matter how often we swear 'never again', we nonetheless find ourselves venturing into the dating and mating field once an appropriate period of mourning has past. Human beings are essentially social animals; most of us need to connect, to interact, to care, to love and have sex. Of course, some people forswear relationships once they've been burnt on the altar of rejection or betrayal, but even these sad souls can usually start again with someone new after either a relatively long time of grieving and/or after availing themselves of therapy or counselling help.

When you start again, however, there are several things to be aware of, especially on the money front.

First, you will necessarily have more Emotional Money Baggage to lug along to your next relationship. How you handle this is up to you. Some people use it as a defence and are therefore unable to trust or put all their emotional eggs in one basket again. Although this is understandable, it is a shame, because a relationship built on mistrust and caution seldom works long term. Other people feel they must form a relationship with someone diametrically opposite from their last partner – they choose a Hoarder rather than a Spender; a Golddigger rather than a Doormat. The only problem is that by choosing the complete opposite, we can often end up in almost the same situation all over again (because the opposite is sometimes only a mirror image). Or, we fling ourselves into a similar relationship to the last one, with someone with the same or similar Money Patterns as our ex, thinking 'this time, I'll win'. Unfortunately, this can set up a combative stance from the beginning and may end in tears relatively soon.

The second thing to be aware of is that fear of failure may make you much more wary of getting in too deep, or may make you want to sign pre-nuptial or cohabitation contracts to an absurd degree, or may make you put off ever committing again. If you feel this way, then you are not ready to have another long-term relationship; you need more time to grieve and to sort your life out as an individual.

It is a very useful exercise to think about your prospective spouse or new live-in partner and try to ask:

- What are their predominant Money Patterns and how do they fit with yours (go back to chapter 2 for more detail)?
- How are they different from your ex?

- How are they similar to your ex?
- Do they have any money addictions?
- Are you playing any power games with each other about money (see chapter 3 for more detail)?
- What do you like about how they are with money?
- What do you not like about how they are with money?

Then you need to decide:

- How do you want money to operate within your relationship?
- How close do you want to be and what kind of money system do you want to operate ('His' and 'Hers', or 'Ours', or a mixture of both)? How intimate do you want to be? Do you want joint savings, a will, pension plans, money goals, or do you want to keep them separate?
- If either of you are bringing a child or children (i.e. stepchildren) to the relationship, how much do you want to share their upbringing and maintenance?
- How open do you want to be about winnings, inheritance, savings, assets, earnings? If you are private about it (or she/he is) what will be the implications?
- What are your long-term goals together as a couple?
- What are your long-term financial goals together? A house in the country? To set up a new business? To retire early? To travel the world? To live a life of luxury? To keep working until you drop? This needs talking about (see chapter 8).

Adopt a positive attitude

The older you get and the more relationships you have, the more Emotional Money Baggage you will necessarily bring with you. Yet this does not spell failure. Indeed, with a positive approach, you can decide to rectify what went wrong in your previous relationship by taking a completely different attitude to money. If you were a victim and a typical Doormat, you can now decide to be in charge as a Planner; if you didn't concern yourself with money as an Ostrich, you can decide to get wise, even be a bit of a Gambler. This is not to say you can change your character – nor should you – but you can consciously decide to work on areas of yourself and money life which caused you grief in your past relationship or marriage in order to make your current relationship a success.

Delia and Michael: starting again with a positive attitude

Delia and Michael are both in their early sixties and have recently married. For both it is a second marriage, although they have both had a few affairs since their first marriages ended. Delia was married for ten years until her beloved first husband died in a road accident when she was thirty. She already had two small children, now in their thirties, and spent their childhood up until their early twenties bringing them up as a lone parent. 'Of course, I had the odd boyfriend, but I felt the children came first. I also worked part-time in a bookshop, so there wasn't much time for anything else really.' Plus, Delia was not sure if she would ever trust any man again, and she felt disloyal thinking about settling with anyone else. Unfortunately, her husband, who had been a self-employed orchestral musician, had died without arranging either a pension or life insurance, and he had substantial debts. 'When he died I was utterly naive about money. I had left that side of the marriage to him. My husband left me with £5,000 of debts and I had to work hard to clear them.' Delia, unused to handling financial matters, moved house to release money to pay off the debts. She took the children out of private schools and sent them to the local comprehensive. She changed all of their habits – food, clothing, holidays – to fit their reduced budget. 'Actually, I felt much happier being in charge of money, although I missed my husband terribly and was angry with him for years for leaving us in the lurch.'

Delia, a regular churchgoer, had met Michael at their local church years earlier. He was married when they first met, but now was also a struggling widower, having lost his wife to cancer in his forties. They had had one daughter, who lived abroad in Australia with her husband and two children. 'Michael was a friend. I knew he was a local businessman, running a successful shoe business, and I thought he was quite well off. After his wife died he employed a housekeeper and everything, although it was only him living on his own. I did wonder why he paid for one when it's so easy to boil an egg.' Over the ten years since Delia's husband's death, love grew gradually between them. Michael eventually proposed late one summer, but Delia was unsure. 'I wanted the children to be completely off my hands before I did anything,' she says firmly, 'plus I didn't really want to lose my independence having found it at last.' Being from an older generation, they found it extremely hard to talk about money together and the subject was seldom raised. 'If we went out for a meal, Michael would pay, and although it was nice to be treated, I felt I didn't want to depend on a man again, just in case it all went horribly wrong.'

Delia's Emotional Money Baggage was making her fearful of trusting and committing, even though Michael ostensibly had plenty of money. The lack of language about money created a barrier to Delia accepting Michael's offer. 'One evening two years ago he came to dinner at my house. I like cooking and couldn't afford to pay for expensive meals out, and Michael blurted out that he wanted me to marry him and he wouldn't take "no" for an answer again.' Delia panicked. She loved Michael and felt she would be happy marrying him if she let herself believe it could work. She was lonely living alone, but the issue of money was the sticking point. She decided to brave it. 'I told him I was scared of depending on him, that we'd never spoken about money properly and I was worried that if I trusted a man again, I would be left in the lurch if something happened.' Delia was amazed at Michael's response. 'His face brightened, you know, it was like the sun coming out. He said he thought my reluctance was based on my not loving him enough. He felt sure he could never replace my late husband. I was so relieved when he said of course we could sort ourselves out financially, we just had to talk about it.'

The wall of fear and mistrust melted. Delia soon discovered that Michael was, in fact, a very different animal from her late husband. As a businessman he was used to dealing with money, making plans, forecasting sales, doing research, implementing budgets, keeping the books. He wasn't frightened of money and could talk about it, it was just he had felt she would find it was too vulgar a subject to raise (he had sensed her reluctance to mention it) and it would sully any romantic feelings for each other. 'He said he wanted to share his life with me, which meant sharing all that he owned, all his worldly goods. I was deeply moved by this and felt, at last, I would be able to let myself go and love him properly.'

They agreed to marry, but Delia stipulated that she wanted everything sorted out fairly and squarely between them first. They spent three months talking through their finances. They agreed their respective children were their own business and both drew up individual wills which reflected this. However, it was agreed they would sell their properties and buy one together jointly which would pass to the other, if one of them died first. 'It was very exciting to be starting again at our age,' says Delia, 'and it really felt like it was laying to rest the ghosts of the past.' Michael let his housekeeper go and Delia taught him some basic cookery even though they continued to live separately. He also agreed that Delia could continue with her part-time work in a bookshop, which she really enjoyed and didn't want to give up. He had no plans to retire until seventy. They sorted out their life insurance and her pension (which was minimal until that point) and put money together into various savings plans. Love blossomed between them as they made their plans, drew up their agreements and bought their house. They married a year later, moving into their new abode after a short honeymoon in the Highlands. 'I never believed I could be this happy,' exclaims Delia, 'not least because I feel the foundations of our marriage are very sound and clear. There are no hidden demons about to jump out at me this time. I'm very lucky to have had this second chance of love.'

Splitting up, divorcing and starting again checklist

- Are there problems about money in your current relationship which you are not mentioning, but which are irking you?
- Do you feel money could drive you apart? If so, how?
- Have you parted from ex-partners/spouses/lovers on bad terms about money?
- Do you have any unresolved issues about money from past relationships which might be colouring your present relationship?
- If you are starting again, what do you never want to repeat about money? How would it be ideally with your new partner/spouse?
- What do you need to do, right now, to improve your Money Relationship with your new partner if you have one?
- If you are single, but burnt by the past, what do you never ever want to repeat again concerning money and love?

Part Four

Stop Fighting about Money

10

Building Your Money Relationship

The greatest discovery of my generation is that human beings can alter their lives by altering their attitudes of mind.

William James

There are several schools of thought about what makes for a healthy and happy relationship. According to some people's way of thinking, a good love relationship should be all harmonious sweetness and light, with partners being able to sit down and talk calmly about problems as and when they arise. As for money fights, well, this seldom happens in these kinds of relationships because the couples are able to relate well and balance out each other when they have opposing viewpoints.

Sounds great, but how many of us really experience this kind of 'ideal' partnership? It sounds more like a dreamy advert for soap suds than the real-life kitchen-sink dramas most of us experience in our everyday lives.

A bland affair

A relationship without any conflict at all is a pretty bland affair. When two people rub up against each other (literally), they create sparks. If a couple never has any arguments it might well be that they are avoiding confronting their differences. Of course, some people absolutely hate arguing and feel they would do anything rather than fight. They might be quite timid, or shy, or feel arguing is impolite, or they dislike aggression. However, avoiding all conflict can lead to a lack of closeness in a relationship because the two people involved never really get to grips with each other as separate individuals. If you don't tussle over what you want, or need or believe in, you don't really have a chance to affect each other's ideas or emotions. You can live like two goldfish in a bowl: co-existing, but seldom touching. This can lead to a very lonely relationship for both of you.

Constant loggerheads

Another school of thought believes that conflict between couples is inevitable, even healthy. How can you put two completely distinct and different people together without there being a chemical reaction, which includes emotional explosions? As for money? Too right it's a subject for wrangling over, as money is all about survival and getting what you want and deserve. Anyway, a good row clears the air, makes you feel closer, sorts out problems. Some couples – who have lasted a long time together – almost think back fondly to their early years of fighting about money, as they have worn each other down, like the sea battering seaside cliffs.

It's true, people influence each other, mellow and grow together over time. But fighting all the time as a permanent way of life can be gratingly wearisome not only for the couple involved, but for everyone else around them. Sometimes these couples are addicted to the drama and adrenaline rushes involved in constant fighting. Some people only feel close through fighting constantly, and it is almost an emotional sado-masochism that goes on, with one battering the other through rows and fights. People who do this a lot often report they enjoy the making up (including passionate love-making) – until the next round of bloody fighting, of course.

If you enjoy arguing as a means of releasing tension, testing the other's commitment, forcing the relationship to change, it can become an addiction. In some cases constant fighting can escalate into physical violence, which is both destructive and dangerous. This should never be condoned by the party who is hit or beaten, especially if there are children in the relationship. This kind of relationship is lonely, too, as trust and intimacy is dissolved through money battles.

The middle way

If you are completely fed up with fighting about money in your relationship, but you nonetheless want and need things to change between you because you are not happy, then you need to find a way of dealing with conflict – constructively. Blandness is pretty boring and fighting is a pretty destructive kind of behaviour, with both parties rehearsing the same old weary arguments and insults. Either feelings are buried deep, emotions are void, or feelings run high, resentments build up, fur flies. There has to be something in between the two extremes of either blandness or all-out war: the middle way. This allows conflict to occur in order to sort out feelings and ideas, but strives to handle conflict constructively.

Nurture your relationship

It may sound like a cliché, but relationships really are like delicate pot plants. They need watering, pruning and feeding. Sometimes they need leaving alone, so they can simply grow; other times, they need repotting, putting in the sunshine or spraying to kill off the bugs. Each pot plant is unique, with its own type of foliage, blooms and berries, flowers and disease. This book can't possibly provide a formula for sorting out absolutely everyone's money fights in detail, but it can suggest positive ways to make things better. The first crucial step is to nurture your relationship, like the proverbial pot plant.

Your relationship is a third entity with a life of its own. This is created when two people come together and fall in love, or learn to love each other over time. As we have seen, relationships can be positive or negative. To flourish positively (and to bring out the best in you both) your relationship needs:

- *time* – to spend with each other, learn about each other;

- *care* – essential for growth, tenderness and sensitivity is important for mutual nurturing;
- *space* – to grow as something special to you as two individuals. You need to give each other space to be yourselves, with different ideas, needs, characters, beliefs, feelings;
- *openness and honesty* – without this, there is no soil out of which your plant of a relationship can grow;
- *trust* – this is crucial, it is like the plantfeed you give your plant during the growing season;
- *respect* – this is like the water you pour onto your plant to give it moisture and life;
- *mutuality* – a relationship out of balance, with one person dominating or controlling the other, will lead to the ultimate death of the plant. It will bolt and literally over-balance, or dehydrate, wither and die. Mutuality, where no one wins or loses, leads to balance and a happy, healthy relationship.

Learn to listen to each other

Crucially, couples need to learn to listen to each other – really listen – in order to nuture their relationship. Few of us do this well, because most of us have never experienced either being listened to properly or listening to someone else. You might have difficulty in getting your partner to talk: they may feel they won't get a fair hearing, so it's pointless to try. It might seem embarrassing, but sometimes you can have a breakthrough with each other if you try to do something differently. Instead of getting into a niggling argument about money, why not try the following exercise instead (you could try it when you are getting on well, rather than when you are at loggerheads).

Listening exercise
Here is an exercise which you can do with your partner (preferably sober) to experience what listening is really like:

1 Get a clock, watch or stopwatch with a second hand.
2 Agree to listen to each other for five minutes without interruption.
3 Sit comfortably facing each other in a room where you won't be

interrupted by either the phone or other people coming in. Set the timer for five minutes.

4   One partner talks for five minutes and the other simply listens. The listener needs to make eye contact with the speaker, but should not interrupt, comment, laugh, nod, agree or prompt. The talker should simply talk.

5   When the time is up, swop over. The first talker should listen while the first listener should talk for five minutes.

6   Compare notes. What was it like for you both to talk and be listened to uninterrupted? What was it like to listen, without interrupting? Take it in turns to say how it felt.

7   Repeat the exercise, this time talking and listening for ten minutes, fifteen minutes, twenty minutes and so on.

8   Compare notes as in 6 above.

This is a useful exercise and will show you both how well you listen (or don't listen) to each other. In future, when you try to talk about money and tempers are fraying, try and take five minutes each just to talk and listen. It can make an enormous difference to how you feel about each other and what you actually 'hear'.

Learn to be emotionally literate

Try not to 'react' if the other says something which provokes you – let it ride and try to listen to the emotions they are trying to communicate underneath their words. This is often called 'emotional literacy'. When we get upset about something – often very trivial – it is because it is literally the tip of the emotional iceberg. Your partner tells you off tetchily for spending too much on some fresh rolls for breakfast. Peeved, because you felt you were doing something nice for you both, you think 'come on, don't be so ridiculous', and you bicker about it, 'at least I'm buying our bloody breakfast, when did you last go out and get some rolls?' Soon you are snapping at each other and all appetite for a cosy breakfast is gone. In fact, your partner, by mentioning the price of the rolls, was probably trying to communicate their anxiety about money or spending.

Another way of responding is to say, 'Yes, I know they're a bit pricey, but I thought we deserved a treat. Are you worried about money at the moment?' Then listen. Often we go into react mode –

our partner says something and we react and soon we are into tit for tat; you did this, I did that. If you try to understand, even if you find what your partner says intensely irritating or annoying, they may well be trying to communicate something to you about their emotional state, you will be on the road to becoming more emotionally literate with each other. This will go a long way to quelling money fights when they are brewing.

Money and feelings

As we have seen throughout this book, money is all about feelings. We attach very strong emotions to money because it is all about:

- survival
- fairness
- self-worth
- self-esteem
- value
- equality
- love – self-love and being able to love and be loved
- self-respect.

Expect money to stir up strong emotions and you won't be surprised when it does. Expect it to be contentious at times, to make you lose your tempers with each other, to make you feel guilty or bad or envious or upset or greedy, and you won't have any nasty surprises. Often we tell ourselves we are cool about money when we are not. You lend £20 to your partner during a night out and they never pay you back. A week later, they borrow another £20, and you soon start feeling aggrieved, but you feel guilty about mentioning it, because, after all, aren't you a lovey-dovey couple? In fact, the person who is borrowing and not taking responsibility is actually Golddigging, and the person who is lending and not mentioning it is being a Doormat. An unequal relationship is being played out and there are plenty of feelings flying around in this kind of situation. The person who feels aggrieved needs to raise the issue and try to get it sorted out because, if they don't, it will escalate into a nuclear explosion somewhere down the line. Equally, the person who is borrowing without caring about the consequences needs to take responsibility and respect the other partner. They need to listen to what their partner has to say and correct the situation. For the aggrieved partner to stay silent because of their fear of the other's reaction is simply to duck out from making the relationship better. And for the constant borrower to avoid their responsibility in paying their way, is to erode the goodwill in the relationship. It takes courage, but ultimately, a relationship can grow if it is challenged in this way. The pot plant is weeded and the emotional fall-out will not have to poison the soil.

Fear of feelings

Our fear of feelings is one of the main reasons some of us avoid rows; our addiction to strong feelings is one of the reasons some of us fight constantly. The trick is:

- to be appropriate about money and let the feelings be whatever they are;
- to accept that you will both have different feelings about money, and that those feelings tell you something not only about your current relationship, but about the past, in terms of your individual Emotional Money Baggage. Then you are in a position to start sorting out what belongs to the past and what belongs to the present (and to you both as separate individuals);
- to separate out your feelings from the issues at hand. If you are angry with each other, that's one thing; but you still have to sort out an unpaid bill or going over your overdraft limit. No amount of shouting or blaming will pay off a debt;
- not to be thrown by your feelings about money, nor avoid relationships altogether, because money always brings up feelings; the art is learning how to identify and handle them as constructively as possible for the good of the relationship as a whole.

Nurture your Money Relationship

As we also saw in chapter 2, love relationships create their own particular Money Relationships. Sometimes these are 'good' in that they are constructive and productive, sometimes they are 'bad' in that the couple live in chaos, constantly fighting over money in a destructive way. Most relationships have a mixture of both good and bad aspects. Nonetheless, if you want to stop fighting about money, you need to nurture your Money Relationship. This will include the following activities.

1   Accept and agree that you have a Money Relationship and that it is something which needs attention (just like your relationship as a whole).

2   Identify, if you can, what Emotional Money Baggage you are both carrying from the past into the current situation (see chapter 1 to remind you of what this entails). Be as open and as honest as you can in talking about this.

3   Write each other a letter. It doesn't have to be long or complicated, but explain what it was like for you about money growing up, what your beliefs, attitudes, ideas are about money ('as for me, money doesn't matter', or 'I think having the same amount to spend is crucial'). Swop letters and read them in private. Meet up, swop back, and see if there are any areas of agreement between you. Also see what is different or contentious.

4   Identify your Money Patterns (see chapter 2 for more on this). This may feel awkward or difficult, especially if you feel ashamed of what you do or how you are. However, it can be a very constructive step forward, especially if you feel your relationship is imbalanced. Talk about your respective Money Patterns with each other. Don't tell each other what you think the other one's Money Patterns are, as this can drive your partner into being defensive; let them identify their patterns for themselves.

5   Similarly, try and identify your own 'patterned streaks'. If you are mainly a Hoarder, but you have Golddigging Ostrich streaks, try and own up and see how you fit together with your partner's patterned streaks. It will help you understand more about why you are in conflict over money.

6   Identify whether your relationship is a Mirror-Image or Chalk-and-Cheese one. This should also give you insights as to why you fight over money. Try and identify where you make assumptions about each other. Perhaps you are wrong? Perhaps you

pigeonhole or punish each other or can't tolerate the other's differences?

7   If either of you is playing money power games or has a money addiction (see chapter 3), try and be as open and honest as you can with each other. This can be very difficult because of the emotions involved, but if you are in a money pickle with each other, you will have to start tackling this aspect of your relationship at some time to avert disaster. You may need to get help, from a counsellor or therapist, money adviser or lawyer at this point to help you sort out your problems as a couple (see pp. 231–7).

Work out what suits your particular Money Relationship

There is so much advice around, not only about how to manage your money sensibly (see Help section for useful books and organisations), but also as to how you should be operating together as a couple. Mention the issue of money and relationships down the pub or at a dinner party and everyone will start laughing, squirming and chipping in their words of wisdom. The thing is, you have to work out what suits your own particular Money Relationship. You are two unique individuals and you fit together in your own unique way. Your Money Patterns and patterned streaks form an original constellation within your particular Money Relationship, so you really have to know yourself and each other well in order to negotiate.

Team work

That said, you need to develop your ability to work as a team. This does not mean that one of you is subsumed under the other as a dependant. It doesn't mean the bigger earner has the last word, either. However, it does mean, that you both operate as individuals, with your own ideas, responsibilities, earnings (or not) and beliefs, and you find the middle ground, where you are able be a team together, solving the money problems which affect your relationship and family life. It's important to remember, especially for women or people who feel they must protect their independence fiercely, that working as a team does not mean disappearing as an individual. To do this effectively, it is important to ask yourselves:

- What are your individual strengths and weaknesses about handling money?
- What are the particular areas of responsibility each of you would like to take on? (he pays for the shopping, she pays for the mortgage, for instance)?
- How do you want to organise your money – separate accounts, joint accounts, or a mixture of His, Hers and Ours?

Co-operation does not mean giving in or being weak. Co-operation means being grown up, learning how to operate within a complexity of emotional and physical demands in modern-day life.

How to reduce money fights

We have seen throughout this book that Flashpoints occur about money for all sorts of reasons. You disagree about spending priorities; you disagree about who controls money and how open you should be with each other. External forces, such as interference from relatives or being made redundant, also increase pressure on your Money Relationship, turning Flashpoints into Money Relationship Crunchpoints. And if you decide to have a baby, pay alimony to an ex or remarry into a new family, money rows can escalate if the groundrules are not sorted out in advance.

Groundrules and boundaries

During dating and mating couples should be looking out for all the warning signs on the money front that they can. This doesn't mean being paranoid, but it does mean being practical. Work out your relationship groundrules as soon as you possibly can. You will need to review and even renegotiate your groundrules each time your situation changes. To do this you need to recognise that:

- relationships are always changing – don't expect things always to be the same;
- you need to agree or negotiate what is appropriate to the situation and moment in your relationship. Review the situation every year;
- set your groundrules – what suits you as individuals. But stay

flexible. If either of you gets too rigid rows will occur because one or both of you is being unreasonable.

- set boundaries – you are both individuals with your own particular needs: your boundaries will reflect who you are. Maybe one of you is happy to lend money to the other and the other one isn't; perhaps one of you wants to save and the other likes to spend. If you have clear boundaries, then you won't need to be defensive or secretive with each other.
- agree ahead of time how you will handle sudden increases or decreases in money, as these can precipitate money fights.

If you want to have a constructive talk with your partner about money, bear in mind the guidelines.

- *Pick your time.* Not late at night, when you've drunk too much, when you are too tired or already arguing about something else.
- *Pick your place.* In private (not in a pub or restaurant) and in peace (not with the TV blaring or the kids screaming).
- *Set an agenda.* Keep your agenda short and manageable. Agree ahead of time what you are talking about and stick to it (don't throw in absolutely everything you want to say about money and/or the relationship).
- *Set a time limit.* An hour or two maximum. Don't put off starting and chat about something else throughout. It's easy to procrastinate. Don't prolong it either.
- *Delegate tasks.* Even if one of you has taken on the role of main money manager.
- *Do your homework.* Find out what your money rights are as individuals and as a couple. If you live together you have fewer rights than if you are married; and women may have different rights to men. It's important to understand the small print of any agreements you have, too, like mortgage or life insurance policies, income support or disability benefits or pensions (private or state). Get legal advice, talk to an Independent Financial Adviser, go to the Citizens' Advice Bureaux (see p. 234).
- *Keep notes.* Always keep a written record of what you have decided to do and who will do it, with a time limit on when it should be done by (but don't keep reminding each other in the interim). Set a date for the next meeting. Keep your notes in a place where you

both have easy access to them or photocopy your notes and have one set each if you live apart.

- *Approach your meeting or money talks positively.* Don't blame each other, such as in 'It's all your fault we're in this mess; if you hadn't left it so long to get the car fixed, it wouldn't have cost so much.' Rather, say, 'Right, we have a problem about paying for the car repair.' Don't go over past history more than once: put it behind you and move on.

- *Don't borrow from each other (unless it is absolutely clear what the groundrules and boundaries are).* Borrowing can set up an imbalance in a relationship if one partner feels the other borrows too much too often, or is taken for granted. Far better to set up a system whereby you each have either the same or similar amount to spend – and then let each other get on with it without comment. If you do borrow, keep a note of it and pay it back within a reasonable amount of time (or the agreed time), otherwise rows will ensue and there will be a lot of ammunition building up for a relationship split in the future.

- *Agree a strategy.* To save or not to save; to buy a house or to continue to rent; to blow money on fun or be sensible for the future; plan for children and marriage or live for the moment. Try and thrash out these bigger questions with each other, otherwise you will fight about money when you come to decide how to spend any you have.

- *Take time out.* If you reach loggerheads during a money talk try not to batter each other into submission, thinking the longer you go on about your point of view the more your partner must agree. Take time out. Agree to have half an hour's break, when you do something else and start again. Or adjourn to another day, when tempers have cooled. Try to use the interim time out to think about what was going on, rather than react. Above all, try not to sulk or take revenge. Be constructive. After all, you were both trying to put your viewpoints across, it's just you couldn't listen to each other. Perhaps try the listening exercise on pp. 212–13 and/or try writing to each other to explain how you see things as on p. 216.

- *Set short-, medium- and long-term goals.* This helps you feel you are moving forward when you get bogged down.

- *Give yourselves a reward.* Pat yourselves on the back when you have made some money decisions without blowing up at each other (too much anyway). Celebrate your achievements.

What's love got to do with it?

Everything. When you nurture your love relationship and tend your Money Relationship you will soon be able to remove your plant from its pot (especially when it grows and gets pot bound) and place it in the sunny garden of your love. It may sound clichéd, but love will flourish when you are able to co-operate well about money, simply because the quality of your life together will improve. Instead of lurching from crisis to chaos and back, you will be able to fulfil your dreams together. This doesn't necessarily mean a *pied-à-terre* in the Bahamas (well, it might to some), but it will mean that the combination of your two hearts, minds and souls has created something positive and fulfilling in the present. Whether you have children, or not, keep parakeets or pet ducks, or simply like surfing (sea or Net) at the weekend, to work together well on the money front so that you can stop fighting about money in an endless, repetitive cycle is to allow for love to flourish and grow. Money can't buy you love, but love can help you create abundance and happiness in life. Which is what really counts.

Appendix:
Money Patterns Quiz

This quiz is designed to help you identify your main Money Pattern. Tick one answer in each section. Read the options and ask yourself which is most like you – it may not fit you exactly, but it may sum up your general attitude to money. Write down your answers in a notebook or on your computer (or scribble them in the book). You may want to do this alone or with your partner – it can be quite fun to do it together (as long as it doesn't spark yet another row). Try and do the quiz when you've got time and are sober. Be as honest as you can about yourself – after all, it's for your benefit.

1 What's your attitude to overdrafts and credit cards?
You
(a) think it's a cheap way to borrow, but always shop around for best deals and pay off at least the minimum (if not all) borrowings monthly;
(b) don't trust them, but seek the best deals and always pay off everything when due;
(c) see them as free money and love them. You're usually up to the limit on more than one card (including store cards). You 'forget' to pay back the minimum and are always trying to extend their limits;

(d) are terrified of them and have a major panic if in the red or can't pay off the full amount on time;

(e) have several, never open statements and forget about borrowings until bailiffs arrive, always opening new accounts for ready cash;

(f) love spending on other people's credit cards, so make sure partners pay at all times. You'd never actually have one yourself, too much of a commitment;

(g) like to help others by paying for their things with your overdraft and credit card – after all you're lucky enough to have them, why not be generous?

(h) can't be bothered with credit cards and overdrafts, all too complicated. Better to pay cash in hand and avoid all this new-fangled electronic stuff;

(i) think credit is spiralling out of control and causing worldwide destruction – you want no part of it.

2 *When buying presents, you*

(a) buy something practical, hard-wearing and value for money with an eye on the price;

(b) buy something in a summer sale or even give away an unwanted Christmas present (they'll never know);

(c) splash out on a real surprise or luxury item – something they'd never buy themselves (or you for that matter);

(d) shop around for ages, trying to find exactly the right thing at the right price and fear the receiver will hate it;

(e) grab something wacky or unusual, but might even forget as there's a game or deal on that demands your immediate cash instead;

(f) only buy presents during seduction or if you feel your partner is losing interest, when they need to be flattered;

(g) save for months and work hard to buy them exactly what they've always wanted (you don't even like it and probably can't afford it), but it's worth seeing them smile;

(h) seldom buy presents because birthdays and Christmas are just a load of hype;

(i) hate all the consumerism and waste at Christmas – you'd rather give someone special a hug instead.

3 What would you do with a £100,000 win? Would you

(a) get financial advice, pay off your mortgage and debts and invest shrewdly?

(b) stash it in the bank and hope no one else knows (don't get financial advice because you can't trust them)?

(c) go wild and splurge on luxury items which you and your loved ones (and everyone in your circle) have always wanted?

(d) have sleepless nights – what if your friends are envious? what if you invest it badly? should you move? should you continue to work? (Money's more trouble than it's worth.)

(e) live like a millionaire till it runs out – you can always get some more somehow?

(f) hoard it if it's yours, spend it if it's someone else's?

(g) have a big party for your friends, buy presents for everyone, buy off your parents' mortgage and spend only a teeny-weeny bit on yourself?

(h) plonk it on a deposit account and forget it's there?

(i) keep a bit for yourself (for essentials), but either share it with friends or give some to your favourite pressure group?

4 A big bill arrives just as you're about to book a holiday. You

(a) pay it on time because you knew it was coming and book the holiday as planned;

(b) only pay the bill at the last minute and put the holiday on hold – you really can't afford it;

(c) book the holiday and put the bill in a drawer (you'll deal with it when you get back);

(d) panic – you knew the bill was coming, but didn't really plan for it. You agonise over whether you can still have a holiday or not;

(e) pay the bill, book the holiday, place a bet or take out a new credit card for spending money;

(f) never pay your bills or for holidays – you make sure someone else pays or you get a freebie;

(g) pay the bill immediately and suggest your partner go on holiday without you – you don't deserve to go;

(h) put the bill in the bin and forget about the holiday (too much bother to organise anyway);

(i) think tourism is destroying the planet; you keep bills to the minimum – so there's no conflict.

5 When planning your career, you

(a) choose one with the greatest salary/wages, best security and perks;

(b) turn down 'risks' and don't change jobs often as you need the security of a good pension, annual increments etc.;

(c) go for glamour, fulfilment or excitement and live on credit – security is secondary;

(d) go for something worthy, but not necessarily well paid;

(e) do what you fancy until you make a killing. Avoid long-term commitment, it doesn't pay;

(f) use your natural assets to get ahead, get perks, and so on;

(g) don't mind what you do as long as you can look after everyone else's financial needs;

(h) just live hand to mouth, without spending or saving much, and don't have a career plan;

(i) don't believe in careers, you follow your bliss in the moment and see what the universe provides next.

6 When you're offered 'something for nothing', you

(a) examine it very carefully looking for the strings attached – and probably turn it down;

(b) grab a good deal when you find one and salt it away for later;

(c) accept it immediately and see if you can get more;

(d) think about it, ask for advice, weigh up the pros and cons and possibly miss it because you were undecided for too long;

(e) take it and sell it to raise cash;

(f) get someone else to buy it for you because you deserve it;

(g) take the deal and give it away to those who deserve it more;

(h) ignore it, you don't need that kind of thing anyway;

(i) try and work out what the catch is, but take it if it's from a fat cat.

7 You've been invited out to dinner and you're broke, so you

(a) go, but negotiate to pay only for yourself;

(b) say you're busy; anyway it's a waste of money as you can eat much cheaper at home;

(c) go and use your plastic to pay – you needed cheering up;

(d) find it hard to decide whether to go or not. If you go, you'll only take cash, but if you don't you'll think you've missed out;

(e) go – and invite everyone else on plastic. It's only money;

(f) go, just as long as your partner goes with you. You'll borrow from someone if you go alone;

(g) go, but you'll just have a glass of water – you don't mind not eating while everyone else does;

(h) hate going out, so you'll ignore the invitation anyway;

(i) go and share someone else's meal – there's always enough to go round as we all consume too much anyway.

8 Your views on the Lottery, prize draws, the Pools and other competitions are

(a) they're a waste of money as the odds are bad;

(b) they're to be avoided, even if the odds are good;

(c) they're great: you love a flutter, someone's got to win, why not you?

(d) you can't decide which offers the best odds, so sometimes you have a go, mainly you don't;

(e) in for a penny, in for a pound – someone's got to win and today's your lucky day;

(f) you inspire others to have a flutter and if they win, you take your cut;

(g) if you're lucky enough to win, you'd give it to someone worse off than yourself or charity;

(h) no one ever wins and you're certainly not joining in the madness;

(i) you don't do the lottery, it's one of the worst aspects of capitalism gone mad.

9 At Christmas you and your partner buy each other presents

(a) you decide a budget ahead of time and stick to it no matter what;

(b) you don't give presents, it's a waste of money;

(c) even if you agree a budget you always exceed it – it's fine to splurge on presents;

(d) you try hard to get value for money so you shop around, but are never sure if you've got it right;

(e) if you remember to buy presents, you buy several extravagant things and let them choose;

(f) you love being given presents, not so keen on buying them (tend to give a 'token' later from the sales);

(g) you give presents to everyone and hate receiving;

(h) Christmas? What Christmas? A load of media hype;

(i) there's more important things to spend your money on – you'd rather spend the pagan winter festival doing something to heal the planet together anyway.

10 Money should be

(a) used wisely, never squandered and made to grow;

(b) saved – you'll need it for a rainy day;

(c) spent – live now, for tomorrow you die;

(d) used for security, although these days that's hard to find as the market's so uncertain;

(e) risked – there's plenty out there just waiting to be taken;

(f) given – to you. You deserve plenty of it and know how to use it;

(g) given away – to others who really need it (you can manage on very little);

(h) ignored – it's nasty stuff;

(i) used to repair all the damage we've done to the planet before it's too late.

Check your scores

Mostly (a)s = Planners
Mostly (b)s = Hoarders
Mostly (c)s = Spenders
Mostly (d)s = Worriers
Mostly (e)s = Gamblers
Mostly (f)s = Golddiggers
Mostly (g)s = Doormats
Mostly (h)s = Ostriches
Mostly (i)s = Eco-Warriors

For a fuller description of these Money Patterns turn to chapter 2.

Further Reading

Money: management and general

Claxton, John, *Managing Your Personal Finances: How to Achieve Your Own Financial Security, Wealth and Independence*, How To Books, 1999

Hall, Alvin, *Money for Life: Everyone's Guide to Financial Freedom*, Hodder & Stoughton, 2000

Rowe, Dorothy, *The Real Meaning of Money*, HarperCollins, 1998

Wallis, Virginia, *The* Which? *Guide to Money*, Penguin, 1999

Money and relationships

Garlick, Helen, *The* Which? *Guide to Divorce*, Penguin, 1992

Pahl, Jan, *Money and Marriage*, Macmillan, 1989

Pahl, Jan, *Invisible Money: Family Finances in the Electronic Economy*, The Policy Press, 1999

Men's and women's relationships

Berne, Eric, *Games People Play: The Psychology of Human Relationships*, Penguin, 1964

Jukes, Adam, *Why Men Hate Women*, Free Association Books, 1993

Mellody, Pia, *Facing Codependence: What It Is, Where It Comes From, How It Sabotages Our Lives*, Harper & Row, 1989

Quilliam, Susan, *Stop Arguing, Start Talking: The 10-point Plan for Couples in Conflict*, Vermilion, 1998

Quilliam, Susan, *Love Coach: No One's Ever Shown You How to Love until Now*, Thorsons, 2000

West-Meads, Zelda, *How To Make Your Man Commit: And What To Do If He Won't*, Hodder & Stoughton, 1999

Managing life, relationships and addiction

Cooper, Cary, L. and Lewis, Suzan, *The Workplace Revolution: Managing Today's Dual Career Families*, Kogan Page, 1993

Fisher, Roger and Ury, William, *Getting to Yes: Negotiating an Agreement without Giving In*, Arrow Business Books, 1981

Useful Organisations

Counselling and therapy

British Association for Counselling
1 Regent Place
Rugby CV21 2PJ
Tel: 01788 550899
Fax: 01788 562189
e-mail: bac@bac.co.uk
Internet: www.counselling.co.uk

Send a s.a.e. for a list of accredited counsellors in your area.

British Association of Psychotherapists
37 Mapesbury Road
London NW2 4HJ
Tel: 020 8452 9823

The British Psychological Society
St Andrew's House
48 Princess Road East
Leicester LE1 7DR
Tel: 0116 254 9568
Fax: 0116 247 0787

e-mail: mail@bps.org.uk
Internet: www.bps.org.uk

Relate
Herbert Gray College
Little Church Street
Rugby CV21 3AP
Tel: 01788 573241 (9 a.m.–5 p.m., Mon.–Fri.)
Internet: www.relate.org.uk

Samaritans
Tel: 0345 90 90 90
e-mail: jo@samaritans.org
or anonymously at:
   samaritans@anon.twwells.com

UK Council for Psychotherapy
167–169 Great Portland Street
London W1N 5FB
Tel: 020 7436 3002
Fax: 020 7436 3013
e-mail: UKCP@psychotherapy.org.uk
Internet: www.psychotherapy.org.uk

Women's Therapy Centre
10 Manor Gardens
London N7 6JS
Advice/information line: 020 7263 6200
Fax: 020 7281 7879

Money addiction, gambling and co-dependency

CODA – Codependents Anonymous
Ashburnham Community Centre
Tetcott Road
London SW10 OSH
Tel: 020 7376 8191 (answerphone information)

Gamblers Anonymous
PO Box 88
London SW10 OEU
Tel: 020 7384 3040

Gamcare
Suite 1
25–27 Catherine Place
London SW1E 6DU
Helpline: 0845 6000 133
Tel: 020 7233 8988
Fax: 020 7233 8977
e-mail: director@gamcare.org.uk
Internet: www.gamcare.org.uk

Promis Recovery Centre
2a Pelham Street
London SW7 3HU
Freefone helpline: 0800 374318
Tel: 020 7584 6511
Fax: 01304 841917
e-mail: robin@promis.co.uk
Internet: www.ftech.net/~promis

Money advice

Citizens' Advice Bureaux – Debt Counselling Service
Freefone: 0800 192 192

Consumer Credit Counselling Service
Freefone: 0800 138 11 11

Money Advice Centres (look up in local phone book)

Legal advice

Law Society
113 Chancery Lane
London WC2A 1PL
Tel: 020 7242 1222

For names and addresses of solicitors only.

Children

British Agencies for Adoption and Fostering
Skyline House
Union Street
London SE1 0LX
Tel: 020 7593 2000
e-mail: mail@baf.org.uk
Internet: www.baf.org.uk

Send A4 s.a.e. plus 80p stamps for general information pack on adoption and fostering.

COTS (Surrogacy)
Lairg
Sutherland
Scotland IV27 4EF
Tel: 01549 402401

Couples Information Pack – send £3.00
Guide to Surrogacy Booklet – send £5.00

Family Rights Group
The Print House
18 Ashwin Street
London E8 3DL
Advice line: 020 7249 0008

Gingerbread
16–17 Clerkenwell Close
London EC1R OAN
Advice lines: 020 7336 8184 (Wales: 01792 648728)
e-mail: office@gingerbread.org.uk
Internet: www.gingerbread.org.uk

Maternity Alliance
45 Beech Street
London EC2P 2LX
Tel: 020 7588 8582

Send a s.a.e. for publications list.

National Childbirth Trust
Alexandra House
Oldham Terrace
London W3 6NH
Tel: 020 8992 8637
Internet: www.nct-online.org

National Council for the Divorced and Separated
13 High Street
Little Shelford
Cambridgeshire CB2 5ES
Tel: 01142 313585

National Council for One-Parent Families
255 Kentish Town Road
London NW5 2LX
Tel: 020 7267 1361

The National StepFamily Association
now incorporated into:

Parentline Plus
520 Highgate Studios
53–79 Highgate Road
London NW5 1TL
Helpline: Freefone 0808 800 2222 for anyone in a parenting role
Textphone: 0800 783 6783
Internet: www.parentlineplus.org.uk

Women

Rights of Women
52–54 Featherstone Street
London EC1Y 8RT
Tel: 020 7251 6577

Free legal advice for women.

Women's Aid Federation
PO Box 391
Bristol BS99 7WS
Helpline: 0345 023468

Men

Families Need Fathers
134 Curtain Road
London EC2A 3AR
Tel: 020 7613 5060

Index

addiction for money
  see money addiction
adoption 160, 234
Aleksander, T. 25, 161
anger 43, 56, 71, 91, 175
attraction 80–1

babies 141, 194
  checklist 205
  planning for 149–50
bank accounts
  joint 105–9
  separate 10, 103–5
Berne, E. 55
blame 175
blind dates 81–2
borrowing from partners 214–15,
  220
boundaries 219

care 212
chalk-and-cheese relationships

39–41, 47, 48, 59, 156, 190
changes in circumstances 172–8
childcare 150, 178
children 234–5
  cost of 142–3, 159–60
class differences 82–3
co-dependency 66–7, 233
co-operation 47, 218
cohabitation 92–5, 96–103, 122
  checklist 118
  contract for 111–18
  paying for 103–9
collusion 61, 137
commitment 97
  fear of 97–9
  money and 93–4
communication 28–9, 45, 110,
  169–70, 200
  lack of 9
competition 56
conflict 43–5, 209–10
control 33, 75, 100, 129, 152

238

Cooper, C. 166–7
COTS 158, 235
counselling 136, 183–4, 231–2
credit cards 9, 93, 104, 188
crunchpoints 8–9, 27, 77
    money relationships 50, 80, 93,
        150–9, 164, 180, 184–5
    splitting up 187–9, 192, 199–200
cultural differences 83–5

dating 77–83, 87–9
    cross-cultural 83–5
    gay and lesbian 85–7
    ground rules for 89–92
dating etiquette 78
    generational differences 79–80
debts 7, 68–9, 93–4, 135
    talking about 110, 149–50
denial 33
dependency 145, 146–8
    fear of 148–9
differences between partners
    acknowledging 48
    respecting 44, 45
disability, effect on relationships
    178–83
divorce *see* splitting up
downshifting 166–9
doormats 35, 56, 58, 134–5, 193

earnings
    talking about 110
    unequal 62, 106, 151, 196–9
eco-warriors 35–6, 59, 179
electronic money 1, 68, 100
    see also credit cards
Elliot, R. 71
emotional hidden agendas 60–1,
    82

emotional literacy 213–14
emotional money baggage 109,
    148, 153–4, 216
    checklist 29–30
    conflicting 131–5
    dating and 78–9, 88
    handling 27–9, 161–3
    and money patterns 58–9
    and splitting up 189–90, 199
    and starting again 201, 202, 204
    understanding 17–24
engagements 124
Equal Opportunities Commission
    196
expectations 82–5, 93
    unreal 195–6

fantasy versus reality 81
fear 43, 91, 136, 147, 168, 175
    of commitment 97–9
    of dependency 148–9
    of feelings 215
    of intimacy 61–2
feelings 214–15
    about dependency 147–50
    about money 42
    about negotiations over money
        91–2
feminism 121
fighting about money 7, 10, 111,
    165
    causes 49–50
    in marriage 130–7
    splitting up 190–3
    and wedding nerves 127–9
financial help 184
    see also money advice
financial inequality 1, 11, 62,
    196–9

financial security 40, 104
first dates 81–2
    expectations 82–5
flashpoints 16, 24, 50, 101, 144–5, 218
flexibility 88
fostering 160, 234
frozen needs 64–6
    in relationships 66–7

gamblers 34, 56, 58, 134–5
gambling 105, 133–5, 136, 233
gay and lesbian relationships 14
generational differences 79–80
goals, life, changes in 165–72
goals, money 50–1, 220
    long-term 114
going Dutch 89–90
golddiggers 34–5, 56, 58, 63, 82, 190
grievances 214–15
    see also resentment
ground rules 218–19
    for dating 89–92

Hall, A. 13
Hardy, T. 119
health, changes in, effect on relationships 178–84
hoarders 33, 58
holding the purse strings 62–4
honesty 212

in-laws 25, 26
independence 102, 104
    of women 85, 12–2, 145–7
    see also dependency
infertility 155–9
insecurity 33

intimacy, fear of 61–2
Ironside, V. 98
isolation 183
IVF (in vitro fertilisation) 155–8

joint accounts 105–9
Jukes, A. 199

language of money 14–15
legal help 184, 219, 234
letter-writing 27–8, 216
Lewis, S. 166–7
life crises 164–5
limit setting 136
listening 88, 170, 175, 212–13
lone parents 25–6, 235, 236
love
    money and 10–11, 45–6, 86, 136, 221
    or need 67–8

marriage 123–4
    money and 119–24, 129–38
    see also weddings
Married Women's Property Acts 120
mating 92–5
mediation 192
men 13, 237
Men's Lib 122–3
mirror-image relationships 36–9, 46–7, 59, 158, 161, 179
money, emotional meaning of 187
money addiction 64–73, 233
money advice 135, 137, 184, 234
money management
    in marriage 129–38
    styles of 99–109, 113

money patterns 31–6, 58–9
   conflicting 44, 102, 130–1,
      156
   identifying 88–9, 110–11, 216
   patterned streaks 36, 39, 216
   quiz 223–8
   starting again 201–2
money relationships 36, 45–51,
   162–3, 170
   nurturing 216–21
   see also chalk-and-cheese
      relationships; mirror-image
      relationships
mortgages 94, 101
Murphy, R. 16
mutuality 212

National Childbirth Trust 150,
   235
negotiation 89–90, 110–11
   feelings about 91–2
non-verbal cues 15, 59, 82, 89

ostriches 35, 58

Pahl, J. 1, 12, 13, 99–100, 120,
   129
parental relationships, effect of
   24–6
parents
   internalised 24–5, 26
   learning attitudes to money
      from 20, 21–3, 40, 41,
      69–70, 105, 132, 134, 154,
      189–90
   role models in talking about
      money 15
patience 88
pin money 121–2, 194, 195

planners 33, 56, 58, 60, 63, 79
positive and negative money
   relationships 47–8, 50
power games 54–64, 217
   checklist 73
power in relationships 11, 102,
   132, 199
pre-nuptial agreements 124–7
pregnancy 143
   feelings about 144
priorities, different 130–3
privacy 12, 13
purse strings 62–4

quizzes
   emotional money baggage 18–20
   money patterns 223–8

redundancy, effect on relationships
   172–5
Relate 117, 136, 153, 192
   survey 10
resentment 56, 90–1, 147
respect 215
responsibility 215
revenge 187
   shopaholism as 71–3, 180
Rowe, D. 11–12

savings 33, 101, 107, 114, 151
secrecy 1, 9, 71
self-esteem 42–3, 59, 154, 178
self-sabotage 71
separate money 10, 103–5
   with joint accounts 105–6
serial monogamy 195
shopaholism 68–71, 135, 180,
   188–9
   as revenge 71–3, 180

as self-sabotage 71
short-termism 195
space 215
spenders 33–4, 58, 93–4
spending
    different priorities in 130–1, 133
    unequal 102, 105, 153
    see also shopaholism
splitting up 187
    checklist 205
    money relationship crunch-points 187–9, 199–200
starting again 200–2
    checklist 205
    positive attitude to 202–5
stealing 65
stepfamilies 25, 160–1, 236
    paying for 137
stress 166–7
surrogacy 158–9, 235
Surrogacy Arrangements Act 1986 158–9

taboo, talking about money as 12, 14

talking about money 12, 13, 14–16, 108, 109–11, 175, 204, 219–20
team work 46, 176, 217–18
time 211
time outs 220
trust 33, 38, 45, 105, 107, 117, 126, 212
Tysoe, M. 81

value 42–3
value for money 33

weddings, and money fights 127–9
withholding money 56
women 236
    earnings 62, 100, 142, 194, 196
    independence 85, 121–2, 145–7
    marriage and property 120
    money management 100
    paying their way 80, 83, 84
    staying single 194
Women's Lib 121
worriers 34, 40, 58–9
worth, sense of 42–3
writing letters 27–8, 216